How to use this Guide

Main route and description of sights

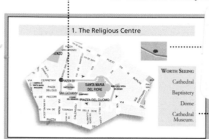

Works of art, sights and areas worth seeing on the itinerary

A number beside the title indicates there is further information on the same subject

Additional information on the traditions and customs of the city. These are found in the itineraries and cover various items of interest.

Plan of churches and monuments visited during the itinerary

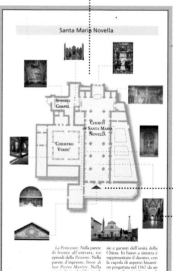

Cuisine -1-

Strange but true, the renowned *bistecca alla fiorentina* is English. Firstly, the word *bistecca* is a corruption of 'beefsteak'; secondly, both the cut and the way of cooking this 'beef chop' came from beyond the English Channel. The steak is "in keeping with the new world of the 18th century, with the philosophie of the Enlightenment, with the increasing use of coal as a source of energy, with the demise of the cuisine of Renaissance and Baroque courts, with free thinkers, with the birth of aristocratic tourism" (M.C. Solemi). Even though today it is considered to be one of the most typical local dishes, it is in fact, both a recent and an imported tradition. The truth is that in Florence, steak was originally cooked by the Florentines for the English tourists. Nor should it come as such a surprise, given that cuisine, like all aspects of culture, is characterized by continual evolution, the ability to absorb and interpret new ideas while abandoning old habits and tastes.

It is therefore difficult to define and itemize 'traditional Florentine cuisine'. Its one outstanding feature is, perhaps, simplicity and sobriety, though according to period and social class, even this is a fairly generalized description. Expensive cuts of meat are not much used; rather the more humble parts, tastily and imaginatively enhanced by the dictates of poverty. In the past, one could even eat fish and eels from the Arno and frogs from the streams. Vegetables and legumes were eaten in such quantity that Florentines were nicknamed 'bean-eaters,' and carefully-tended

vegetable gardens prospered both inside the city walls and in the surrounding countryside. The close relationship between town and country was therefore continually evident at table too, exemplified in the case of wine. Aged in barrels in villas dotting the hillsides, it was then brought to the cellars of the palazzi where the owners lived in the city. It was sold to the public in flasks, from characteristic little windows made in the imposing façades of noble residences during the 16th century: one can still be seen in Palazzo Bartolini Salimbeni Vivai, on Via del Giglio, #2 , in the form of a miniature, rusticated doorway; and another, close to the junction of Via della Spada and Via delle Belle Donne, still even has the opening hours engraved in marble. Some of the taverns won lasting fame: the one run by the Bertucce family was already long-established at the time of Lorenzo the Magnificent. Many had curious and picturesque names: the *Fico* (Fig) the *Porco* (Pig), the *Malvasia* (Malmsey wine), the *Vinegia* (Grape vine). Food was also available from itinerant stall holders who sold *castagnaccio*, baked apples and pears and even, in the Piazza della Signoria of the 19th century, *maccheroni* with cheese and pepper. Bread rolls filled with tripe and other offal can still be bought today from hand carts in the streets of downtown. Now becoming a rarity on the other hand, are the fried-food shops, once found in the streets of working class areas. Here, 'old-fashioned' fast-food consisted of fried polenta, rice fritters, *roventini* (pork blood puddings, served hot with a sprinkling of Parmesan cheese), *cecina* (chick pea paste), *castagnaccio* (a cake made from chestnut flour, flavored with rosemary leaves and sprinkled with pine nuts and raisins) and *coccoli* (plain salted fritters, made from bread dough).

Main entrance

Location of the works of art inside the building

La Pentecoste. Nella parete di fronte all'entrata, tre episodi della Passione. Nella parete d'ingresso, *Storie di San Pietro Martire.* Nella parete destra, *La Chiesa militante e la Chiesa trionfante,* ove è esaltato il ruolo dei domenicani come guardiani della vera fede contro le eresie e garanti dell'unità della Chiesa. In basso a sinistra è rappresentato il duomo, con la cupola di aspetto bizantino progettata nel 1367 da un gruppo di artisti fra i quali lo stesso Andrea. Nella parete sinistra, *Trionfo di San Tommaso d'Aquino.* Nella scarsella, *San Jacopo*

Reference

Location of area on the map at back of guide

Street name

borgo la croce; ☞ T6/H5.

Map reference

T.6   T.5   H   5

Florence

Mandragora

©1998 **La Mandragora srl**
50122 Firenze, piazza Duomo 9

Edited by	*Alberto Anichini, Sandra Rosi*
Texts	*Paolo de Simonis, Gian Bruno Ravenni,*
	Claudio Rosati
Traslation	*Eve Leckey*
Graphic design	*Lorenzo Gualtieri*
DTP	*Franco Casini*
Photographs	*Archivio Mandragora, Andrea Bazzechi,*
	Stefano Cellai, Nicola Grifoni, Liberto Perugi,
	Press Photo, Antonio Quattrone, Archivio FMG
Colour separation	*Studio Leonardo Firenze*
Printed by	*Giunti Industrie Grafiche*

ISBN 88-85957-23-4

This book is printed on paper TCF
(total chlorine free)

Introduction

According to statistics produced by UNESCO, 60% of the world's most important works of art are located in Italy and approximately half of these are in Florence.

These stark and startling figures give us cause to reflect on two facts: the vast range of choices available to the visitor and, at the same time, the problems - mainly economic and organizational - arising from the management and preservation of such a heritage. We should not therefore be surprized when occasionally we are denied the pleasure of admiring certain paintings and sculptures mentioned in the guides, due to restoration, nor when the façade of some historic palazzo or famous church is obscured by tarpaulins and scaffolding for the same reason. Nor should we complain too much about the opening hours - often quite limited, it is true - of museums and churches; although these have been extended in recent years, the continual increase in the flow of tourists (now about 6 million a year, in other words 15 times the city's own population) imposes urgent new requirements.

It is important that anyone visiting Florence for the first time should try to look beyond the various inevitable difficulties to understand the character of this city with its wealth of history and culture, yet so solemn and haughty, and to observe closely its inhabitants with that singular Florentine blend of proud aloofness and biting wit. Without such a mental predisposition even the best-intentioned visitor may remain disappointed. There is no point in trying to absorb the art and history if one does not also relate it to the present, to trace those links which can help us better understand the world in which we live. In contradiction of a famous Latin motto it has been said that "history is bunk". It is however, pointless to stand before the David or the Primavera at best appreciating them aesthetically, at worst in order to boast feebly "I've seen it". To lack an understanding of the economic, social, political and cultural contexts which produced such works is to remain a victim of the consumer syndrome which is one of the worst aspects of contemporary life.

The authors have therefore tried, we hope successfully, not only to describe the works of art, but also to provide some food for thought, some lively and curious insights as well as useful information of all kinds. And they sincerely hope that your first trip to the city, sadly often limited to only a few days, might be enjoyable enough to encourage other, more leisurely visits.

The Publisher

Florence: how to use this guide

As with any world-famous tourist centre, a vast amount has been written and published on the city of Florence. The visitor who buys this guide will no doubt have selected it from a vast range of similar titles, basing his choice on several positive factors: the substantial content, the stylish production, the wealth of new and attractive illustrations and, last but not least, the excellent value for money. In the hope that such favourable first impressions will be confirmed by use and leisurely reading, we would like to briefly mention the criteria adopted in compiling the guide, and suggest various ways of using it effectively.

First and foremost the guide is intended to be an introduction to the history and city of Florence. Thus the main monuments and works of art are described fully and precisely while, however, seeking to avoid filling the pages with a plethora of imposing names in heavy print as in so many other books on the same subject.

The description of the city is arranged according to a series of itineraries to be followed on foot, a method now both popular and practical. As can be seen from the sketch maps at the beginning of every chapter, all the itineraries are circular and all begin and end in Piazza del Duomo or Piazza San Giovanni. Such a system, altogether new in a guide to the city, is both practical and stimulating. On the one hand, the visitor avoids following the same route in both directions and on the other, it enables him to swap from one route to another as he wishes, since they may occasionally intersect or run close to each other. In any case the itineraries clearly consist of a series of suggestions and may only be followed in their entirety by that fortunate minority who, as well as being physically and psychologically prepared to set out on some quite long and demanding walks, have at least a week available to do so. The brief paragraphs in italics, highlighting descriptions of monuments in an itinerary, are intended mainly for these visitors. Those who are limited to a period of only two or three days will find handy abbreviated alternatives suggested on the inner cover, providing a broad overview of the city's artistic and historic heritage.

The itineraries - each introduced by a brief description of the most important characteristics of the route - are supplemented by a series of brief essays covering subjects ranging from history of art to economics, from urban development to the Renaissance, from cookery to folklore. These also contain descriptions of areas or museums which lie outside the historic centre, or which are only mentioned briefly in the itineraries. Some of these essays describe events in the life of the city - events which are often only described in a separate introduction, removing them therefore from their true context and consequently often ignored or not fully appreciated by the reader. References from

both the itineraries and the essays to the main text are always indicated by the symbol ☛.
The guide also contains an A-Z of Useful Information which is
well worth reading before setting out to discover the city. The information provided here is based on direct experience, however
we would not wish to claim that it is entirely without omissions,
gaps or even errors. We would therefore be most grateful to re-
ceive, via the publisher, any additions, comments or inaccuracies.
To complete the guide are a glossary of art and historical terms
(for those who would like or need to improve their knowledge of
an often unfamiliar terminology), an index of place names and
monuments, and an index of artists mentioned in the text giving
birthplace and, where possible, the year of birth and death. Lastly, a word about the illustrations: the volume contains over 700
images which are merely a foretaste of all that is described or
mentioned in the text. These are only intended to help the visitor
immediately identify a specific work of art or building, and are
not intended for the detailed study and appreciation which only
a specialized work can satisfy.

The Authors.

Contents

Religious architecture -1-

Romanesque. Romanesque architecture spread throughout Europe from the end of the 10th century during a period of economic, political and cultural recovery which was most evident in the renewed growth of the cities. The Romanesque cathedral is, in fact, symbolic of the revival of urban society in western Europe. A reinterpretation of the Christian basilica, the style consists of a subtle organization of space and form, creating the light and dark effect known as *chiaroscuro*. The heavy stonework is arranged in tiers, often with open arcades. At the end of the 11th century, first in Burgundy and then in Lombardy, stone vaults were introduced into Romanesque churches: these replaced the earlier wooden ones and required highly sophisticated construction techniques, which are now lost to us.

Florentine examples of Romanesque architecture have a particular elegance and linearity, almost representing a form of 'medieval classicism.' A typical feature of Tuscan Romanesque is the facing in white marble and green and black serpentine.

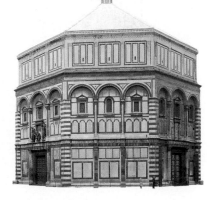

Baptistery of San Giovanni
First mentioned in records in 897, the building was altered and another order added at the beginning of the 11th century. The crowning lantern dates from 1175. The external decoration, consisting of geometric patterns in green and white marble, was made between the 11th and the 13th centuries.

The Church of San Miniato al Monte
Built on the site of an 8th-century church dedicated to Saint Minias, the present church was begun in the early 11th century and finished almost a century later. The interior is in the form of a basilica and is on three levels: the presbytery is raised above the main body of the church while the crypt lies beneath.

The Badìa Fiesolana
The Romanesque façade of the church dates from the 12th century. It is set into the larger and unfinished façade made when Cosimo the Elder decided to enlarge the church during the first half of the 15th century.

Santi Apostoli
Dating from the late 11th century, the church's Romanesque façade was restored during the 1930's.

Gothic. Gothic architecture was first introduced to Italy at the beginning of the 13th century by the Cistercian monks of the Abbey of San Galgano, near Siena. The Gothic style developed from a building technique which is based on an ogival vault resting on a pointed arch. This design, which has a greater load-bearing capacity than the rounded arch, also had the effect of lightening the stone structure, giving a vertical, upward lift to the building and allowing the insertion of large stained-glass windows. Compared to French Gothic, the Florentine style made limited use of the possibilities offered by the new technique and the churches of the important mendicant orders which were being built just outside the city walls at the time, preserved the classical features so characteristic of the city's art and architecture.

**The Cathedral
of Santa Maria del Fiore**
The cathedral, designed by Arnolfo di Cambio, was begun on September 8, 1296. The first three bays were completed in 1364. In 1378, the vault of the central nave was finished, and the side aisles in 1380. The interior has three naves divided by clustered pilasters supporting ogival arches and vaults.

Santa Maria Novella
Begun by the Dominican friars, Sisto and Ristoro, the church was founded in 1278 and built during the first half of the 14th century. The interior, in the form of a Latin cross, has three naves divided by clustered pilasters supporting ogival arches and vaults.

Orsanmichele
Originally a grain warehouse, the structure was built between 1337 and 1380; the upper floors were added later. It was converted to a place of worship in the late15th century. The Gothic mullioned openings on the ground floor are decorated with attractive stonework tracery and have small statues in the springers of the arches.

Santa Croce
Building was begun by Arnolfo di Cambio in 1295 and was completed in 1385 after his death. The interior has three naves divided by octagonal pilasters supporting wide, pointed arches. The roof above the central nave has exposed truss beams.

Santa Trinita
Originally built by the Vallombrosan monks in the 11th century, the church was rebuilt in Gothic style in the 14th century.

1. **The Religious Centre**

Andrea Pisano, relief panel from Giotto's bell tower. Museo dell'Opera del Duomo.

Piazza del Duomo and Piazza San Giovanni combine to form a single urban entity: the historic, religious heart of Florence, linked by Via de' Calzaioli to the city's civic centre in Piazza della Signoria.

In Roman times, the area lay at the north-eastern limit of the city, and was enclosed within defensive walls which ran along the north side of the present square, behind the apse of the cathedral. The city's population gradually dwindled during the early Middle Ages and consequently the city walls were reduced, leaving the area outside their perimeter.

It was precisely in this period, during the 6th and 7th centuries, that the first Christian temples were built. The Baptistery and the ancient Cathedral of Santa Reparata (demolished in 1275 to make way for Santa Maria del Fiore) were built on top of Roman foundations, the remains of which were discovered during recent archaeological excavations.

The Cathedral of Santa Maria del Fiore was begun by Arnolfo di Cambio in 1296, when medieval Florence was at the height of its expansion with approximately 90,000 inhabitants. It was during this period that the piazza began to take shape: houses and structures built close to the Baptistery were torn down, and the level of the sur-

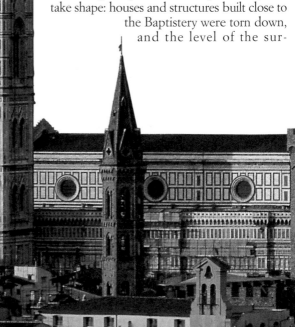

Andrea della Robbia, the Agnus Dei, *emblem of the Wool Guild.*

rounding streets was lowered to create more space around the religious buildings. Later, towards the end of the 14th century, several towers near the cathedral were demolished for the same reason. Almost entirely occupied by the massive structure of Santa Maria del Fiore, the piazza assumed its present appearance towards the end of the 19th century. The marble façade of the cathedral was finished in 1887, and in 1895, the area behind the apse of the Baptistery was enlarged by moving back the façade of the Archbishop's Palace, thus creating today's Piazza San Giovanni.

Bernardo Daddi, Madonna della Misericordia *(detail of the fresco), Bigallo Museum.*

Restoration workshop of the Opera del Duomo in Via dello Studio.

Left, detail of the 19th-century façade of the cathedral. Right, general view of the buildings.

Bernardino Poccetti, drawing of Arnolfo di Cambio's façade. Museo dell' Opera del Duomo.

CATHEDRAL OF SANTA MARIA DEL FIORE

502 feet long, 125 feet wide at the aisles and 295 feet at the transept, the cathedral (or *Duomo*) of Santa Maria del Fiore is the fourth largest Christian church, preceded only by St Peter's in Rome, St Paul's in London and the cathedral of Milan. Entirely decorated in pink, white and green marble, the church has a majestic and harmonious air, despite a conglomeration of different styles, from its foundations to the 19th-century additions.

With a capacity of up to 30,000 people, the church was conceived by Arnolfo di Cambio as a vast, covered piazza where the entire population of the city could gather. In fact, it was here that Dante's *Divine Comedy* was read out to large, enthusiastic crowds.

The city council commissioned Arnolfo "to prepare models or plans to rebuild Santa Maria Reparata with such great and sumptuous magnificence that man's industry and power could not surpass it in beauty and size." Work began in 1296, but was interrupted at the beginning of the 14th century by the death of the architect. Building began again under Giotto (1334-1337), followed by Andrea Pisano (1337-1348), and finally by Francesco Talenti (1349-1359), who altered the original plans. The area of the apse, with the tribunes and the drum of the dome, was completed in 1421. The construction of the dome, designed by Filippo Brunelleschi, was finished in early 1436. The church was solemnly consecrated that same year, on March 25th — the first day of the year according to the old Florentine calendar. The lantern, in the form of a small temple, was raised in 1446 and in 1468, some 172 years after building had started, Verrocchio crowned it with the large gilt sphere and bronze cross.

Façade. The original façade, of which Arnolfo di Cambio had build almost half, was never completed, and was demolished in 1588. The sculptures which decorated it

Picturesque transport by horse and carriage in front of the cathedral. Below, the baptistery, cathedral and bell tower seen from Piazza San Giovanni.

are now housed in the Museo dell'Opera del Duomo. Designed by architect Emilio De Fabris, the existing façade was added in 1887. The bronze doors, made by Augusto Passaglia and Giuseppe Cassioli, are also 19th-century.

Right side. The first two bays constitute the oldest part of the cathedral. In the second is a door, known as that of the *campanile* or bell tower, with a *Madonna and Child* in the lunette (currently under restoration) and *Christ Blessing* in the tympanum above,

both by the school of Andrea Pisano (1290-1349).

Beyond the next two bays, near the apse, is the *Porta dei Canonici* (late 14th century) in Florentine Gothic style, with a delicate decoration of marble inlay by Giovanni d'Ambrogio and Piero di Giovanni. In the lunette is a *Madonna and Child* (1396) *and Angels* (early 15th century), attributed to Niccolò di Piero Lamberti.

Apse. The apse consists of four tribunes and three minor apses radiating out from the large, octagonal drum which supports the dome. From the corner of Via del Proconsolo and Via dell'Oriuolo, there is an excellent view of the apse and the immense ribbed dome, "which soars to the sky and has a shadow wide enough to cover all the people of Tuscany," as described by Leon Battista Alberti, the famous architect, mathematician and humanist.

Detail of the central doorway. The present façade (1887) was designed by Emilio De Fabris.

1. The Religious Centre

WORTH SEEING

Cathedral

Baptistery

Dome

Museo dell'Opera del Duomo

Two views of the cathedral interior. It took 172 years to complete the building, the fourth largest Christian place of worship.

Left side. Passing around the apse, we come to the *Porta della Mandorla,* the last and perhaps the most beautiful of the doors to be made. The name derives from the almond-shaped pinnacle containing a relief sculpture of *Our Lady of the Assumption* (1414-1421), probably the greatest work of Nanni di Banco. In the lunette is a mosaic *Annunciation* (1491), by Domenico Ghirlandaio. Before returning to the front of the cathedral, we reach the *Porta di Balla* (late 14th century). The name originates from the proximity to Via dei Servi, previously known as 'Borgo di Balla,' being the area where the bales of fabric were brought to be stretched and dried in the airing sheds belonging to the Wool Guild.

Inner façade. Impressive in its vastness and austerity, the interior is in the form of a Latin cross and is divided into three aisles linked by ogival arches rising from imposing clustered pilasters. A long gallery runs above the central nave.

Above the central doorway of the inner façade is the *Clock for the Canonical Hours* (1443), painted by Paolo Uccello and

Paolo Uccello,
equestrian monument
to Giovanni Acuto
(John Hawkwood).

Paolo Uccello,
clock face.

recently restored. In the lunette beneath is the *Coronation of the Virgin,* attributed to Gaddo Gaddi (early 16th century). In the small arches on either side of the lunette are *Musician Angels* (late 16th century), by Santi di Tito.

On the inner façade are three circular *stained glass windows* made to a design by Lorenzo Ghiberti. These represent one of the few surviving pictorial works by the artist who, between 1434 and 1455, supervised the making of all the stained glass windows in the cathedral, with the exception of the four mullioned windows in the side aisles dating from the end of the 14th century.

On the right of the inner façade is the *tomb of Antonio Orso* (1321), by the Sienese sculptor, Tino di Camaino. In 1312, Orso, at the time Bishop of Florence, defended the city against the imperial army of Henry VII of Luxembourg.

Right nave. In the first bay is a medallion depicting *Filippo Brunelleschi* (1446), by Andrea Cavalcanti (known as Buggiano). Further on is a 16th-century wooden tabernacle with a *statue of a prophet* – either Isaiah or Daniel – probably by Nanni di Banco (1380/90-1421). On the same wall is a tondo with a fictive portrait of *Giotto* (1490), by Benedetto da Maiano.

The ceremony of the Scoppio del Carro *(Explosion of the Cart) which takes place on Easter Sunday.*

Andrea del Castagno, equestrian monument to Niccolò da Tolentino.

In the second bay is the entrance to the crypt of the ancient cathedral of Santa Reparata, discovered beneath the paving of the cathedral during excavations begun in 1966. St Reparata was an Early Christian martyr of the 3rd century. In Florentine iconography, she is represented holding the palm of martyrdom and a book, also sometimes with a dove coming from her mouth, representing the soul leaving the body. Displayed in the crypt are Roman and medieval relics discovered during the work of excavation, as well as numerous 13th- and 14th-century tombstones. In 1972, the tomb of Filippo Brunelleschi was discovered, engraved with the following epitaph in Latin: *Corpus magni ingenii viri Philippi Brunelleschi florentini* ("body of the great genius, Filippo Brunelleschi, Florentine").

In the third bay is an attractive stained glass window with

Six Saints, designed by Agnolo Gaddi and dated 1494; a statue of the prophet *Isaiah* (1427), by Bernardo Ciuffagni; and a pair of frescoed *tomb monuments* (first half of the 15th century), by Bicci di Lorenzo. In the fourth bay is a bust (1521) of the philosopher *Marsilio Ficino* (1433-1499), by Andrea Ferrucci.

Dome. The entrance to the stairway leading up into the immense dome (299 ft high) is at the end of the right nave. The first part of the ascent (463 stairs altogether) leads to a gallery; from here the climb leading to the lantern which crowns the dome becomes more demanding. One is rewarded, however, with a splendid panorama of the city and surroundings.

The vault is decorated with a *Universal Judgment* (1572-1579), painted by Giorgio Vasari and Federico Zuccari, recently restored.

The circular stained glass windows inside the drum were made from designs by the following artists: Ghiberti (*Presentation at the Temple, Ascension, Christ in the Garden*), Donatello (*Corona-*

View of the cathedral dome from Via dei Servi.

Above: *School of Giotto,* Madonna and Child, *part of a fresco now lost.*

Domenico di Michelino, The Divine Comedy illuminates Florence.

Brunelleschi's dome

Ludovico Cigoli (second half of the 16th century), cross section of the dome. Uffizi, Gabinetto dei Disegni e Stampe.

At the end of the 14th and beginning of the 15th centuries, the Florentine Republic was developing into a regional state. The city's new role also brought about changes to its most important building, the cathedral. It was begun in 1296 by Arnolfo di Cambio, who intended it to be a sort of enormous hall, capable of accommodating the city's entire population. In 1367, it was decided to enlarge Arnolfo's plan, both in size and in height. The structure neared completion towards the end of the century, with the building of the 180 ft high octagonal drum across the naves. Now the cathedral only lacked a dome to finish it, and in 1418 a competition for its design was announced. Normally in the 14th century a wooden framework was put into place first to support the brickwork structure of a domed roof. This was then dismantled once the masonery had been strengthened. This technique was impracticable for Santa Maria del Fiore as, to make a wooden rib capable of spanning a chasm almost 150 ft in diameter – the measurement of the area to be covered – required an immense amount of wood. Moreover, it is possible that workmen capable of making such a huge wooden structure were no longer to be found in Florence. Filippo Brunelleschi took part in the competition presenting a revolutionary plan which replaced the timber framework with a self-supporting structure of wood and brick. During the months of October and November 1418, he had already experimented with the new method, making a scale model in rough brickwork. The structure of the dome consisted of a double shell, supported by eight main ribs – visible on the outside, dressed with white marble – and sixteen internal ribs, all interconnected in order to bear the lateral thrust of the structure. Work began on August 7, 1420 and was completed in 1436, closing the last ring at a height of almost 300 feet. In the same year Filippo designed the lantern which not only crowns the structure but also stabilizes it with its weight. It was put into place, slightly altered, in 1446. In order to put this new technique into practice, Brunelleschi had had to revolutionize construction methods, using all the experience he had gathered in artists' and craftsmen's workshops. He had to create machines, tools and even a new system of working.

Giuliano da Maiano, wood inlay in the Sacristy.

tion of the Virgin), Paolo Uccello (*Resurrection* and *Nativity*) and Andrea del Castagno (*Deposition).*

Below, in tabernacles at the bottom of the transept arches, are eight 16th-century statues of the *Apostles.*

In the centre of the transept is the octagonal marble choir. The elegant railing is made of marble carved with *bas-reliefs* by Baccio Bandinelli and his pupil Giovanni Bandini (1547-1572). Some have been removed and are displayed in the Museo dell'Opera.

In the middle of the choir is the main altar, also by Bandinelli, with a *Crucifix* by Benedetto da Maiano.

Tribunes and sacristies. Radiating from the transept are the three tribunes. Each of these are divided into five chapels illuminated by beautiful 15th-century *stained glass windows.* The tribunes are separated by two sacristies known respectively as the Sacrestia dei Canonici (Canon's Sacristy), to the right of the main altar, and Sacrestia delle Messe (Mass Sacristy), to the left. Their bronze doors are decorated with bas-reliefs and in the timpani are glazed terracotta sculptures by Luca della Robbia (mid-15th century).

The walls and cupboards in the Sacrestia delle Messe are finely decorated with wood inlay by Giuliano da Maiano. It was here that Lorenzo the Magnificent took refuge on April 26, 1478 when, during Easter celebrations in the cathedral, he and his brother

Giuliano – who died from stab wounds – were attacked by conspirators led by the Pazzi family.

In front of the altar in the central tribune is a bronze *urn*, one of Lorenzo Ghiberti's greatest works, containing relics of St Zenobius (1430-1440), the first bishop of Florence. On the floor in the left tribune is a bronze meridian sundial made by Paolo dal Pozzo Toscanelli (mid-15th century). The summer solstice is marked by a ray of sun which enters through a hole in the dome and falls on the sundial.

Left nave. In the fourth bay, near to the exit from the dome, is Domenico di Michelino's painting *The Divine Comedy illuminates Florence.* It was commissioned by the Opera del Duomo in 1465 to celebrate the second centenary of Dante's birth, a belated homage to the poet from the city that sent him into exile.

In the second and third bays of the left aisle are two large frescoes: the equestrian monument to *Sir John Hawkwood* (1436), the English soldier and commander in the Florentine army from 1377 to 1434, by Paolo Uccello; and, in the second, Andrea del Castagno's painting of *Niccolò da Tolentino* (1456), commander of the Republican army in the battle of San Romano (1432). Fur-

Luca della Robbia, Angel candle bearer.

Giotto's bell tower and the elegant mullioned windows on the first floor (below). Above, detail of the elaborate corbels which support the terrace.

Stained glass window in the drum of the dome portraying the Nativity, *designed by Paolo Uccello.*

ther ahead is a bust of the organ builder, *Antonio Squarcialupi* (1490), by Benedetto da Maiano.

GIOTTO'S CAMPANILE

The elegant campanile, or bell tower, has a square ground plan (47 ft square and 278 ft high), and is faced with colored marble: white from Carrara, pink from Siena, and dark green from Prato. Giotto began work in 1334, but was only able to complete the first level before his death in 1337. The work was taken over by Andrea Pisano who followed Giotto's design on the second level but modified it on the next two, introducing two pilaster strips on each side as well as niches with large statues. In 1348, Andrea was dismissed by the Opera del Duomo. No further progress was made for two years, during the dreadful outbreak of the Black Death, which reduced the city's population by two-thirds. Francesco Talenti took over in 1350 and built the last three levels, completing the building in 1359.

The sculptures are not merely decorative but form an integral part of the campanile's structure. The present sculptures are copies, the originals having been removed between 1965 and 1967 to be displayed in the Museo dell'Opera. The hexagonal reliefs which decorate Giotto's lower level represent the *Creation of Man* and the *Labours of Man.* The panels (1437-1439) on the side facing the cathedral are by Luca della Robbia, while the others are attributed to Andrea Pisano himself. The diamond-shaped panels of the next level are also by Pisano, apart from the *Sacraments,* which are attributed to Alberto Arnoldi. The niches on the level above house statues of *Patriarchs, Kings, Prophets* and *Sibyls* (1419-1436), by Donatello, Nanni di Bartolo and others.

A climb of 414 steps brings us to the top of the campanile, where one can enjoy a wonderful view of Brunelleschi's dome, the city and surrounding countryside.

BAPTISTERY OF SAN GIOVANNI

The Baptistery of St John was built on foundations dating from the Roman epoch, and some of the original marble from these buildings was used in its construction. During the

Middle Ages, it was believed to have been a temple to Mars, later transformed into a church. In fact, its origin is doubtless related to that of the old cathedral of Santa Reparata: the baptismal font of early Christian churches was always built outside, in the area immediately in front of the church. The present appearance of the building is the result of work carried out between the 11th and 13th centuries. In 1059, it was reconsecrated by Pope Niccolò II, and in the 12th century it was entirely clad with inlayed green and white marble from Prato. Towards the mid-12th century, the third level of marble panels was added and the pyramid-shaped roof and lantern (1174) were built. In 1202, the original semi-circular apse was replaced with the current rectangular one. The Baptistery, under the patronage of the Calimala Guild, was enhanced by important works of art, the most notable of which are the *bronze doors* depicting biblical scenes.

South Door. The door facing the Loggia del Bigallo is the oldest, as well as being a splendid example of Gothic sculpture. It was made by Andrea Pisano who completed it in 1330. It is divided into twenty-eight panels. The eight lower panels represent *Humility* and the *Theological and Cardinal Virtues.* The twenty panels above illustrate *Episodes from the Life of St John the Baptist*, the patron saint of Florence. The bronze frieze which

frames the door is a later addition (1452-1462), designed by Vittorio Ghiberti. Above the door is a bronze sculpture of *St John the Baptist, the Executioner and Salome*, by Vincenzo Danti.

North Door. Currently the main entrance to the Baptistery, facing Via Martelli. The door is by Lorenzo Ghiberti, who worked on it between 1403 and 1424, assisted by Masolino da Panicale, Donatello, Michelangelo and Paolo Uccello. The eight lower panels depict the *Evangelists* and the four *Fathers of the Church.* The twenty panels above illustrate *Scenes from the New Testament.* Over the door is a bronze group depicting *St John the Baptist between the Levite and the Pharisee,* by Giovan Francesco Rustici.

Gates of Paradise. The East Door is more commonly identified by Michelangelo's admiring description. Lorenzo Ghiberti worked on them from 1425 to 1452, and they are without a doubt his greatest masterpiece. Made of bronze and gold leaf, the doors are divided into ten large panels, each containing Old Testament scenes in bas-relief. Reading from top to bottom and from left to right these are: *The Creation and Expulsion from Paradise; Cain and Abel; Noah's Sacrifice and Drunkenness; Abraham and the Angels and the Sacrifice of Isaac; Esau and Jacob; Joseph sold and recognized by his Brethren; Moses receiving the Tablets of Stone; the Fall of Jericho; Battle with*

Alternately pointed and curved windows in the baptistery (above, seen from the Bigallo Loggia).

The south door, by Andrea Pisano.

The north door, by Lorenzo Ghiberti.

Lorenzo Ghiberti, the east door which Michelangelo called the 'gate of Paradise'.

Donatello and Michelozzo, detail of the tomb of the antipope, John XXIII: the theological virtues.

Above, the mullioned windows around the gallery; below, the apse and the mosaics in the vault.

the Philistines; *Solomon and the Queen of Sheba.* The frames consist of twenty-four small niches containing figures of biblical characters and twenty-four tondi containing the busts of artists who were contemporaries of Ghiberti. His own self-portrait is to be found fourth from the top in the inner row of the left leaf. Above the door is a copy of a marble sculpture by Andrea Sansovino, *Christ and John the Baptist* (1502). The bronze panels of the doors are also copies. The originals were damaged by the flood of 1966 and some are still being restored, while the others are on display in the Museo dell' Opera.

Interior. Octagonal in shape, the Baptistery consists of a lower order with large, monolithic columns taken from the ruins of Roman buildings and an upper order, consisting of the gallery, with elegant mul-

lioned windows and pilaster strips. Above the gallery is the attic floor on which rests the vast octagonal pyramid of the roof, entirely covered with mosaics. The walls are decorated with geometric patterns in white and green marble (11th-12th centuries). The pavement, similar to that of San Miniato al Monte, is made of marble inlay with oriental-style motifs; opposite the east door is a an inlay (*opus tassellatum*) representing the Sun and the signs of the zodiac (mid-11th century).

The most striking feature of the interior are the mosaics in the dome, apse and gallery. The mosaics above the altar are the oldest. Begun before 1226 by the Franciscan monk Jacopo da Torrita, they represent a large wheel supported by four figures of Atlas kneeling on Corinthian capitals. In the centre of the wheel is the *Lamb of God* surrounded by prophets and patriarchs, and to the sides are the *Madonna and Child and St John the Baptist.* The double archway is decorated with motifs of foliage and busts of *Christ, Mary, Apostles* and *Prophets.*

Work on the mosaics in the vault was already under way in 1270, and was finished during the first half of the 14th century. The work was carried out by Venetian craftsmen in the Byzantine style, working to designs by Florentine artists

Christ in judgement (right) and details of the mosaics in the vault and apse (left and below).

(Coppo di Marcovaldo, Meliore, Cimabue). The decoration is divided into six sections: in the upper band, around the lantern, are stylized plant motifs with grapevines, deer and peacocks. In the next band is Christ among the Seraphim and the angelic hierarchy. The section above the apse is almost entirely filled by a large figure of *Christ in Judgment* with scenes from the Universal Judgment on either side. In the other five sections, reading from top to bottom, are *Genesis, the Story of Joseph, Stories of Mary and Christ, the Story of John the Baptist.*

The Baptistery also contains several other works of art: to the right of the apse is the *Tomb of Baldassarre Costa*, the Antipope John XXIII who was deposed by the Council of Constance (1414-1418) and died in Florence in 1419; both Donatello and Michelozzo worked on the monument (1421-1427). On the left of the south door is a marble *baptismal font* (1371) with six panels in bas-relief illustrating baptismal scenes and attributed to the school of Andrea Pisano.

Opposite the entrance to the Baptistery, on the corner of Via de' Calzaioli, is the Loggia del Bigallo.

LOGGIA DEL BIGALLO

This small building and loggia were constructed during the mid-14th century for the Misericordia. It was probably designed by Alberto Arnoldi, the

head of the cathedral works. In 1425, it became the seat of the Confraternity of the Bigallo, a welfare institution founded by St Peter Martyr in 1244.

The Loggia consists of two large arches with wrought iron decorative work. The floor above has elegant mullioned windows with trefoiled arches and is decorated with 14th-century sculptures. The Confraternity put lost and abandoned children on display beneath the Loggia, in the hope that they might be reclaimed.

This small museum, which is only open during the Christmas festivities, contains Florentine paintings from the 13th to the 16th centuries. In the Sala dei Capitani is a most interesting detached fresco of the *Madonna della Misericordia* (1342) which has the oldest known view of Florence in the background.

Leaving the Loggia del Bigallo, we continue along the right side of the cathedral. On the opposite corner of Via de'

The Bigallo Loggia which houses the Bigallo Museum.

Bernardo Daddi, the Virgin Enthroned, *Bigallo Museum.*

Maestro del Bigallo, Crucifix.

The Cathedral, Baptistery and Bell Tower

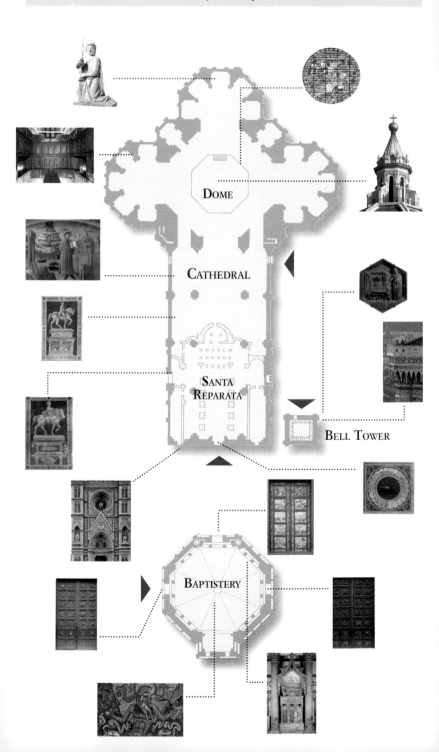

Niccolò Gerini and Ambrogio di Baldese, Charity, *fresco in the Bigallo Museum.*

Calzaioli *is the* Palazzo dell'Arciconfratèrnita della Misericordia, *(Brotherhood of Mercy), the seat of the religious institute founded by St Peter Martyr in 1244. The building was donated to them in 1576, restored by Alfonso Parigi in 1578 and then altered by Stefano Diletti in 1781. The palazzo houses the Brotherhood's important archive and a small museum with paintings, statues and liturgical items.*

Continuing along the right side of the square we come to Palazzo dei Canonici *(Canons' Palace), on the corner of Via dello Studio, designed by Gaetano Baccani (1792-1867); at the corner of Via dell'Oriuolo, at no. 10, is the 17th-century* Palazzo Strozzi di Mantova. *Immediately after, behind the cathedral, is the building which houses the Museo dell'Opera di Santa Maria del Fiore (Cathedral Museum).*

Museo dell'Opera di Santa Maria del Fiore

Better known as the museum of the Opera del Duomo, the institution created at the end of the 13th century to supervise the construction of the new cathedral. Housing works of art formerly located in the cathedral, baptistery and campanile, the museum was opened in 1891 in premises belonging to the Opera since the beginning of the 15th century. Representing all the most important periods in the history of Florentine art, the outstanding collection makes this one of the most important museums in Italy. The rooms were renovated and rearranged after the flood of 1966.

Courtyard and entrance. To the left in the courtyard are two Roman sarcophagi, dated 2nd-3rd century AD; these were situated on either side of the South Door of the Baptistery until the flood of 1966. On the right are large marble figures by Girolamo Ticciati (1676-1740), which once were part of the Baroque altar in the Baptistery. The ticket office is in the entrance hall and displayed here are a bust of *Filippo Brunelleschi* by Andrea Cavalcanti (1412-1462), and two 16th-century marble bas-reliefs (formerly located in the chancel of the cathedral), by Baccio Bandinelli and Giovanni Bandini. In the lunettes over the doors are two glazed polychrome terracottas, commissioned by the Opera from Andrea della Robbia. The first, representing *Eternity between two worshipping angels,* has a plain background and is by the workshop; the second representing the *Madonna and Child with two angels* (1489), has a scenic background and is by the artist himself.

Andrea Cavalcanti, bust of Brunelleschi.

Girolamo Ticciati, John the Baptist, *Museo dell'Opera del Duomo, courtyard.*

Monte di Giovanni, Adam and Eve, *illuminated initial in an antiphonal.*

Detail of a Roman sarcophagus dated 2nd-3rd century A.D.

Luca della Robbia, processional cross.

Michelangelo, Pietà.

Arnolfo di Cambio, Madonna and Child *(below right).*

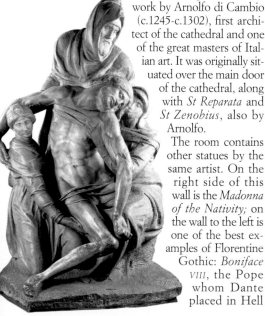

Salette brunelleschiane. From the entrance hall we enter two small rooms dedicated to Filippo Brunelleschi. Displayed here are the death mask of the artist, various wooden models and some tools and apparatus which illustrate the methods of construction used in the building of the dome.

Sala della Facciata. The next room is dedicated to the original façade of the cathedral. Displayed here are sculptures removed from the façade when it was demolished in 1587, and a 16th-century drawing by Bernardino Poccetti illustrating its original appearance. On the wall opposite the entrance, on the left, is a *Madonna and Child,* better known as the 'Madonna with the eyes of glass.' This highly articulate sculpture is a late work by Arnolfo di Cambio (c.1245-c.1302), first architect of the cathedral and one of the great masters of Italian art. It was originally situated over the main door of the cathedral, along with *St Reparata* and *St Zenobius,* also by Arnolfo.

The room contains other statues by the same artist. On the right side of this wall is the *Madonna of the Nativity;* on the wall to the left is one of the best examples of Florentine Gothic: *Boniface VIII,* the Pope whom Dante placed in Hell

as he had supported the Neri faction of the Guelph party. Among the monuments which later adorned the façade, the statues of *St Luke* by Nanni di Banco and *St John the Evangelist* by Donatello are of particular importance. Both these powerfully expressive sculptures date from the early 15th century and were placed in niches on either side of the main door.

Sala dei Corali. Displayed in this room are four splendid 16th-century *choir books.* In the other cases are various items of religious art. Of particular interest are the 16th-century *chasuble,* embroidered in gold, which belonged to Cardinal Alessandro Farnese; a *processional cross* in gold-plated copper decorated with blue enamel, attributed to Luca della Robbia; a *crosier,* a beautiful example of early 15th-century Florentine goldsmiths' work which belonged to the first archbishop of Florence, Amerigo Corsini.

Ottagono delle oreficerie. Next we enter the Octagon where beautiful examples of goldsmiths' work are dis-

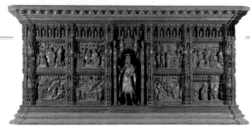

Andrea del Verrocchio and others, silver altar frontal with Stories of John the Baptist.

played, especially some splendid *reliquaries* dating from the 13th to 16th centuries.

Saletta della Pietà. Halfway up the stairs leading to the first floor is a small room containing Michelangelo's *Pietà* (1550-1555). Made in Rome many years after the *Pietà* in St Peter's, this was one of the great artist's last sculptures.

The marble group, which Michelangelo had actually intended for his own tomb, was brought to Florence in 1674 by Grand Duke Cosimo III. According to Giorgio Vasari, the figure of Nicodemus, bearing Christ, is a self-portrait. The drama of the work is emphasized by Michelangelo's famous *non finito* (unfinished) technique, leaving parts of the sculpture barely roughed out. The piece was finalized by a student, Tiberio Calcagni, who completed the figure of Mary Magdalen.

Sala delle Cantorie. Located on the first floor, this room houses the two beautiful marble choir galleries formerly situated above the sacristy doors in the cathedral, removed in 1688 on the occasion of the marriage of Ferdinando II. The *choir gallery* (1431-1438) by Luca della Robbia is on the entrance wall: inspired by Psalm 150 in the Psalms of David, the work expresses a serenely tranquil view of life and demonstrates fine delicacy in the treatment of feelings and emotions. On the opposite wall is the *choir gallery* (1433-1439) made by Donatello. The exquisite image of

cupids dancing and playing behind a row of columns, decorated with mosaic, strongly shows the influence of the style and motifs of classical antiquity which Donatello had studied during a trip to Rome with Filippo Brunelleschi.

Beneath the *choir stall* is another sculpture by Donatello, the *Mary Magdalen.* A later work by the artist, the strength and dramatic realism it conveys are impressive. The wooden statue was restored after the 1966 flood, returning it to its original colors.

Also housed in this room are the sixteen statues which were once in the niches of the second order of the campanile, now replaced with copies. As well as works made between 1342 and 1350 by Andrea Pisano and workshop (the *Tibertine Sibyl, David, Solomon,* the *Persian Sibyl,* and four *Prophets*), there are important statues by Donatello (including *Habakkuk*, nicknamed 'lo zuccone' or 'pumpkin head,' and *Jeremiah*) and by Nanni di Bartolo (*St John the Baptist* and *Abdia*).

Sala delle Formelle. Located to the left of the

Donatello, Saint John the Evangelist.

Luca della Robbia, Choir galleries. *Above, detail of the bas-reliefs.*

Lorenzo Ghiberti, panel on the 'Gate of Paradise' with Scenes from the Creation.

Donatello, Mary Magdalen.

Andrea Pisano, panels from Giotto's bell tower portraying the art of Weaving, Legislature *and* Navigation.

Sala delle Cantoric, the Bas-Relief Room houses the *panels* removed from Giotto's bell tower and replaced with copies between 1965 and 1967. They are displayed in their original sequence. Some of the hexagonal ones from the lower order (c.1348-1350) were made by Andrea Pisano to designs by Giotto, while the last five, representing the arts, sciences and industries (1437-1439), are by Luca della Robbia. The diamond-shaped panels from the upper order are by the school of Andrea Pisano (allegories of the planets, virtues and liberal arts), and by Alberto Arnoldi (the Holy Sacraments).

Sala dell'Altare. The entrance to the Altar Room is also from the Sala delle Cantorie. Displayed here, as well as Ghiberti's bronze panels removed from the Gates of Paradise, is a magnificent silver altar frontal which also came from the Baptistery. In a large case in the centre of the room are four of Ghiberti's gilded bronze panels (*Story of Joseph, Story of David, Cain and Abel,* and *The Creation*). Recent restoration has returned these magnificent works to their original splendor. Applying the very finest gold leaf, the artist succeeded in achieving both depth and a pictorial quality.

On the walls are 14th- and 15th-century panel paintings from the Tuscan school, and a series of twenty-seven silk panels embroidered in gold: these decorated the liturgical vestments, known as "St John's," with *Stories of St John the Baptist and Christ.* The panels, designed by Antonio del Pollaiolo, were made by Florentine, French and Flemish embroiderers between 1466 and 1480, and were recently restored.

Also in this room are several attractive sculptures by the Sienese artist Tino di Camaino (such as the bust of a *Woman with Cornucopia*), and Andrea Pisano (a statuette representing *St Reparata and Christ Blessing*).

At the far end of the room is the *silver altar frontal*, originally in the Baptistery and a magnificent example of the skills of the city's gold and silversmiths. Commissioned by the Calimala Guild, who paid

the vast sum of 40,000 florins for the piece, it was begun in 1366 and completed in 1480. It was displayed over the font in the centre of the Baptistery twice a year, to celebrate the week of Epiphany and for the feast day of St John the Baptist on June 24. The altar frontal consists of twelve panels in silver and enamel representing *Scenes from the Life of John the Baptist*. Many of the most important artists of the day worked on it at one time or another, including Andrea del Verrocchio, Antonio del Pollaiolo, Bernardo Cennini and Michelozzo, who made the small statue of the saint in the centre. On top of the altar is a richly decorated *Cross* (1457-1459) made of laminated silver and enamel, by Antonio del Pollaiolo, Betto di Francesco and Bernardo Cennini. Preserved inside is a piece of wood from the True Cross, brought from Constantinople in 1545.

Turning to the right out of the museum, we continue around the cathedral. At no. 28 is Palazzo Nicolini, *originally Palazzo Nardini del Riccio, built during the 17th century on the site of Donatello's house. Facing the cathedral between Via de' Servi and Via Ricasoli are several old houses; no. 5 and no. 7 (the* Casa dell'Opera di San Giovanni*) are both*

15th-century. The statue of the saint over the doorway of the latter is a copy of the original by Michelozzo, now in the Bargello Museum.

We cross the piazza at the junction with Via Martelli, keeping to the north side of the Baptistery. Close to the north door, crowned by a cross, is the Column of St Zenobius, *a bishop of Florence in the 5th century. Erected in 1384, it commemorates a miracle reputed to have taken place when the saint's remains were moved from San Lorenzo to Santa Reparata. Legend has it that a dead elm tree on this spot spontaneously broke into full leaf as his body was carried by it.*

Behind the apse of the Baptistery, between Via Cerretani and Via de' Pecori, is the immense structure of the Archbishop's Palace. *Originally built during the Middle Ages, it was partially rebuilt by Giovanni Antonio Dosio in the 16th century. The façade was moved back in 1895 to enlarge Piazza San Giovanni. Incorporated into the back of the palace which faces onto the long and narrow Piazza dell'Olio, is the little Romanesque church of* San Salvatore al Vescovo *(10th century). The attractive façade is original but the interior, closed to the public, was heavily altered in the 18th century.*

Luca della Robbia, detail of the Choir gallery.

14th-century Byzantine art, mosaic panel.

Centre, Donatello, Habakkuk *(nicknamed 'Zuccone'); below, façade of the church of San Salvatore al Vescovo.*

The origins of the Renaissance -3-

Donatello (1386-1466)
"For these Florentine masters of the beginning of the fifteenth century were no longer content to repeat the old formulae handed down by medieval artists. Like the Greeks and Romans, whom they admired, they began to study the human body in their studios and workshops by asking models or fellow-artists to pose for them in the required attitudes. It is this new method and this new interest which makes Donatello's work look so strikingly convincing". (E. Gombrich)

With Donatello, sculpture discovers a dramatic and realistic style which becomes most obvious when compared with the solemn Gothic statues aligned around the exteriors of the great cathedrals. Of humble origins, the artist learned his craft in the workshops during the late 14th century and was one of Ghiberti's assistants in making the bronze reliefs for the Baptistery doors (1404-1407). He introduced the atmosphere and images of working-class Florence to the figurative arts of his day, representing human emotions and situations with startling effectiveness. He always remained a man of the people, even when, as a respected artist, he worked for Cosimo the Elder. A contemporary of his, Vespasiano da Bisticci, relates the following story: "Since Donatello did not dress as Cosimo thought suitable, Cosimo gave him a red cloak and hood and had a coat made for under the cloak, dressing him as new from head to foot. He sent them to him one feast day so that he could wear them. He only wore them once or twice and then put them away, not wanting to wear them again and saying that they were too fine for him".

David.

St John the Evangelist (1404-1414). The statue was originally located alongside those of Arnolfo di Cambio and Nanni di Banco on the old Gothic façade of Santa Maria del Fiore, demolished in 1587. Despite the clearly Gothic style, the realistic and humane elements are more pronounced in Donatello's work.

St George. Commissioned from Donatello in 1416 by the Armourers Guild for the church of Orsanmichele. "Donatello's *St George* stands firmly on the ground, his feet planted resolutely on the earth as if he were determined not to yield an inch. His face has none of the vague and serene beauty of medieval saints — it is all energy and concentration. He seems to watch the approach of the enemy and to take its measure, his hands resting on his shield, his whole attitude tense with defiant determination". (E. Gombrich)

The choir gallery (1433-1439). The problem of mathematical perspective was developed by Donatello with these figures in flattened relief, where depth is projected onto the slender slab of marble. "Donatello seems to have set himself a difficult task in trying to transmit the impression of real movement to the dance of his putti. They are not moving in only one direction, for while the figures in the foreground are clearly going from right to left, those behind are running in the opposite direction. A fray of chubby arms and legs fills the entire space". (C. Avery)

Mary Magdalen (1453-1455). "At first sight the image is terrifying. The wrinkled face and sunken eyes, the skinny limbs covered with dark, leathery skin, resemble an Egyptian mummy. But for a Christian, the message is not pessimistic: it is through the consumption and hardship to which Mary Magdalen has deliberately subjected her body, which originally was an object of desire, that her spirit is strengthened and ennobled". (C. Avery)

The "Scoppio del Carro"

While the traditional tournament of Florentine football (☞ p. 136) suffered a lengthy interruption and has undergone considerable changes, the explosion of the cart, celebrated on Easter Saturday, has remained largely unchanged.

"The little 'dove' arrives, hits the side of the cart, pauses a moment, then moves back again rapidly, flying towards the high altar. 'Its flying to the altar like a bride!' cry the countryfolk. There is a thud... The cart disappears amidst a thick, white smoke which slowly rises into the air. 'Hurray! The harvest will be the best ever!'" Thus in the 1870|s, Yorick, a noted journalist and humourist, described a |flight| of the dove-shaped rocket along a wire, straight down the central aisle of the cathedral, to ignite the |cart| in front of the Baptistery. The behaviour of the |dove| - zealous, sluggish or even a failure - was considered to be an omen for the harvest and from the early hours of the morning, labourers from the surrounding countryside crowded into the piazza along with the Florentines. The tradition begins with a certain Pazzino del Pazzi, a crusader who is reputed to have been the first to climb the walls of Jerusalem to liberate the Holy Sepulchre. He was rewarded with three splinters from the stone of the walls and these he carried back to Florence. On Easter Saturday a spark was

drawn from the stone to light a fire which was carried in procession to Santa Maria del Fiore. The 14th-century historian, Giovanni Villani recounts that, "The Florentines ordered that this holy fire should be spread throughout the city. As the centuries passed, the 'holy fire', originally simply a large torch, developed into a "festive cart, such as was used in those times," wrote Giuseppe Conti, "all gilded with various figures and carvings cleverly and expertly arranged, decked out with fancy fireworks, bangers, Catherine wheels and the very biggest and best of rockets". In 1679, the cart collapsed of old age while it was being pulled to the cathedral by two pairs of white oxen suitably adorned, as still occurs today. The present cart was built at the expense of the Pazzi family in 1765 and consists of three levels: painted on the first are the coats of arms of the various districts of the city; the second displays the Pazzi coat of arms and the third is decorated with gilded masks.

In Florence the ceremony of the 'new fire' was transformed into a spectacular event during the Renaissance when triumphs and feasts came into fashion and, until the 17th century, the cart still carried a brazier from which coals were distributed to the population and used as a talisman against hail and lightning.

The origins of the Renaissance -1-

"The Italians of the fourteenth century believed that art, science and scholarship had flourished in the classical period, that all these things had been almost destroyed by the northern barbarians and that it was for them to help to revive the glorious past and thus bring about a new era. In no city was this feeling of confidence and hope more intense than in the wealthy merchant city of Florence, the city of Dante and of Giotto. It was there, in the first decades of the fifteenth century, that a group of artists deliberately set out to create a new art and to break with the ideas of the past". (E.H. Gombrich)

Filippo Brunelleschi (1377-1436)

Vasari began his account of the life of Filippo Brunelleschi thus: "There are many men whom nature has made small and insignificant, but who are so fiercely consumed by emotion and ambition that they know no peace unless they are grappling with difficult or indeed almost impossible tasks and achieving astonishing results".

It was by studying the techniques used in the buildings of ancient Rome when he visited the city with Donatello, that Brunelleschi succeeded in resolving apparently impossible problems such as the construction of a self-supporting dome as vast as that of Santa Maria del Fiore (☞ p. 26). It was he who gave shape and form to the sprawling clutter of medieval Florence, reforming, without destroying, areas and buildings and creating the image of the Renaissance city. His knowledge was founded on an awareness of the laws which objectively govern the vision of space, beyond one's individual perception. Through experimentation, Brunelleschi formulated a method of mathematical perspective, the first to conceive architectural space as the result of precise mathematical relationships between the various elements of the buildings. It is from precisely this concept of space that the unmistakable purity of his style derives.

The portico of the Spedale degli Innocenti. Begun in 1419. Here Brunelleschi reorganized the space in front of the church of Santissima Annunziata, drawing his inspiration both from the porticoed square of antiquity and from 14th-century Florentine loggias.

Sacrestia Vecchia, San Lorenzo (1419-1428). "A perfectly square hall with a dome above: four plain panels on which the sense of space, external and internal, is represented proportionally: four large arches represent the horizon; rising above these is the curve of the dome, which repeats the contours of the four perpendicular spaces in a circular contour" (G.C. Argan).

The Pazzi chapel
Commissioned by Andrea Pazzi, work on the chapel was begun between 1429 and 1430. "We see at once that it has little in common with any classical temple, but even less with the forms used by Gothic builders. Brunelleschi has combined columns, pilasters and arches in his own way to achieve an effect of lightness and grace which is different from anything that had gone before" (E.Gombrich).

2. The Area of San Lorenzo

This itinerary around the north-western part of the historic centre covers an area which once lay outside the city limits, incorporated only when the commune of Florence constructed its first ring of defensive walls (1173-1175). San Lorenzo – the first Christian church on the north side of the Arno – was built here during the 4th century, and remained the city's cathedral until the 8th century. The name of the street that we take from Piazza del Duomo, 'Borgo' San Lorenzo, is an indication of its original position outside the walls. In fact, before the city limits encompassed a larger area, the name *borgo* referred to the shanty-towns which proliferated along the roads leading into the city and at the gates. In the 13th century, mendicant orders such as the Dominicans, Franciscans, Augustinians, Carmelites and Servites established them-

Michelangelo, Day.
San Lorenzo, New Sacristy.

FLORENTIAE·CIVITAS

Detail of the Florentine coat of arms in semi-precious stone. San Lorenzo, Chapel of the Princes.

selves here. Unlike the Benedictines who preferred solitude, these orders chose to work within the community, especially in the poorer, more densely-populated areas, "to give help to the unfortunate and, at the same time, see to their religious education" (F. Cardini). In doing so, they hoped to counter the effect of heretical movements which, during the 12th century, had gained considerable influence here.

A billowing sail, symbol of good fortune and the emblem of Giovanni Rucellai. Façade of Santa Maria Novella.

In the 15th and 16th centuries, these 'new' areas became, along with San Marco, the heart of Medicean Florence. Cosimo the Elder, and later Lorenzo the Magnificent, gradually deprived the old republican aristocracy of its power, at the same time indirectly altering the importance of certain areas of the city. As symbols of medieval and republican Florence, the Duomo and Palazzo Vecchio diminished in importance, while San Lorenzo, which had become the Medici family church, and Palazzo Medici-Riccardi on Via Larga (*today's Via Cavour:* ☞ *pp. 72-73*), the real seat of political power in the 15th century, became more prominent.

Under the patronage of the Medici and their allies the Rucellai family, the greatest artists of the day – from Brunelleschi to Masaccio, from Paolo Uccello to Leon Battista Alberti and Michelangelo – worked on the churches of San Lorenzo and Santa Maria Novella, creating some of their most magnificent works of art.

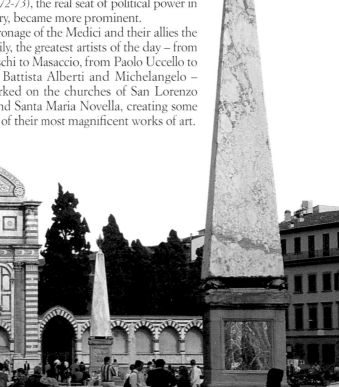

The lively market of San Lorenzo.

Bacio Bandinelli, monument to Giovanni dalle Bande Nere. Right, detail of the base with battle scenes.

Leaving Piazza San Giovanni, we cross over to Borgo San Lorenzo: here begins the lively street market that occupies much of the surrounding area. At the end of this short, busy street is Piazza San Lorenzo.

PIAZZA SAN LORENZO

This square not only represents some of the most characteristic and colourful aspects of Florentine life, it is also one of the most interesting historically and architecturally.

At no. 6, facing the church of San Lorenzo, is the *Ximenes Observatory*, founded as an astronomical observatory by the Jesuit Father Leonardo Ximenes in 1755, and today an important meteorological and seismological centre. The observatory, which houses two important libraries, is located in a monastery which originally belonged to the Jesuits, though it later became a charity school run by Piarist monks.

2. The area of San Lorenzo

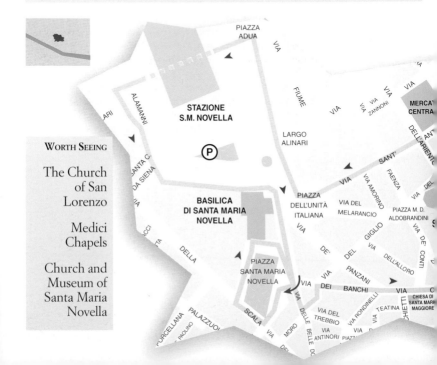

The harmonious interior of the church of San Lorenzo, designed by Filippo Brunelleschi.

Further ahead, at the corner of Via Ginori and Via de' Gori, surrounded by market stalls, is a statue by Baccio Bandinelli of *Giovanni dalle Bande Nere* (1540), a mercenary soldier and the father of Cosimo I de' Medici. Around the pedestal are bas-reliefs of battle scenes.

On the north-east side of the piazza, where one of the most characteristic and animated areas of Florence begins, are several 15th- and 16th-century buildings. One of the most striking is *Palazzo Lotteringhi della Stufa*, with its large, colonnaded roof terrace and the family coat of arms sculpted in *pietra serena* on the façade.

Church of San Lorenzo

This is the second most important church in Florence after the cathedral. Consecrated in 393 by St Ambrose, Bishop of Milan, it was Florence's cathedral until the 8th century. Rebuilt in Romanesque style, it was reconsecrated in 1059.

From the early 15th century onwards, the Medici family had the church entirely rebuilt, and today nothing remains of the earlier structure. The history of the church was thereafter closely linked to both that of the Medici family and the city's political fortunes.

After 1418, the wealthiest families of San Lorenzo, primarily the Medici, assumed the expense of renovating the church. Giovanni di Bicci de' Medici, father of Cosimo the Elder, financed the building of a sacristy and a chapel. The project was entrusted to Filippo Brunelleschi, who had recently presented his plan for the dome of Santa Maria del Fiore. Filippo completed his design for the sacristy in 1421, the year in which Giovanni di Bicci, who had run a prosperous trading business since 1397, was elected *gon-*

View of Piazza San Lorenzo. In the centre is Palazzo Lotteringhi della Stufa (15th-16th century).

The exterior of San Lorenzo. Although various plans were drawn up (including one by Michelangelo), the façade was never decorated.

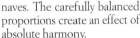

Domenico Ghirlandaio,
Saint Antony with
Saints Lawrence and
Julian.

Michelangelo,
wooden model for
the façade of San
Lorenzo, Casa
Buonarroti.

faloniere (a high ranking city official). Upon his father's death in 1429, Cosimo became head of the family and assumed complete responsibility for the building of the church. The work continued somewhat slowly, not only because Brunelleschi was working on the Cathedral dome but also because in 1444, Cosimo initiated the building of his palazzo on Via Larga (now Via Cavour). On Brunelleschi's death in 1446, the project was taken over by Antonio Manetti the Younger, who completed the interior in 1461. The façade remained undecorated however, and although various designs were proposed, including one commissioned by Pope Leo X from Michelangelo (the wooden model of which is in the Buonarroti Museum), none was ever realized. During the next century, the fortunes of the church became ever more closely bound to those of the Medici family, who transformed it into a grandiose family mausoleum and commissioned Michelangelo to construct the New Sacristy and the Laurentian Library.

Interior. Brunelleschi based his design on Florentine Gothic churches with three aisles and chapels on both sides of the transept. Departing from this model, however, he highlighted the horizontal lines by making a flat caisson ceiling over the central nave, with a corresponding straight entablature along the top of the arches which separate the

Rosso Fiorentino,
The Betrothal of the
Virgin.

Filippo Lippi,
Annunciation
(Martelli chapel).

naves. The carefully balanced proportions create an effect of absolute harmony.

The church houses a wealth of extremely important works of art. In the second chapel of the right nave is the *Marriage of the Virgin* (1523), by Rosso Fiorentino, one of the early Florentine mannerist artists "so richly inventive," wrote Vasari, "that in his pictures he never left any space over, and he carried out everything with so much grace and facility that it was a marvel".

Between the last chapel and the right transept is a *marble tabernacle* (mid-15th century), by Desiderio da Settignano.

Beneath the last two arches of the central nave are two *pulpits*. These were Donatello's last works and were finished by his pupils, Bertoldo di Giovanni and Bartolomeo Bellano.

The *high altar* (1787) was made by the Opificio delle Pietre Dure, to a design by Gaspare Maria Paoletti.

In the first chapel on the left of the transept is a *Madonna and Child,* a late 14th-century wooden sculpture attributed to Giovanni Fetti.

In the second chapel is an

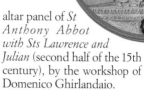

altar panel of *St Anthony Abbot with Sts Lawrence and Julian* (second half of the 15th century), by the workshop of Domenico Ghirlandaio.

Old Sacristy. The entrance to the Sacrestia Vecchia, built by Brunelleschi between 1421 and 1426, is from the left transept. The structure consists of a perfect cube, topped by a dome formed of segments outlined by *pietra serena* ribs, and ending in an apse with the same structure. It is a masterpiece of the early Florentine Renaissance in which, for the first time, the artist achieves his ideal of perfectly geometrical architecture. All the various elements are separated in precise and harmonious proportion to each other, including minor details such as doors and windows "which become an integral part of the composition, while introducing the human element" (A. Chastel).

The fine *bas-reliefs* (1443-1444) which decorate the sacristy are by Donatello, who was also responsible for: the frieze of cherubs and seraphim around the walls; the bronze doors and the lunettes above with *Sts Cosmas and Damian* (the patron saints of the Medici), on the right and *Sts Lawrence and Steven* on the left; the four tondi of the *Evangelists* on the walls; and the *Scenes from the Life of St John the Evangelist* in the pendentives.

The bust of *St Lawrence* to the right of the entrance, previously believed to be by Donatello, is now attributed to Desiderio da Settignano.

In the centre, beneath a marble tablet, are the tombs (1434) of *Giovanni di Bicci de' Medici* and his wife, *Piccarda Bueri*, by Andrea Cavalcanti.

On the left, made of porphyry and bronze engraved by Verrocchio, is the elegant *funereal monument* (1472) *to Piero and Giovanni de' Medici*, sons of Cosimo the Elder.

Represented on the ceiling of the apse is the passage of the sun between the constellations. Astronomers have deduced that it shows the sky above Florence on the night of July 4, 1442, proof of Cosimo's interest in astrology.

Returning to the church, in the Martelli Chapel (the last in the left aisle before the transept) is a lovely altar panel of the *Annunciation* (mid-15th century), by Filippo Lippi.

In the last bay of the left aisle is a fresco of the *Martyrdom of St Lawrence* (1565-1569), by Agnolo Bronzino. *To the left of the front of the church is the entrance to the cloisters. In the far corner is a*

Old Sacristy, interior.

Donatello, tondo with a bas-relief of the Martyrdom of Saint John the Evangelist *in the Old Sacristy.*

Tondos in the cornice, attributed to Donatello.

The cloister of San Lorenzo (right) and the monumental stairway in the Laurentian library.

monument (1560) to Paolo Giovio, *Bishop of Como, by Francesco da Sangallo.*

From the cloisters we enter the Laurentian Library.

LAURENTIAN LIBRARY

The Biblioteca Medicea Laurenziana was founded by Cosimo the Elder, a great bibliophile, and was enlarged by his son Piero and later also by Lorenzo the Magnificent. It houses one of the most important Italian collections of manuscripts. When the Medici were banished from Florence in 1494, the library was saved by the Dominican monks of San Marco, who moved it to their monastery. In 1508, Cardinal Giovanni de' Medici, later Pope Leo X, acquired it and moved it to Rome. It was returned to Florence in 1523 by another Medici pope, Clement VII, who commissioned Michelangelo to design and build suitable housing for it. Work was begun in 1524 and the project was finished by Bartolomeo Ammannati and Giorgio Vasari, who completed it according to the original plan.

The Church of San Lorenzo

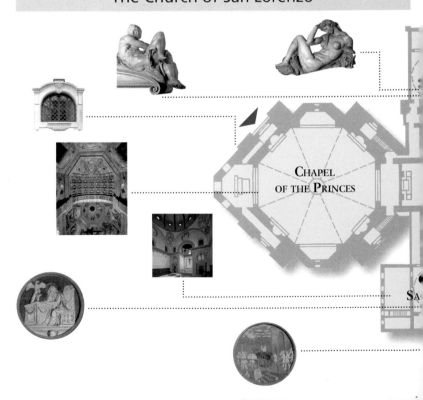

CHAPEL OF THE PRINCES

SA

Interior of the Laurentian Library. Founded by Cosimo the Elder, many rare manuscripts are housed here.

In the vestibule is the highly original staircase, formed of three separate flights, built by Bartolomeo Ammannati to Michelangelo's design. This leads into the reading room. The atmosphere of imposing solemnity here is created by the simple, linear style of decoration intended to facilitate concentration and study. The splendid, carved wood *ceiling* (1549-1550) is by Giovanni Battista del Tasso and Antonio Carota, while the terracotta floor (which repeats the ceiling's motifs)

was made to a design by Tribolo between 1549 and 1554 by Santi Buglioni, the last representative of the Della Robbia workshop. The twenty-eight desks and chairs are by Ciapino and Battista del Cinque.

Leaving the cloister, we cross the square and follow the right side of the church, then bearing left into Via del Canto de' Nelli, until we reach Piazza Madonna degli Aldobrandini. The entrance to the Medici Chapels is here from the apse of the church.

Below, Laurentian codex with a portrait of Lorenzo il Magnifico in the margin and the Medici coat of arms below.

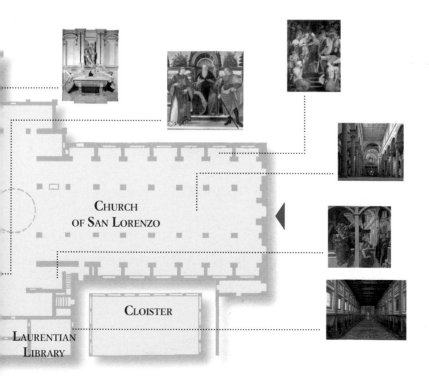

CHURCH OF SAN LORENZO

CLOISTER

LAURENTIAN LIBRARY

Michelangelo, the tomb of Lorenzo, duke of Urbino.

View of the Chapel of the Princes from Piazza Madonna degli Aldobrandini, where the entrance is. Above, the vault, frescoed in the early 19th century.

MEDICI CHAPELS

The Medici Chapels include the Chapel of the Princes (Cappella dei Prìncipi) – the mausoleum of the Medici family – and Michelangelo's New Sacristy.

Chapel of the Princes. Cosimo I conceived the idea of this self-glorifying monument to the Medici dynasty after the defeat of Siena (1555) and the establishment of the Grand Duchy of Tuscany. The building, designed by architect Matteo Nigetti, was initiated by Ferdinando I. Work on this rare example of Florentine Baroque was begun in 1605, and completed in 1640 with the imposing roof resembling the dome of Santa Maria del Fiore.

The visit begins in the large *crypt,* made in 1508 to a design by Buontalenti. Beneath the low ceilinged, ribbed vault are the tombs of the Grand Dukes of the Medici and Lorraine dynasties. Under the crypt, in an area closed to the public, are the *tombs of Cosimo the Elder and Donatello.*

A stairway on the right leads up to the chapel itself. The large, octagonal room completely occupies the dome, frescoed in 1828 by Pietro Benvenuti with *Stories from the Old and New Testaments*, *Evangelists* and *Prophets.*

The walls are entirely decorated with precious stone and marble like some magnificent funerary mantle. The decoration was carried out by the Opificio delle Pietre Dure, founded in 1588 for this very purpose. This is the greatest example of the skill and expertise of the Opificio, which worked on the chapel for more than three centuries. The cladding and inlay of the walls was carried out during the 17th and 18th centuries, the altar was assembled in 1939 using panels of various periods, and the mosaic pavement, also in semi-precious stone, was begun in 1874 and finished in 1962.

Around the walls are the *coats of arms* of the sixteen cities which formed the Tuscan Grand Duchy. These elegant mosaics in lapis lazuli, mother-of-pearl and coral, were made in the 17th century.

In the niches above the sarcophagi are a gilded bronze statue of *Ferdinando I* (1626-1632) by Pietro Tacca, and a partially gilded statue of *Cosimo II* (1626-c.1642), by Pietro and Ferdinando Tacca.

Behind the altar are the Reliquary and Treasury Chapels. These house a collection of precious reliquaries and religious items dating from the 15th to the 18th centuries. To the left of the altar is a particularly beautiful *crosier* (1520) in gilded silver, donated to the church by Leo X.

New Sacristy. A narrow corridor leads from the Chapel of the Princes to Michelangelo's Sacrestia Nuova. Although the name distinguishes it from Brunelleschi's Old Sacristy, it is in reality the

Michelangelo, Night *(right). The sculpture, with the figure of* Day, *decorates the tomb of Giuliano de' Medici, duke of Nemours (below).*

mausoleum of Lorenzo the Magnificent's family.

Michelangelo repeated Brunelleschi's square-shaped plan with a dome, but in emphasizing the effect of light and dark and by playing on the contrast between the white of the marble and the dark grey stone of the ribs, he created an atmosphere of powerful solemnity. The large marble statues which dominate the chamber exude the same melancholy.

Commissioned by Leo X, Michelangelo began working on the sacristy in 1520. In 1527, however, the Medici were ousted from Florence and the Republic was restored: the artist interrupted work on the building to reinforce the city's defensive walls in anticipation of a siege by the army of Charles V. Upon the return of the Medici in 1531, Michelangelo resumed work on the sacristy, continuing until 1534 when he left for Rome. In the 1550's, Giorgio Vasari and Bartolomeo Ammannati completed the interior, arranging the statues as they remain today.

To the right of the entrance is the unfinished *tomb of Lorenzo the Magnificent and his brother Giuliano,* who was assassinated as a result of the Pazzi Conspiracy in 1478. On top of this simple tomb is a delicately sculpted and

most moving *Madonna and Child,* made by Michelangelo in 1521. On the two sides are saints *Cosmas* (1537) and *Damian* (1531). The former was sculpted by Giovanni Angelo Montorsoli, the latter by Raffaello da Montelupo, both pupils of Michelangelo.

Also on the right wall is the *tomb of Giuliano, Duke of Nemours,* son of Lorenzo the Magnificent (d.1516), dressed in a suit of armour. On the sarcophagus are statues of *Day* on the right, and *Night* on the left. The meaning of the allegory was explained by Michelangelo himself as follows: "Night and Day are speaking and saying, 'We have with our swift course brought the Duke Giuliano to death; it is therefore just that he take vengeance upon us as he does, and the vengeance is this: that we having slain him, he thus dead has taken the light from us and with closed eyes has fastened ours so that they may shine forth no more upon the earth. What

The arms of the city of Florence in semiprecious stone inlay, Chapel of the Princes.

Below, the Chapel of the Princes; on the left, Virgin and Child *by Michelangelo.*

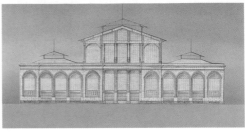

Plan of the central market. Reconstruction of a period drawing (1874).

Food stalls (on the ground floor) and fruit and vegetable stalls (on the first floor) inside the central market.

would he have done with us then while he lived?'"

On the opposite wall is the tomb of *Lorenzo, Duke of Urbino*, nephew of Lorenzo the Magnificent, represented as a pensive warrior. Beneath are statues of *Dawn* (1531) and *Dusk* (1531-1532).

On the altar are two marble candelabra and an elegant bronze *Crucifix*, attributed to Giambologna.

From the Medici Chapels we return to Via del Canto de' Nelli and turn left into Via dell'Ariento. Passing the stalls where clothing and leather goods are sold, we arrive at the Central Market.

CENTRAL MARKET

The Mercato Centrale was the largest structure made of steel and glass to be built in Florence during the late 19th century. Inside, a series of wide aisles outlines a network of right-angled 'alley-ways' where a thriving food market is still held. (Bread, meat, fish, cooked meats, cheese and milk are on the ground floor, while fruit and

vegetables are sold on the upper floor.) It was built as part of a campaign to improve the hygiene of the working class areas of the city, which were frequently afflicted by contagious diseases and tuberculosis.

Facing the entrance to the market is Via Sant'Antonino, a narrow and lively little street with brightly-coloured shops and some interesting palazzi. At no. 11, after the junction with Via Faenza (which leads to the medieval Porta Faenza and now ends at the 16th-century Fortezza da Basso: (☞ p. 246), is the curious Palazzo dei Cartelloni (placards) built by Giovan Battista Nelli at the end of the 16th century for the mathematician and student of Galileo, Vincenzo Viviani. Its name is derived from the two large marble inscriptions which cover much of the façade.

Via Sant'Antonino leads to Piazza dell'Unità, *where there are two large hotels and* Palazzo Cerretani *on the right. In the middle of the square is an obelisk, erected in 1882 in memory of those who fell in the Italian War of Independence.*

Opposite, across Via Panzani and Via degli Avelli, the apse and bell-tower of the church of Santa Maria Novella can be seen. Until the 13th century, the axis of the church was east-west and thus it originally faced today's Piazza dell'Unità.

Florentine cookery-1-

Strange but true, the renowned *bistecca alla fiorentina* is English. Firstly, the word *bistecca* is a corruption of 'beefsteak'; secondly, both the cut and the way of cooking this 'beef chop' came from beyond the English Channel. The steak is "in keeping with the new world of the 18th century, with the philosophy of the Enlightenment, with the increasing use of coal as a source of energy, with the demise of the cuisine of Renaissance and Baroque courts, with free thinkers, with the birth of aristocratic tourism" (M.C. Salemi). Even though today it is considered to be one of the most typical local dishes, it is in fact, both a recent and an imported tradition. The truth is that in Florence, steak was originally cooked *by* the Florentines *for* the English tourists. Nor should it come as such a surprise, given that cuisine, like all aspects of culture, is characterized by continual evolution, abandoning old habits and tastes. It is therefore difficult to define and itemize 'traditional Florentine cuisine'. Its one outstanding feature is, perhaps, simplicity and sobriety, though according to period and social class, even this is a fairly generalized description. Expensive cuts of meat are not much used; rather the more humble parts, tastily and imaginatively enhanced by the dictates of poverty. In the past, one could even eat fish and eels from the Arno and frogs from the streams. Vegetables and beans were eaten in such quantity that Florentines were nicknamed 'bean-eaters,'

and carefully-tended vegetable gardens prospered both inside the city walls and in the surrounding countryside. The close relationship between town and country was exemplified in the case of wine. Aged in barrels in villas on the hillsides, it was then brought to the cellars of the palazzi where the owners lived in the city. It was sold to the public in flasks, from characteristic little windows made in the imposing façades of noble residences during the 16th century: one can still be seen in Palazzo Bartolini Salimbeni Vivai, on Via del Giglio, in the form of a miniature, rusticated doorway; and another, close to the junction of Via della Spada and Via delle Belle Donne, still even has the opening hours engraved in marble. Some of the taverns won lasting fame: the one run by the Bertucce family was already long-established at the time of Lorenzo the Magnificent. Many had picturesque names: the *Fico* (Fig) the *Porco* (Pig), the *Malvasìa* (Malmsey wine), the *Vinegia* (Grape vine). Food was also available from stall holders who sold *castagnaccio*, baked apples and pears and even, in the Piazza della Signoria of the 19th century, maccheroni with cheese and pepper. Bread rolls filled with tripe and other offal can still be bought today from stalls in the city centre. Now becoming a rarity on the other hand, are the fried-food shops, once found in the streets of working class areas.

'Old-fashioned' fast-food consisted of fried polenta, rice fritters, chickpea pies, *castagnaccio* (a cake made from chestnut flour, flavoured with rosemary leaves and sprinkled with pine-nuts and raisins) and *coccoli* (plain salted fritters, made from bread dough).

The busy, narrow street of Sant'Antonino, linking the areas of San Lorenzo and Santa Maria Novella.

Market stall in San Lorenzo.

Palazzo 'dei Cartelloni' (Placards) (Giovan Battista Nelli, 17th century) in Via Sant'Antonino.

THE STATION OF SANTA MARIA NOVELLA

To the right of Piazza dell'Unità is the extensive square of the Santa Maria Novella railway station — one of the most important examples of rationalist architecture in Italy. It was built between 1933 and 1935 to a design by the *Gruppo Toscano*, headed by Giovanni Michelucci.

Extremely simple in style with pure lines, it is attractively faced with *pietra forte*, in clear contrast to the architectural fabric of the old part of the city, generally built in *pietra serena*. Indeed, as the writer Emilio Cecchi maintained, the station represents "an intelligent architectural statement" which, without conceding any stylistic compromises, has achieved a form which comfortably introduces a modern dimension to the city of the Renaissance.

Highlighting the interior is a series of vertical glass panels which start opposite the apse of Santa Maria Novella, continue upwards and then across the ticket hall, and finally descend to end at the platform roofing. Considerable attention was given to the internal, decorative detail: the benches, drinking fountains and baggage racks attached to the columns were all made in bronze.

Crossing Piazza dell'Unità towards the apse of the church of Santa Maria Novella, we then turn left along Via degli Avelli (the 'avelli' are the tombs along the right side of the church) leading into Piazza Santa Maria Novella.

PIAZZA SANTA MARIA NOVELLA

One of the loveliest squares in the city, Piazza Santa Maria Novella came into being during the last decade of the 13th century, when the city council demolished a rather squalid group of buildings in order to clear space in front of the church then under construction.

The piazza took on its present appearance in the 1930's, when the paving was lifted and the central fountain and triangular beds of grass were put in. Supported by Giambologna's bronze tortoises, the marble obelisks were erected in 1608 as boundary markers for horse and carriage races instituted by Cosimo I in 1563.

Giovanni Michelucci and others, the station of Santa Maria Novella (1933-1935).

The apse of the church of Santa Maria Novella seen from the station (left). Below, a view of the façade of the church.

On the south side of the square is the 15th-century *loggia* of the former San Paolo Hospital, founded in the 13th century. Suppressed by Grand Duke Pietro Leopoldo in 1780, it subsequently became a Leopoldine school for teaching young boys a craft or skill. Between the arches are glazed terracotta medallions by Andrea della Robbia (second half of the 15th century).

At the corner of the piazza with Via della Scala is a large tabernacle with a copy of a *Madonna and Child with Saints*, by Francesco d'Antonio (14th-15th century).

Deviating very slightly along Via della Scala, at no. 16 we find the famous Santa Maria Novella *Officina profumo-farmaceutica* (perfumery and pharmacy) founded by the Dominican monks of the church in 1612. In 1866, the pharmacy passed to the state and was taken over by Cesare Augusto Stefani, nephew of the last pharmacist monk, Damiano Beni. Since then, Stefani's descendants have continued making their soaps, lotions and perfumes to the original recipes of the monks.

CHURCH OF SANTA MARIA NOVELLA

When the Dominican monks came to Florence in 1219,

they took over the little church then known as Santa Maria delle Vigne ('in the Vineyard') for its rural surroundings. From 1278 onwards, they began to convert the original structure into the present monastery and church of Santa Maria Novella. The building of the monastery complex – the largest in the city – was initially undertaken by two Dominican architects, Fra' Sisto and Fra' Ristoro. Later directed by their fellow monks, Fra' Jacopo Talenti and Fra' Giovanni da Campi, work was completed during the mid-14th century.

Façade. When the church was consecrated in 1420 by Pope Martin V, only the façade had yet to be completed. In 1458, Giovanni di Paolo Rucellai commissioned Leon Battista Alberti to finish the job. Alberti made use of the existing Gothic elements of the 14th-century façade, and succeeded in creating a harmonious Renaissance style. By carefully respecting the proportions of the various sections of the façade and by continuing the original use of coloured marble (white and dark green) typical of Tuscan Romanesque architecture, old and new were successfully blended together. Alberti re-

The perfumery and pharmacy of Santa Maria Novella in Via della Scala.

The main door of the church of Santa Maria Novella, in typically Renaissance style.

The tympanum of the church, decorated with a radiant sun, symbol of the Dominicans.

Detail of the stained glass in the apse.

The volute on the right side of the façade of Santa Maria Novella. Invented by Alberti, this architectural feature was widely used for many centuries.

worked mainly the upper part of the façade, framing the existing circular window in a tripartite design, divided vertically by striped pilaster strips. To disguise the roof there is an up-turned volute on each side, an original motif which was frequently imitated throughout the Renaissance and Baroque periods. In the triangular pediment is the image of the shining sun, the symbol of the Dominican order. In the lower part of the façade is the majestic and somber doorway in classical style.

Interior. The church is in the form of a Latin cross, more than 325 feet long and almost 200 feet wide at the transept. The three naves have ogival cross-vaults and are divided by clustered pilasters in *pietra serena*.

It is worth devoting some time to a visit, as the church contains works by some outstanding artists, including Giotto, Andrea Orcagna, Filippo Brunelleschi, Domenico Ghirlandaio, Filippino Lippi and Masaccio, who here painted the *Trinity*, one of the great masterpieces of Western art.

On the inner façade is a stained glass window with *The Virgin En-*

throned, made to a design attributed to Andrea di Buonaiuto (14th century), who also painted the frescoes in the Spanish Chapel. On the right is a fresco of the *Annunciation* by a 14th-century Florentine painter; on the left, another painting of the *Annunciation* (16th century), by Santi di Tito.

In the second bay of the right aisle is the *tomb of Beata Villana Betti* (1451), by Rossellino and Desiderio da Settignano. On the altar is a *Nativity* (1573), by Giovanbattista Naldini.

In the sixth bay is the entrance to the Cappella della Pura, built after 1473 to house a reputedly miraculous image of the Madonna. According to legend, the Madonna appeared to two children who were playing in front of the church, and invited them to come home with her to wash themselves. Florentine mothers still worship her to this day.

At the end of the aisle, a flight of stairs leads into the 14th-century Rucellai Chapel. On the altar is a marble statue of the *Madonna and Child* (mid-14th century), by Nino Pisano.

On the far right of the transept is the Bardi Chapel. To the right of the entrance, on a pilaster predating the church itself, is a 13th-century relief of *St Gregorius blessing the founder of the chapel*. On the walls are the remains of 13th-century frescoes. On the altar is a

Madonna of the Rosary (1570), by Giorgio Vasari.

Next we come to the Strozzi Chapel, decorated with *frescoes* by Filippino Lippi, painted between 1489 and 1502. On the far wall is the *tomb of Filippo Strozzi* (1491-1495), by Benedetto da Maiano. The design of the stained glass window lighting the chapel is also attributed to Lippi, one of the earliest Florentine mannerist painters.

In the sanctuary's main chapel – that of the Tornabuoni family – one finds a cycle of paintings (1485-1490) by Domenico Ghirlandaio. In the vault are the *Evangelists*; on the left wall, *Scenes from the Life of the Virgin;* on the right, *Stories of St John the Baptist*, and on the far walls, the *Coronation of the Virgin with Saints* and *Stories of the Saints*, including *St Dominic burning heretical books* and *The Death of St Peter Martyr*, a priest who vigorously fought heresy in Florence. Many of these religious paintings contain portraits of important Florentines of the day: on the far wall members of the Tornabuoni family, who donated the works, are seen worshipping. Their representation in the frescoes and the fact that the

Tornabuoni family was related to the Medici, outraged Savonarola who condemned the cycle as an example of frivolous and profane art.

The wooden *choir stalls* beneath the frescoes are by Baccio D'Agnolo (late 15th century), but they were considerably altered by Vasari in 1566.

On the altar is a bronze *Crucifix*, by Giambologna (1529-1608).

Next is the Gondi Chapel (1503), decorated in black and white marble and red porphyry and designed by Giuliano da San Gallo. The *Crucifix* here is the only wooden sculpture ever to have been made by Brunelleschi.

On the ceiling are the remains of 13th-century frescoes by Byzantine artists. These are some of the oldest wall paintings to be found in Florence.

Continuing along, we arrive at the Gaddi Chapel. On the altar is a mannerist painting of *Christ performing a miracle*, by Agnolo Bronzino (1503-1572).

At the left side of the transept, up some stairs, is the Strozzi di Mantua Chapel. The walls are entirely decorated with frescoes by Nardo di Cione. Painted between 1350 and 1377, they

Domenico Ghirlandaio, The Birth of the Virgin, *Tornabuoni chapel in Santa Maria Novella. On the left, the interior of the church.*

Domenico Ghirlandaio, Visitation. *Santa Maria Novella, Tornabuoni chapel.*

Nardo di Cione, Bishop Saint, *detail of the frescoes in the Strozzi chapel.*

*Andrea Orcagna,
polyptych of the
Risen Christ, Santa
Maria Novella,
Strozzi chapel.*

*Stained glass
window in the apse.*

represent *Paradise* (on the left), the *Universal Judgment* (in the middle) and *Hell* (on the right). The choice of subject here is proof of how popular Dante's work had already become shortly after his death in 1321. Dante himself is shown in prayer on the left of the far wall.

The splendid altarpiece by Andrea Orcagna – brother of Nardo – depicts the *Risen Christ giving the Keys to St Peter and the Book of Knowledge to St Thomas,* and *Madonna, St John the Baptist and other Saints* (1357). Painted shortly after the dreadful epidemic of the plague which swept through Europe between 1348 and 1350, reducing the population of Florence alone by two-thirds, the significance of the painting was quite clearly intended to indicate that Christ, in strengthening his Church after the devastation, invested the Dominicans (represented by St Thomas) with special authority.

Leaving the Strozzi di Mantua Chapel, the 14th-century sacristy is on the right, attributed to Fra' Jacopo Talenti but altered in the 17th-18th centuries. The large wall cupboards were made by Guerrino Veneziani to a design by Buontalenti (1593). To the right of the entrance is a marble *lavabo* in a glazed terracotta niche by Giovanni della Robbia (1498); to the left is another marble *lavabo* dated early 18th century. Over the door

is the large *painted Cross* by Giotto (finished before 1312), currently under restoration (1997).

In the third bay of the left aisle is the most important work in the church: the renowned fresco by Masaccio of the *Trinity with the Madonna, St John and the Lensi Donors in Prayer.* Here, the artist applied the rules of mathematical perspective established by Brunelleschi to create an entirely original optical effect, so that, as Vasari wrote: "the surface looks as if it is indented". The figures are simple, yet majestic; their realism is profoundly human and dramatic, quite unlike the delicate grace of Gothic art. Applying the rules of perspective, Masaccio placed man as a corporeal being at the centre of the universe.

To the left of this masterpiece is *St Lucy with the Donors*, by Davide Ghirlandaio.

By the next to last pilaster of the aisle is a marble *pulpit* by Brunelleschi, made in 1462 by his adoptive son, Andrea Cavalcanti.

Leaving the church, we turn to the right: entrance to the cloisters and the Museum of Sacred Art (Museo d'Arte Sacra) is down a few steps to the left.

CLOISTERS AND MUSEUM OF SACRED ART

Green Cloister. One enters the Chiostro Verde from the

Masaccio, the Trinity with Mary and Saint John flanked by the doners, members of the Lenzi family. *One of the supreme masterpieces of painting.*

corridor. Built by Fra' Jacopo Talenti who began work in 1332, it was frescoed in the first half of the 15th century by Paolo Uccello and others, using the green and reddish tints which gave the cloister its name. The most important paintings are those by Uccello himself, on the entrance wall of the cloister. Starting from the far wall we see: the *Creation of the Animals, Adam and Eve* and *Original Sin*; continuing to the right: *the Labours of the Prisoners* and *Cain and Abel*; next, *Lamech and Noah's Ark.* The *Flood* and *Drunkenness of Noah* are masterpieces by Uccello, combining fantasy with a sophisticated use of perspective.

Spanish Chapel. The Cappellone degli Spagnoli is reached from the cloister, on the side opposite to the entrance. Previously the chapter room of the monastery, in the 16th century Eleonora de Toledo, wife of Cosimo I, assigned it to the Spanish members of her entourage. The chapel gives the impression of being extremely large due to its carefully studied proportions. At the end of the 19th century John Ruskin wrote: "It will literally seem to you one of the grandest places roofed without a central pillar that you ever entered. And you will marvel that human daring

ever achieved anything so magnificent".

Built by Fra' Jacopo Talenti, beginning in 1343, it consists of a rectangular hall, with a single cross vault supported by wide arches resting on low corner pilasters set into the walls, and an apse with an altar.

The vault and walls are entirely decorated with a grand fresco cycle (1367-1369) by Andrea di Buonaiuto, which exalts the role of the Dominicans in the struggle against heresy. The cycle, portraying allegories of religious dogma intended to educate the people, clearly demonstrates the intellectual and doctrinal nature of the Dominican order, so different from the practical and fervent nature of the Franciscans who preferred to decorate their churches with scenes from the life of their founding saint.

Illustrated in the vault are *The Voyage of St Peter, Resurrection, Ascension* and *Pente-*

The 14th-century 'Chiostro Verde', an imposing structure of low arches.

The Spanish chapel, frescoed by Andrea di Bonaiuto (later 14th century).

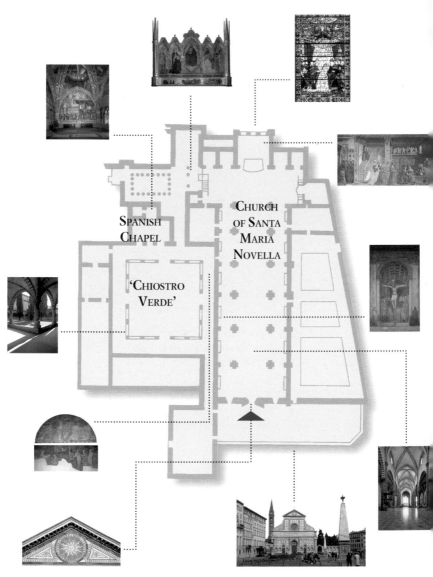

cost. On the wall opposite the entrance are three scenes from the *Passion.* On the entrance wall are *Scenes from the Life of St Peter Martyr.* On the right wall are the *Militant Church and the Church Triumphant*, emphasizing the role of the Dominicans as guardians of the faith against heresy, and of church unity. Low down on the left is an image of the cathedral with a Byzantine style dome, designed in 1367 by a group of artists which included Andrea di Buonaiuto himself. On the left wall is the *Triumph of St Thomas Aquinas.* In the apse is *St James heals a cripple*

(1592), by Alessandro Allori.

Cloister of the Dead. Beside the Spanish Chapel is the small Chiostro dei Morti, already in existence before the arrival of the Dominicans and altered in the mid-14th century.

Museum of Sacred Art. Entrance from the Green Cloister. Housed in two rooms which were previously the monastery's refectory and vestibule, the museum contains *paintings*, *reliquaries*, *church ornaments and vestments* belonging to the church of Santa Maria Novella.

Large Cloister. Near to the museum is the original entrance to the monastery's Chiostro Grande, which today forms part of the buildings occupied by the school for Carabinieri. The buildings around the cloister are medieval.

Popes' Chapel. On the first floor above the cloister, accessible only with permission from the police headquarters, is the Cappella dei Papi. The name derives from the fact that the Medici Pope Leo X stayed there when visiting Florence in 1515. The chapel was decorated for the occasion with a *Coronation of the Virgin*, by Ridolfo Ghirlandaio and a splendid *Veronica*, by Pontormo.

After visiting the Dominican complex, we cross the piazza in the direction of Via de'

Banchi. From here we turn almost immediately right onto Via delle Belle Donne, arriving shortly after at the Trebbio Cross. *Supported by a granite column, the stone cross was erected in 1338 to commemorate a confrontation which occurred in 1244, between the Dominicans, defending church orthodoxy, and a group of northern heretics.*

Turning left again onto the last, twisting part of Via del Moro, we then turn right into Via de' Banchi, arriving at the junction of Via de' Cerretani. Interestingly, the term 'cerretano' *(which became* 'ciarlatano' *in Italian and* 'charlatan' *in French and English), is derived from the name Cerreto Guidi, a Tuscan village whose inhabitants were renowned as peddlers.*

Continuing along Via de' Cerretani in the direction of

Paolo Uccello, the Drunkeness of Noah, *a scene from the fresco cycle. Santa Maria Novella, 'Chiostro Verde'.*

Paolo Uccello, Creation *and the* Temptation of Adam and Eve, *scenes from the fresco cycle. Santa Maria Novella, 'Chiostro Verde'.*

The Trebbio cross.

the Cathedral – where we end our walk – we find, on the right, the narrow piazza of Santa Maria Maggiore, with the church of the same name.

CHURCH OF SANTA MARIA MAGGIORE

This is one of the oldest churches in the city. Founded in the early 11th century, it was rebuilt in Gothic style in the mid-13th century by the Vallombrosan monks. It still has the original pre-Romanesque bell tower set into the façade. Set high on the bell tower is a *bust* of a woman from the late Roman era, nick-named 'Berta'.

The interior is Cistercian in style, with three aisles divided by Gothic arches resting on square pilasters.

On the inner façade and the first pillar on the right are late 14th-century frescoes, attributed to Mariotto di Nardo.

History -1-

From the Roman city to the rise of Cosimo the Elder

Florence was founded by the Romans during the spring festival of *Floralia* in 59 BC, at a ford across the river, in the valley of the Etruscan settlement of Fiesole. The town grew considerably during the 2nd and 3rd centuries AD, though with the crisis of the Roman Empire, it once again dwindled to little more than a village. A battleground in the war between the Greeks and Ostrogoths, it was sacked by Totila, king of the Goths, then reconquered by the Byzantine empire in 550. In 570, it fell under the dominion of the Lombards who, however, chose Lucca as the seat for the Duchy of 'Tuscia,' as it was more distant from the Byzantine territories, lying on the Adriatic side of the Appenines. It was not until the beginning of the 9th century, during the reign of Charlemagne, that Florence began to flourish again, and a century later the Margrave Ugo reinstated it as the administrative headquarters of Tuscany. At the beginning of the 12th century, independent civic institutions began to take form, and the first Florentine consuls were nominated in 1138. At the same time, Florence began to extend its control over the surrounding area. In

The fleur-de-lys emblem of the city of Florence on the façade of the palazzo of the Butchers' Guild in Via Orsanmichele.

Over the altar in the second chapel on the right is *St Rita of Cascia* by contemporary Florentine painter Primo Conti, signed and dated 1949.

In the main chapel, behind the presbytery, is the fresco cycle *Herod orders the slaughter of the innocents*, (late 14th century) attributed to Nardo di Cione or Spinello Aretino.

In the chapel on the left is a magnificent wood polychrome bas-relief dated 13th century, representing the *Madonna Enthroned with Child,* attributed to Coppo di Marcovaldo; on either side are panel paintings by his workshop.

The sacristy leads out to the 16th-century cloister, decorated with early 17th-century frescoes.

Leaving Santa Maria Maggiore, we continue to the right along Via de' Cerretani, which brings us back to Piazza San Giovanni.

1125, the Florentines conquered Fiesole. By now, however, the city was dominated by aristocratic factions at war between themselves: this led to the development of the 'tower society' as the opposing factions built mighty fortified tower-houses for defensive purposes, one of the most characteristic features of the 13th-century city. In an attempt to bring these internal divisions to an end, in 1207 the consuls were replaced by a *Podestà*, the first being Gualfredotto. From the end of the 12th century to the beginning of the 13th century, the Guilds – powerful trade corporations – came into being. The oldest is the Merchants Guild, the *Calimala*, followed by the Bankers and Moneychangers, the Wool and the Silk Guilds. Both the economy

The florin, first minted in gold in 1252.

and the population of the city began to expand rapidly; just outside the walls working-class areas grew up where, during the 13th century, the mendicant religious orders built their main churches — Santa Croce, Santo Spirito, Santa Maria Novella. In the mid-13th century the most important currency in the economy of medieval Europe came into being: the *fiorino*, or florin. The *popolo* or 'common folk,' merchants and guildmembers, began to take part in the political life of the city, gradually undermining the feudal-based power of the aristocracy. It was during this period that the Florentine nobility divided into the Guelphs, loyal to the Pope, and the Ghibellines, on the side of the Emperor. In 1250 the Guelphs, now allied with the *popolo*, succeeded in expelling the

Ghibellines. In 1260, at Montaperti, they were defeated by the Sienese Ghibellines, allied with Manfred, King of Sicily. Six years later, however, when Manfred was killed at the battle of Benevento, the Guelphs returned to power. On June 11, 1289, the Florentines took Arezzo at the battle of Campaldino. The differences between nobility and '*popolani*' now became critical. The victory of the latter is represented by the *Ordinances of Justice* (1293) written by Giano della Bella, which excluded the old nobility from the government of the city. The struggles within the Guelf faction now led to its division into the *bianchi* (whites) who were in favour of coming to an agreement with the Ghibellines and jealous of the Pope's autonomy, and the *neri* (blacks) who fervently supported papal jurisdiction. In 1302, with the help of Charles of Valois, brother of the king of France, the *neri* drove the *bianchi* out of Florence. Despite the fact that Florence was now an important economic power, the city had little real political influence and was vulnerable to the stormy international climate. The beginning of the Hundred Years War and the failure of Edward III, king of England, to repay his enormous debts accumulated with Florentine banks, brought about the collapse of numerous banks and businesses. The city elected the French noble, Walter of Brienne, Duke of Athens, as Lord of Florence but a year later, in 1343, an insurrection by the citizens led to his expulsion. In 1348, Florence, which now had approximately 80,000 inhabitants, was struck by the Black Death. In just two years, the population was reduced to around 25-30,000 people. In the years following this disaster, the social conflict became more pronounced. Between 1375 and 1378 the 'War of the Eight Saints,' in which Florence opposed the Pope, led to the uprising of the *Ciompi*, the wool

carders, representing the city's chief industry. Once the rebellion had been put down, power returned to the wealthy families. The city again divided into two factions: members of the old oligarchy and the Wool and Silk Guilds gathered around the Àlbizzi family; the lower classes instead supported the Medici who originated from the Mugello and had recently become rich as a result of aggressive commercial and financial dealings. By now, the republic was growing into a regional state: Pisa was conquered in 1406 and the following year, Livorno, thus providing access to the sea. However, the Florentines now had to struggle to defend their new position against the Duke of Milan, who wished to extend his territories towards the south. The city emerged victorious but exhausted and weakened from the war, and once again internal political conflicts came to the fore. In 1433, Rinaldo degli Àlbizzi managed to exile Cosimo the Elder, head of the Medici family, only to see him return to Florence in triumph a year later.

The glory and decline of the Medici

The Medici family were originally from the area of the Mugello. Their wealth, however, was the result of various successful financial operations undertaken by Giovanni di Bicci (1360-1429), father of Cosimo the Elder. At the end of the 14th century, Giovanni founded the Medici bank which rapidly became one of the foremost in Europe. It was with Cosimo that the 'Medici rule' began, although officially the Florentine constitution remained unaltered. In fact Cosimo wielded his influence from his new palace, designed for him by Michelozzo, on Via Larga (Palazzo Medici-Riccardi, ☞ p. 70-72) while Palazzo Vecchio, seat of the supreme magistrature, was gradually reduced to a purely representative role. Cosimo was succeeded by his son Piero, known as 'the Gouty' (1416-1469) who found himself faced with a crisis caused by the failure of some European sovereigns to repay money lent by Florentine banks. On his death his son, Lorenzo the Magnificent (1449-1492), assumed power. Having narrowly escaped assassination in a conspiracy organized by his rivals, the Pazzi, in 1478, Lorenzo, an important patron of the arts, succeeded with a finely-balanced political policy in not only consolidating the prestige of Florence, but also the supremacy of his family. On his death the internal struggles became ever more bitter and in 1494 his successor, Piero, was driven out of the city for not having effectively resisted Charles VIII, king of France, who had marched on Tuscany with his troops. A new republic now came into being, inspired by the oratory of the Dominican monk, Girolamo Savonarola who was, however, excommunicated by Pope Alexander VI, and condemned to death for heresy in 1498. Some fifteen years later, in 1512, Lorenzo's two sons, Giovanni (1475-1521) the future Pope Leo X, and Giuliano, Duke of Nemours (1479-1516) returned to Florence under the protection of the Spanish army. Lorenzo di Piero (1492-1519), Duke of Urbino, to whom Machiavelli dedicated *The Prince*, was nominated steward of the city. On his death, his son Alessandro (1510-1537) and Cardinal Ippolito (1511-1535) took over the city's government; but the power of the Medici was now concentrated in Rome, and in 1523 Giulio (1478-1534) the son of Lorenzo the Magnificent, was appointed Pope with the name of Clement VII. In 1527, Emperor Charles V occupied and sacked Rome in revenge for the Pope's alliance with France. The Florentines seized the opportunity to drive the Medici out of the city again and restore the republic. To little avail though, for when Charles made his peace with the Pope in 1529, he laid the city under siege. Barricaded behind the fortifications designed by Michelangelo, the Florentines resisted the imperial siege for eleven months, but were finally overwhelmed. The Florentine state thus became a duchy in 1532 with Alessandro once more at its head. His rule was not destined to last for long: in 1537 he was assassinated by his cousin Lorenzino and with his death the direct lineage of Cosimo the Elder came to an end. To avoid the Florentine state becoming absorbed into the empire, the citizens acclaimed the youthful Cosimo (1519-1574) as Duke — the son of Giovanni dalle Bande Nere from the younger branch of the Medici family. Once the republicans, lead by the Strozzi family, had been defeated, Cosimo set about consolidating his power. In 1555, he conquered Siena, Florence's ancient rival for supremacy of the region, and in 1569, with the Pope's blessing, he became Grand Duke of Tuscany. Cosimo was succeeded by Francesco (1574-1587) and then by Ferdinando I (1587-1609). It was during this period that important infrastructural initiatives and improvements destined to shape the Tuscan countryside and influence its economy even today, were carried out. The port of Livorno was built and a series of river ports was created along the banks of the Arno. With Cosimo II (1609-1621) the dynasty began to fall into decline. Within the context of a Europe now dominated by large nation states, little Tuscany, with its neglected and outdated industry, dwindled in significance. After Cosimo II came Ferdinando II (1621-1670), Cosimo III (1670-1723) and lastly Gian Gastone (1723-1737) who died without heir, thus bringing the dynasty to an end.

The city walls

The Roman walls. According to tradition, Florence was founded in the spring of 59 BC, during the *ludi florales*, at a ford over the river where a a few years later a bridge would be built. The line of the Roman walls is still recognizable in the quadrangle formed by Piazza del Duomo, Piazza San Firenze, Piazza Santa Trìnita and the extreme western end of Via dei Cerretani. The *cardo* (north-south axis) and the *decumanus* (east-west axis) crossed in today's Piazza della Repubblica, where the Roman Forum once stood. The city grew rapidly, and in the 2nd century AD already counted some 10,000 inhabitants.

The Byzantine walls. With the crisis of the Roman Empire, Florence experienced a long demographic decline. Between 541 and 544, the Byzantines turned it into a sort of fortified stronghold, constructing a new ring of walls considerably smaller than the Roman ones. In any event, the city probably had no more than 1,000 inhabitants at the time and could not have defended a larger enclosure.

The Carolingian walls. Not until the 8th and the 9th centuries did Florence, as indeed most of Europe, begin to recover from the long crisis following the fall of the Roman Empire. The population of the city began to increase again, and in the 9th century reached 5,000 inhabitants. A new enclosure for the city was therefore built at the end of the 9th and beginning of the 10th centuries. The east-west limit extended once more to the previous Roman walls, while to the south (in the direction of the Arno) the axis followed Borgo Santi Apostoli – Via Lambertesca. To the north, the Carolingian circle of walls ended on the southern side of Piazza del Duomo.

Matilda's walls. In the mid-11th century, the seat of the Tuscan Marquis was moved from Lucca to Florence. The city, which now had some 20,000 inhabitants, was in a phase of expansion and development which, in Dante's time, would turn it into one of the few large European cities. Thus, in 1072, Countess Matilda ordered the construction of a new defensive ring, Dante's 'cerchia antica,' which followed the line of the Carolingian walls, but now extended to the north to encompass all of Piazza del Duomo.

The fifth ring. Although it was not until 1183 that the Emperor officially grant-

ed Florence autonomy of government, the Florentines had already been establishing their own institutions for several decades. Political autonomy was the logical consequence of a continually expanding economy and population. The city now had over 30,000 inhabitants, and houses now extended beyond the gates along the approach roads, still identifiable by the name *Borgo* (☞ pp. 182-183). In 1172, the commune decided to build a new and much larger circle of walls, which would encompass a total area of eighty hectares — three times that enclosed by Matilda's walls. Begun in 1173, the work was completed just two years later. For the first time, the walls took in the Oltrarno area, even though only with a wooden palisade.

The sixth ring. In the year 1200, the city's population had grown to 50,000; in 1260 this had become 75,000; in 1280, 85,000 and in 1300 it had reached 95-100,000. In all of Europe only Paris was larger, with its 200,000 inhabitants. Consequently, at the time of Dante, the Florentines decided to build a new ring of walls which would be able to accommodate this rapid rate of growth. Be-

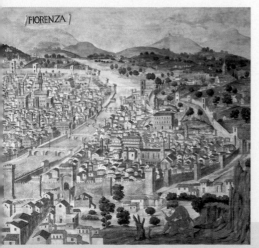

tween 1284 and 1333 therefore, some 8,500 meters of wall were built, enclosing an area of 430 hectares (more than five times the area within the fifth walls). The line followed that of today's boulevards, or inner ring road, built by architect Giuseppe Poggi when Florence was capital of Italy (1865-1871), demolishing the 14th-century walls. Some sections of the walls are still intact however, as well as the most important gates which were saved as monuments: Porta a San Gallo, Porta a San Frediano, Porta San Niccolò (the only gate which has not been lowered) Porta Romana, Porta a San Gallo, and Porta alla Croce.

The optimistic expectations of the Florentines proved, however, to be mistaken. In 1348, fifteen years after the building of the walls, the dreadful outbreak of the Black Death swept through Europe, killing two-thirds of the city's population. Not until the late 18th century would the population recover numerically.

The San Giorgio gate (above left). One of the towers in the city walls which climb from San Niccolò to the Belvedere fort (above right). A view of part of the sixth ring of walls (centre, above). The 'Catena' (Chain) map. 'Firenze com'era' Museum.

3. The Area of the Medici

The area covered by this itinerary was once leafy, open countryside, an area well-suited by its tranquil nature to the work and needs of monks, artists and scientists — a place of peaceful isolation surrounded by orchards and gardens. Indeed, the monasteries of San Marco and Santissima Annunziata first came into being as small oratories outside the original town walls, in an area named Cafaggio on the edge of the Mugnone river. The buildings now occupied by the Academy Gallery and the Opificio delle Pietre Dure were also once monasteries. Even when the area was later enclosed by the city walls, it remained peaceful and unspoiled, and many artists including Rosso Fiorentino, Pontormo and Franciabigio chose to live or to set up studio there. In San Marco, both art and religion are celebrated in Fra' Angelico's frescoes. On the corner of Via Giusti is the house of Andrea del Sarto, who created some of his most important works in the nearby Santissima Annunziata. Some of the most exceptional artists learned their skills in the Medici's Accade-

Above, Michelangelo, David. Galleria dell'Accademia. Above right, water jar with Aphrodite and Phaon, Archaeological Museum.

mia degli Orti, and innovative architectural projects, destined to become the stylistic cornerstones of the Renaissance, first came into being here: Palazzo Medici, the Spedale degli Innocenti, the Rotonda of Santa Maria degli Angeli. Meanwhile, the Casino dei Medici was the scientific laboratory of the Prince of the Studiolo, Francesco de' Medici (1541-1587), while opposite San Marco, Cosimo I created a botanical garden, at one time among the most important in Europe. Thus, following the building of their palace on Via Larga (today's Via Cavour), the Medici also took cultural possession of the whole area, asserting their power and creating an image for themselves at the same time. The work of Michelozzo, Cosimo's chosen architect for his own residence as well as San Marco and Santissima Annunziata, is an example of their expansion and dominance. Towards the end of the last century, the area changed completely. No longer an artistic laboratory, it became a distinguished conservator of the past, in particular with its splendid museums, the most famous of which is the Academy housing the *David,* the most venerated cult figure in the ritual of the modern tourist.

*Michelozzo, Palazzo
Medici Riccardi, façade.*

*Palazzo Medici
Riccardi, Medici coat
of arms on the corner
of Via Cavour and
Via de' Gori.*

Leaving Piazza del Duomo,
we enter Via Martelli. Originally this street was much narrower, but it was widened by
moving back the right-hand
side to bring it into line with
Via Cavour, further ahead, as
part of the urban reorganization which took place when
Florence was capital of Italy
(1865-1871).

A house belonging to the
Opera di San Giovanni *at no.
3 still maintains some 14th-cen-
tury features; on the façade is
the coat of arms of the Calimala
guild. At no. 7, a copy of the
Martelli coat of arms, sculpted
by Donatello, can be seen (the
original is at no. 22r, Via Cerretani). On the corner of Via de'
Gori is the* Oratory of San
Giovannino *(some original
Gothic windows can be seen
along the side). In 1579, the
church was renovated in mannerist style by Bartolomeo Ammannati, and completed by Alfonso Parigi in 1661.*

*Palazzo Medici-Riccardi is lo-
cated immediately after the
junction with Via de' Gori, at
the beginning of Via Cavour.*

PALAZZO MEDICI-RICCARDI

"This is too big a house for
such a small family," Cosimo
the Elder is reputed to have
said when he took up residence here in 1462. The Riccardi family, on the other
hand, considered it too small
when they bought it in 1670,
and consequently enlarged it,
adding seven windows to each
floor on the right-hand side as
well as a doorway and window

on the ground floor. The original square-shaped structure
thus became rectangular. The
new stonework was impecca-
bly integrated with the old, but
the part which was added is
clearly identifiable by the Riccardi family's emblem of keys,
seen in the tondi above the
mullioned windows.

The first real example of a
Renaissance mansion, it was
long subject to the alternating
political fortunes of the
Medici: confiscated in 1509, it
was returned to them in 1512,
but was again abandoned by
the owners in 1527. In 1531,
Alessandro moved back again,
only to be murdered there.
Works by the most outstanding artists – Michelozzo, Donatello, Gozzoli, Michelangelo – were kept there, and
among the illustrious guests
were Galeazzo Sforza, Emper-
or Charles VIII, and Charles V
of France. In 1540, Cosimo I
decided that Palazzo Vecchio
was more suitable a residence
for his position as Duke, and
thereafter less important members of the Medici family lived
there. Until 1814, it was maintained by the Riccardi family,
who then sold it to the government of the Grand Duchy.
The administrative offices of
the Province of Florence are
now housed here.

Exterior. Built by Michelozzo
between 1444 and 1462, the
original façade on Via Cavour
had two asymmetrical doorways and ten mullioned windows with rounded arches on

*Benozzo Gozzoli,
detail of the fresco
cycle in the chapel of
Palazzo Medici
Riccardi.*

*Palazzo Medici Riccardi,
first courtyard.*

each of the two floors. The arches on the corner with Via de' Gori were open, forming a public loggia; these were later closed and Michelangelo's famous 'kneeling' windows with a lowered ledge were inserted. This architectural feature would subsequently be repeated on buildings for several centuries. Another feature frequently adapted and repeated is the style of the stonework, consisting of graduated rustication, heavy at the lower level, becoming smooth at the top.

The building is completed by Michelozzo's classical cornice, decorated with acanthus leaves, rosettes and dentils.
First courtyard. Entrance is from the large doorway perfectly centered to the arches around the courtyard and the entrance to the garden behind. The arches of the portico continue uninterrupted around the corners. Above are a deep frieze, mullioned windows on the first floor and a loggia on the second. The eight *medallions* (1491) attributed to

3. The area of the Medici

Bertoldo (a pupil of Donatello, and Michelangelo's *maestro*) are all that remain of the original decoration of the portico. On the walls, large baroque frames contain archaeological fragments collected by the Riccardi family.

Benozzo Gozzoli Chapel. The first flight of stairs on the right leads to the chapel, one of the most splendid Florentine Renaissance works of art. Michelozzo was responsible for the design and the fittings: the carved and gilded ceiling, inlayed pews, the pavement decorated with marble and porphyry. Benozzo Gozzoli's fresco cycle of *The Journey of the Magi* (1459) actually represents the visit of Emperor John VIII Paleologus to Florence in 1439. Gozzoli's supreme narrative ability is evident in both the scenery and his treatment of the figures. Bernard Berenson wrote of the artist: "Benozzo was gifted with a rare facility not only of execution but of invention, with a spontaneity, a freshness, a liveliness in telling a story that wakes the child in us, and the lover of fairytales". The altarpiece is a copy, believed to be contemporary, of the original by Filippo Lippi.

Benozzo Gozzoli, details of the fresco of the Journey of the Magi in the chapel.

Gallery. Returning to the courtyard, the second flight of stairs on the right leads to the gallery on the first floor, an impressive example of Florentine baroque by Pier Maria Baldi. Originally, special large cupboards here housed the family's collection of gems, coins, medals and small bronzes. The ceiling is frescoed with the *Apotheosis of*

the Medici (1682-1683), by Luca Giordano, a celebration of the Medici dynasty with mythological overtones.

Second courtyard. Located here are the remains of Michelozzo's loggia and an 18th-century Italianate garden, salvaged in 1911 when the entire building was restored. Further work carried out in 1996 brought the beautiful old paving to light.

VIA CAVOUR

The presence of Palazzo Medici-Riccardi at the beginning of Via Cavour set the tone for the subsequent development of Via Cavour as a showpiece for the most important Florentine families, who built their town houses there. Some of the most important are: at no. 4, the 17th-century *Palazzo Covoni*, designed by Gherardo Silvani, with attractive decorations in bronze and stone on the façade (note also the heraldic symbols on the main balcony and the ornate iron work on the ground floor windows); at no. 18, *Palazzo Bastogi*, built by Ferdinando Ruggieri around 1740 for Senator

Piazza San Marco and the façade of the church. In the foreground is a statue of General Manfredo, a hero of the Italian Risorgimento.

Roberto Capponi; at no. 22 and 24, *Palazzo Bartolomei*, also by Silvani, with attractive 'kneeling' windows, now housing the Bank of Naples.

The *Biblioteca Marucelliana*, founded by Francesco Marucelli, is at no. 43. In 1703, this noted scholar and bibliographer left a considerable bequest for the creation of a library, open to the public and housing his own collection of books, totaling approximately 40,000 volumes. The building was finished in 1747 and today the library contains over 500,000 books and journals.

Just beyond the Biblioteca Marucelliana, to the right of Via Cavour, is Piazza San Marco.

PIAZZA SAN MARCO

For centuries this area of the city has been the center of the arts, sciences and religion in Florence. In the 13th century, a small Vallombrosan oratory existed here, becoming, during the Renaissance, a monastery famous for the works of Fra' Angelico. In their private gardens on the left side of the church, the Medici created an Arts Academy where masters including Donatello, Michelozzo, Pollaiolo, Verrocchio and Michelangelo learned their skills. The Academy established by the Grand Dukes on the corner of Via Ricasoli, still active today, may be considered the natural heir of the Medici Academy. To the right of the church, where today the university headquarters are located, an enclosure for rare and exotic animals was made during the 16th century, and in the same period one of the first botanical gardens was created just a few yards ahead.

On Via Cavour, no. 51 is the *Palazzina della Livia*, which Pietro Leopoldo had built for his lover, Livia Malfatti Raimondi, a ballerina from Rome. The design is of a transitional nature, imitative in style, yet a prototype for future houses. Built by Bernardo Fallani between 1775 and 1780, on the one hand it is a late and somewhat weary repetition of the proportions and decorative elements (triangular tympanum, roundels with bas-reliefs, corbels, cornices and pilasters) of Renaissance buildings; on the other, it may be considered to have provided the model for the numerous bourgeois villas which appeared at the end of the 19th century in the new suburban areas created when Giuseppe Poggi demolished the old city walls as part of the programmed of urban expansion. Today it houses the military Officer's Club.

Deviating just briefly from our route we come to two more interesting buildings. Slightly further ahead, at no. 57, is the Casino Mediceo. *Designed by*

The 'Palazzina della Livia', designed by Bernardo Fallani (1775-1780).

Via Cavour: the façade of Palazzo Bartolommei, by Gherardo Silvani (17th century).

The loggia of San Matteo now houses the Academy of Fine Arts.

The interior of the church of San Marco.

The monastery library. Below, a view of the monastery and bell tower of San Marco.

Bernardo Buontalenti for Prince Francesco, built over the Medici gardens, the Casino was originally a laboratory for the Prince's alchemical and mechanical experiments. Its purpose, requiring large open spaces, is evident from the structure consisting of only two floors, yet extending horizontally. Buontalenti's lively imagination is visible in the decoration of the windows and doorway; a typical example in the latter is the little monkey's face peeping out from under a shell.

Turning left onto Via Salvestrina, on the corner with Via San Gallo (at no. 74) is the harmonious building of **Palazzo Pandolfini**. Its style and origins owe more to Rome than to Florence, as it was commissioned by the papal prelate Giannozzo Pandolfini. The palace was almost certainly designed by Raphael; however, due to his numerous projects in Rome, he delegated the task of overseeing its construction to Giovanfrancesco da Sangallo after 1520. With its airy elegance, the building appears rather unusual amidst the Renaissance buildings of Florence; it consists of two elements which are separated by a rusticated doorway and are yet harmoniously linked by the tabernacle-style windows.

To the north, Via San Gallo ends in the spacious Piazza della Libertà, a vast 19th-century creation surrounded by porticoed buildings. On the south side of the piazza is the **Porta San Gallo**, a remnant and re-minder of the 14th-century city walls; opposite is the triumphal arch built in honour of Francesco Stefano, the first Grand Duke of the Lorraine dynasty (☛ p. 123). Designed in 1745 by the architect J.N. Jadot of Lorraine, it is crowned by an equestrian monument to Francesco Stefano, by Giovan Battista Foggini.

CHURCH OF SAN MARCO

"Invest 10,000 florins in a monastery for the city": this was the penitence Pope Eugene IV imposed on Cosimo the Elder to make amends for his "dishonestly acquired" wealth. Thus Michelozzo was commissioned to build one of the first cloistered structures of the Renaissance, at the same time enlarging the existing Gothic-Romanesque church dating from the late 13th century. Beato Angelico, Fra' Bartolomeo, Bishop of Florence St Antonino, and Savonarola all lived and worked in this monastery.

Façade. Michelozzo's original design for the façade was altered in 1780 by Fra' Gioacchino Pronti, who rebuilt it in rather somber Baroque style. The bas-relief on the attic story representing *St Antonino blessing the City of Florence* also dates from this period.

Interior. The church consists of a single nave with no side aisles and was renovated on several occasions: by Giambologna (principally the side chapels) at the end of the 16th century, and in the

The Sant'Antonino cloister. Right, tabernacle of the Linen Drapers guild.

late 17th century by Pier Francesco Silvani (the tribune and ceiling).

On the inner façade is a large *Crucifix* by the school of Giotto. At the first altar on the right is *St Thomas in prayer* (1593), by Santi di

The Church of San Marco

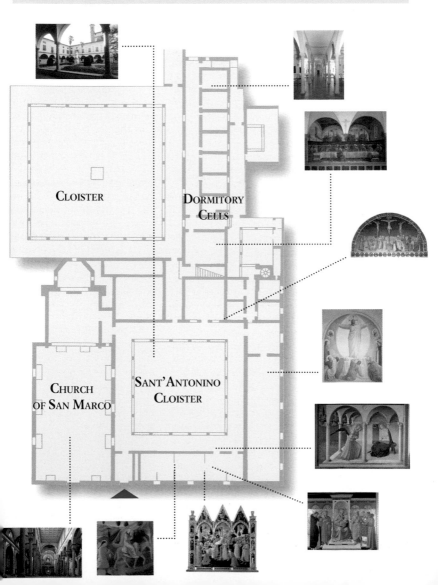

CLOISTER

DORMITORY CELLS

CHURCH OF SAN MARCO

SANT'ANTONINO CLOISTER

Fra' Angelico,
Transfiguration.
Below, the Annalena
*altar piece and, on
the right, the*
Lamentation, *both
also by Fra' Angelico.*

Tito; on the second altar is a *Madonna with Saints* (1509), by Fra' Bartolomeo.

At the end of the nave is the sacristy designed by Michelozzo. This contains valuable church ornaments and vestments dating from the 15th to the 18th centuries, and a sarcophagus with a bronze statue of *St Antonino,* attributed to Giambologna. Also by Giambologna is the Salviati Chapel on the left-hand side of the church, decorated with beautiful bronze bas-reliefs.

Leaving the church, immediately on the left is the entrance to the Museo di San Marco.

SAN MARCO MUSEUM

"It is as if all the sugar in the world had been concentrated in one place". Thus commented Bernard Berenson when, after World War I, all of Fra' Angelico's Florentine works were brought together in the monastery commissioned by Cosimo and built by Michelozzo between 1437 and 1452. Beato Angelico, wrote Berenson, "was the typical painter of the transition from Medieval to Renaissance. The sources of his feelings are in the Middle Ages but he enjoys his feelings in a way which is almost modern; and almost modern also are his means of expression".
Ground floor. In the cloister of Sant'Antonino are several frescoes by Poccetti and other 16th- and 17th-century artists. Outstanding, however, is Fra'

Angelico's *Crucifixion with St Dominic.*

From here, we enter the spacious Ospizio dei Pellegrini (Pilgrims' Lodgings) where works by Fra' Angelico, previously in the Academy and the Uffizi, are now housed. Displayed in this room are: the *Deposition* (1432), with what is believed to be a portrait of Michelozzo, seen in the man with a black turban; the *San Marco Altarpiece,* which the Medici commissioned for the main altar of the church, seriously damaged by 19th-century restoration (the background has one of the most fascinating landscapes ever painted by the artist); the *Linaiuoli Altarpiece* (1433-1434) with twelve musician angels around the frame — the most reproduced of all Angelico's figures; the *Triptych of St Peter Martyr* (before 1429); the *Annalena Altarpiece* (after 1434), the first to show Renaissance influences; the *Universal Judgment* (1431), still

completely medieval in concept, as can be seen from the rich use of brocades and gold; thirty-five *Scenes from the Life of Christ* decorating a cupboard intended for silverware; a *Deposition* (1440).

More works by Angelico are in the chapter room, on the other side of the cloister (a large fresco of the *Crucifixion)* and in the Sala del Lavabo (three *lunettes* and two *panel paintings*, displayed with some of Paolo Uccello's minor works). From here we enter the large 14th-century refectory, housing works by 17th- and 18th-century artists, while displayed in the two rooms opposite are works by Fra' Bartolomeo and Alessandro Baldovinetti. Also from the chapter room we reach the small refectory, with a *Last Supper* (c.1480) by Domenico Ghirlandaio, rich in symbolism and perfectly adapted to the structure of the room.

First floor. The monks' cells

lining three sides of the cloister of St Antonino form the backdrop to the famous fresco cycle which Fra' Angelico painted for the specific purpose of aiding and encouraging meditation. While Fra' Angelico was doubtless responsible for the overall scheme and the sketches, various assistants clearly helped in painting the frescoes.

Immediately opposite the top of the stairs is the renowned *Annunciation* (1442), where the two figures, beneath a classic Renaissance loggia, are arranged on a diagonal axis. On the wall opposite is a *Crucifixion with St Dominic,* and to the left of the *Annunciation* the first corridor begins. The cells on the left are decorated with masterpieces which may be attributed almost entirely to Fra' Angelico. The most important frescoes here are: the *Deposition* (cell 2); the *Annunciation*

Three more works by Fra' Angelico: above, the Annunciation: *above left, the* Universal Judgement; *below, the* San Marco altar piece.

Fra' Angelico, the Flight into Egypt.

Fra' Angelico,
Annunciation.

Domenico
Ghirlandaio, Last
Supper.

Fountain in the
Botanical Gardens.

Fra' Angelico,
Crucifixion with Saints.

the entrance to the library. Divided by two rows of slender columns, this magnificent hall was designed by Michelozzo for the hundreds of volumes collected by the humanist Niccolò Niccoli. A splendid collection of antiphonaries, graduals, missals and choir books, all beautifully decorated with miniatures, is housed here.

(cell 3); the *Crucifixion* (cell 4); the *Transfiguration* (cell 6); the *Crowning with Thorns* (cell 7); the *Coronation of Mary* (cell 9). At the end of the corridor is the cell which was once Savonarola's. Two 13th-century bibles in Latin are displayed here. On the right of the corridor, in cell 25, is the *Madonna of the Shadows*, one of Angelico's most famous works. Some medieval wall paintings were recently discovered beneath the floor of cell 22. These can be seen reflected in a fixed mirror.

The three cells at the end of the second corridor were the Prior's quarters; the novices were housed in those facing onto the cloisters, where the image of the *Crucifixion with St Dominic* is repeated.

Benozzo Gozzoli almost certainly worked in the cells on the left side of the third corridor, and the *Adoration of the Magi* – in the second of the cells reserved for Cosimo the Elder – is also probably by him. On the same side of this corridor is

To the right of the church of San Marco is Via Giorgio La Pira (this then becomes Via Lamarmora and leads to one of the avenues created at the end of the 19th century). At no. 4 Via La Pira are the first three sections of the Natural History Museum. The entrance to the fourth, the Giardino dei Semplici *(Botanical Gardens), is from no. 3 Via Pier Antonio Micheli (next street on the right).*

NATURAL HISTORY MUSEUM

The humanist philosophy, as followed by the Medici, was just as concerned with the creations of nature as with those of man's own invention, and this aspect of Medicean interests gave rise to various collections which developed into a group of museums unique in Italy. The Natural History Museum (Museo di Storia Naturale) is divided into four sections: the Museum of Mineralogy and Lithology, the Museum of Geology and Paleontology, the Botanical Museum, the Giardino dei Semplici (Botanical Gardens). **Museum of Mineralogy and Lithology.** An offspring of the

Lorenzo Monaco, Annunciation.

Pacino di Buonaguida, Lignum vitae, detail.

Michelangelo, Saint Matthew. Below, Michelangelo, David, detail.

Medici collections, the museum has approximately 40,000 items, including an enormous topaz (333 lbs.) and 5,000 samples of minerals from the island of Elba.

Museum of Geology and Paleontology. The museum has almost 300,000 exhibits. Most spectacular are the examples of mammals from the Tertiary period, including the original skeleton of *Oreopithecus bambolii,* an anthropomorphic monkey discovered in layers of lignite in an area near Grosseto.

Botanical Museum. This is one of the most important in Italy. The herbaria, collections which were created in the 16th century by Andrea Cesalpina, today consist of approximately four million samples from all parts of the world. The collection also contains wax models, plant fossils, seeds and pollens, and a tropical herbarium with 300,000 samples of plants from Somalia and Ethiopia, unique in the world.

Giardino dei Semplici. Created by Cosimo I in 1545, these botanical gardens were at their height during the 18th century. Covering over 26,000 square yards, with hot and cold houses, the gardens now contain approximately 7,000 samples of arboreal and herbaceous plants. The oldest trees were planted in the 19th century, except for a yew tree, which was planted in 1720. The collection of azaleas is a delight to see when blooming in the springtime.

From the Botanical Gardens we *head back towards the cathedral and, crossing Piazza San Marco, we take Via Ricasoli. The Galleria dell'Accademia is on the left, at no. 60.*

ACADEMY GALLERY

Grand Duke Pietro Leopoldo founded the Galleria dell'Accademia in 1784, leaving a considerable endowment of classical paintings to the newly-formed school of art created to consolidate the city's various drawing schools. This valuable patrimony was intended to provide the students with models. During the 19th century, sculptures were added to the collection, and when the *David* was brought here from Piazza Signoria, the Academy became increasingly identified as 'the museum of Michelangelo' and of his artistic circle.

The former hospital of San Matteo was taken over and remodeled to house the Academy. Overlooking Piazza

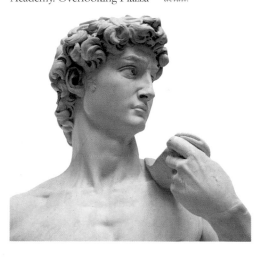

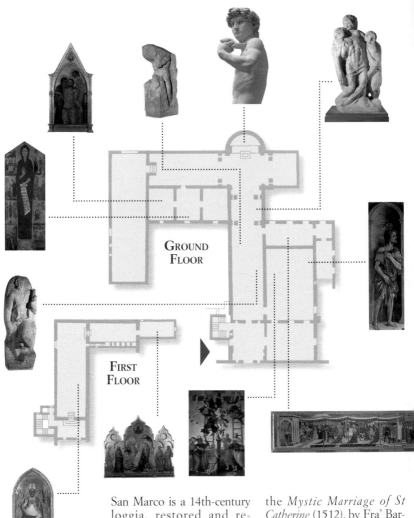

San Marco is a 14th-century loggia, restored and re-opened in 1935, which was also part of the hospital. In the lunettes over the two doors are glazed *bas-reliefs* by Andrea della Robbia.

Sala del Colosso. Our visit starts in the Colossus room, in the middle of which stands a plaster model of the *Abduction of the Sabine Women* by Giambologna (the marble statue is in the Loggia dei Lanzi). On the walls are early 16th-century Florentine paintings, including the *Mystic Marriage of St Catherine* (1512), by Fra' Bartolomeo; and a *Deposition* begun by Filippino Lippi and finished after his death (1504) by Perugino, possibly assisted by Raphael.

The Gallery. Dominating the gallery are the four large *Prisoners* (1530) and *St Matthew* (1505). These are magnificent examples of Michelangelo's immensely expressive *non finito* (unfinished) technique, which had its roots in neo-Platonic philosophy. As Giulio Carlo

Pontormo, Venus and Cupid

Argan explained, "the meaning of the figures is no longer evident in their symbolism, but must be sought in the act of their creation, in the impression left by the artist's anguish expressed in every stroke of the chisel. The figure is merely a finishing point: an idea finally achieved as the result of a painful process of liberation".

Michelangelo created the *Prisoners* for the tomb of Pope Julius II, but the original project was later modified and the statues remained in Florence. *St Matthew,* with statues of the other eleven apostles, was intended to decorate the chapels in the choir of the cathedral.

Beside the *Bearded Prisoner* is the *Palestrina Pietà.* This dramatic work – the only by Michelangelo to lack full documentation – dates from around 1550. The figure of Christ appears to be fully expressed, while in contrast, those of the Virgin and Mary Magdalen have a more dramatic and sculptural quality.

Tribuna del "David". The neoclassical tribune (De Fabris, 1882) at the end of the gallery houses the renowned *David* (1502-1504). Michelangelo sculpted the figure from a block of marble which Agostino di Duccio had abandoned forty years earlier as being impossible to work. The young David – symbolizing the triumph of intelligence and courage over brute force, with which the Florentines liked to iden-

tify themselves – was one of the most popular subjects of Florentine art at the time.

Irving Stone described the work as being "...the incarnation of everything Lorenzo de' Medici had been fighting for, that the Plato Academy had believed was the rightful heritage of man [...] a glorious creation capable of beauty, strength, courage, wisdom, faith in his own kind [...] the most fully realized man the world had yet seen, functioning in a rational and humane world". It was precisely for this symbolic value as a defender of freedom that the thirteen-foot statue was located in front of Palazzo Vecchio, where it remained until 1872 when a copy was put in its place. It took a week for the masterpiece to reach the Academy, and a railway wagon running on iron tracks with points was specially designed to transport it.

Florentine paintings contemporary to Michelangelo's work are in the two vestibules off the tribune. On the right is a lovely *Venus* (c.1532), painted by Pontormo from a drawing by Michelangelo. On the left we see represented the two different influences in late 16th-century Florentine painting: the sophisticated late-mannerist style – the *Disputation* by Carlo Portelli – and the opposing, controversial return to a simpler style (*Christ entering Jerusalem*, by Santi di Tito).

Sale fiorentine. From

Andrea Rico da Candia, Madonna and Child.

Lorenzo di Bicci, Saint Martin. *Left, Filippino Lippi,* Mary Magdalen.

Above, the 'Adimari Cassone' (wedding chest). Right, Atlas, *one of Michelangelo's 'prisoners'.*

Giovanni da Milano, Pietà.

Michelangelo, the Palestrina Pietà.

the right of the gallery we enter the 'Florentine Rooms,' where one finds an excellent collection of 15th-century Florentine painting. Of particular note are: the *Adimari chest*, an excellent example of secular Renaissance art by Giovanni di ser Giovanni (Masaccio's half-brother) depicting a wedding procession with the Baptistery in the background; the *Trinity with Sts Benedict and John Gualberto*, by Alessio Baldinovetti; a *Thebaid*, considered to be by Paolo Uccello for its rich composition and perspective; a *Madonna and Child with the young St John and two angels* (c.1470), one of Botticelli's last works; a carefully crafted *Madonna of the Sea* (1470), possibly the work of the young Filippino Lippi.

Gipsoteca Bartolini. At the end of the left wing of the tribune is the 'gallery of plaster casts,' where the models used by Lorenzo Bartolini (1777-1850) for his sculptures – mainly portraits – are housed.

Sale Bizantine. On the left of the same wing are the Byzantine Rooms, so named because important paintings pre-dating Giotto are displayed here. The panel painting of the *Magdalen* surrounded by eight small images of scenes from her life is by the Maestro della Maddalena. The *Madonna Enthroned with Child and*

Four Saints, dated last decade of the 13th century, is by the Maestro di San Gaggio. The paintings by Taddeo Gaddi and Ber-nardo Daddi are similar in style to Giotto's work.

First floor. An extremely interesting collection of Florentine 14th- and 15th-century paintings is exhibited in the rooms on the first floor, opened in 1985. Important works here are those by Lorenzo Monaco (two *Crucifixions,* an *Annunciation,* and the *altar-step* painted for Santa Trìnita) and the collection of polyptychs. Exhibited in the third room are late-Gothic panel paintings and a collection of rare 16th- to 18th-century Russian icons.

Leaving the gallery, we continue in the direction of the cathedral. On our left we come to the small Piazza delle Belle Arti. At no. 2 is the Luigi Cherubini Conservatory of Music.

LUIGI CHERUBINI CONSERVATORY OF MUSIC

Dedicated to Florence's most famous musician, the Conservatorio di Musica houses a

valuable collection of musical instruments, initiated by Ferdinando I (1663-1713) and subsequently increased. Of particular note are some Stradivarius violins, an Amati cello, a Del Mela upright piano and a Floriani spinet. The Conservatory is presently closed to the public.

Turning to the left immediately after the square, we enter Via degli Alfani. At no. 78 is the Opificio delle Pietre Dure, one of the most unusual museums in Florence.

OPIFICIO DELLE PIETRE DURE

Created by Ferdinando I, the Workshop and Museum of Semi-precious Stone was founded on September 3, 1588 for the purpose of coordinating the various court craftsmen who were already working on the Chapel of the Princes in San Lorenzo. At first, the Opificio was housed in the Casino at San Marco and then in the Uffizi; in 1796, it was transferred to the old monastery of San Niccolò in Cafaggio. It is therefore more of a workshop than a museum, housing items which were made here by the craftsmen, but which, for various reasons, were never consigned to the client. Amongst the items ex-

hibited are an extensive collection of samples of minerals and gems, items made with semi-precious stone inlay and scagliola, decorative painted stonework, a graphic display of the procedures, and many of the tools used in the craft.

Continuing in the same direction along Via degli Alfani, we reach the junction with Via de' Servi. Looking to the right we enjoy a wonderful view of the cathedral dome, as this straight, narrow street emphasizes the perspective and volume. Turning to the left, we come to Piazza Santissima Annunziata.

PIAZZA SANTISSIMA ANNUNZIATA

"An extended Renaissance courtyard": this is the most frequent and apt description of this square which, in fact, represents one of the most sublime pieces of planning ever carried out by Brunelleschi. The sense of spaciousness is enhanced by the lofty arcading: although the portico on the left was made between 1516 and 1525 by Antonio da Sangallo the Elder and Baccio d'Agnolo, it had formed part of Brunelleschi's original plan. The view straight down Via de' Servi to the Cathedral dome is spectacular and behind, on a perfect axis with it,

Gerolamo Della Valle, semi-precious stone mosaic sunflower. Above left, semi-precious stone inlay, designed by Giuseppe Zocchi (18th century).

Domenico Remps, Tromp l'oeil still life.

Fountain on the right side of Piazza Santissima Annunziata cast, with its matching pair, by Pietro Tacca (1629).

Customs and festivals -3-

San Giovanni (St John's Day). "When springtime comes along, gladdening the entire world, every Florentine begins to prepare for the joyful feast of St John," wrote the historian Goro di Stagio Dati at the beginning of the 15th century. Celebrations for the city's patron saint were proclaimed a month in advance by the *podestà*, and on June 24 the *Signoria* received homage from the cities and castles under the dominion of the Florentine Republic. The popular *palio dei Bàrberi* was held too: riderless Barbary horses started from a bridge known as *alle Mosse* (*mossa* in old Italian meant the parting signal, and still today a *mossiere* starts the *palio* held in Siena). The finish line was in Piazza San Pier Maggiore (☞ page 228). Inspired by classical examples, the *palio dei Cocchi* was more aristocratic, introduced by Cosimo I in 1563. Chariot-like carts, drawn by

Fireworks on the Santa Trìnita bridge, by Thomas Patch.

two horses, competed in Piazza Santa Maria Novella racing around two pinnacles which were at first temporary wooden structures, until replaced in 1608 by the existing ones (☞ p. 55). Fire has always been a feature of St John's eve. Flames of celebration were lit on the towers, along the walls and in the piazzas, while bowls filled with fat were lit and hung on the façades of houses and palazzi. During the second half of the 16th century, these fires were replaced by fireworks lit on the tower of Palazzo Vecchio. In 1827, the rockets and Catherine wheels were moved from there to the Carraia bridge and the public watched from the banks of the Arno while the river was filled with richly decorated boats. Today, sophisticated displays of fireworks take place from the most panoramic point in the city — Piazzale Michelangelo. The ideal place from which to see this spectacular exhi-

16th-century 'kneeling window', palazzo Budini Gattai, designed by Ammannati.

is the dome of Santissima Annunziata, made by Alberti.

In the center of the piazza is the equestrian statue of *Ferdinando I*, by Giambologna, completed in 1608 by Pietro Tacca. It was cast from the bronze cannons of Turkish warships captured by the Knights of St Steven during the expedition to Bona in Africa, as poetically recorded in the inscription on the horse's belly: "Of the metal wrested from the ferocious Thracian enemy". On the base is the emblem of Ferdinando (a swarm of bees

around the queen, symbol of innate superiority): the staggered arrangement of the sixty bees gave rise to the legend that it is impossible to count them.

Pietro Tacca also made the two *fountains* (1629) with sea monsters and imaginary figures, originally intended for the city of Livorno.

PALAZZO BUDINI GATTAI

The problem of completing the fourth side of the piazza (on the corner with Via de' Servi, on the left, coming

bition, which starts around 10 pm, is from the banks of the river.
A reminder of Florence's past glory and splendor, instead, is the great procession in historic costume which winds through the city before the final game of 'Florentine Football'.

The festival of the 'Rificolona' in an 18th-century print. ('Firenze com'era' Museum).

Rificolona. Fire, although in the more modest form of a candle lit inside a paper lantern (the *rificolona*), is also part of another important Florentine festival which takes place on the evening of September 7. Throughout the city various celebrations and plays are held, especially for children, who parade through the streets carrying a little lantern on the end of a stick. Now a lively market of natural products and wholefoods, the Rificolona was originally a fair held in Piazza Santissima Annunicata.

The women of the Casentino and Pistoia areas once brought the dried mushrooms and woven cloth they produced to sell here, sleeping in the loggia and the cloisters of the church before returning home. "They sing hymns to Our Lady in their harsh vernacular," wrote Marco Lastri in 1821.

Rough and unsophisticated, the haughty townspeople christened them the *fierucolone*. Their peasant dress was an object of derision for young Florentines, and Giuseppe Conti wrote in 1899 that "the *rificolone* were large dolls made of paper, caricatures of the peasants from the mountains, with a candle under their petticoats".

San Lorenzo (St Lawrence's Day). Another ancient tradition is still celebrated during the hot Florentine summer, on August 10, in the piazza in front of the church of San Lorenzo. The founding of the church and the feast of its patron saint was first celebrated in 1421, with a meal of pastry cornets, peaches, walnuts and fennel.

The culinary aspect of the day's festivities could also be seen in the bakers' shops which were adorned with imaginative decorations made from pasta. Now, on the evening of August 10, Florentines and tourists alike gather in the piazza, where brightly honourfavored stalls (organized by a special committee) offer free portions of pasta with meat sauce, drinks and large slices of watermelon.

from the Cathedral) was resolved between 1563 and 1574 by Bartolomeo Ammannati, using a daring and unusual contrast of honourfavors between the red of unfaced bricks and the grey of stone. One of the greatest examples of Ammannati's talent, the building is remarkable for its originality and rich decoration, especially on the façade facing Via de' Servi. The first floor loggia, beneath the rustication framing the window on the façade against the piazza, creates a central focus which distracts from the doorway on the right, the only feature to have remained of a previous design.

Spedale degli Innocenti

"Agatha Emerald is the name of the first female baby to be left at our hospital on Friday at 12 o'clock of St Agatha's Day". In fact, on January 25, 1445, the 'spedale' devoted entirely to abandoned babies (or Innocents) opened its doors, almost thirty years after the Silkmakers Guild had agreed

The revolving stone grate where abandoned babies were left.

Façade of the Spedale degli Innocenti. In the foreground is the statue of grand duke Ferdinando I.

Over the main entrance is a fresco by Bernardino Poccetti (16th century); the tondos by Andrea della Robbia portray new-born babies in swaddling, the symbol of the institute.

Below, the 'Rificolona' fair, held on 7 September in Piazza Santissima Annunziata.

to finance it. It was designed by Filippo Brunelleschi, who drew up a plan which was innovative both in its practical arrangement and in its architectural style. Breaking with the traditional plan of medieval hospitals, he created a single complex, not unlike a miniature city, where every area was intentionally planned with a specific function.

His decision to revive, after centuries, the classic element of the column with base and capital seen in the delightful, airy portico, was equally revolutionary and inspired. Indeed it is recognized as representing the birth of Renaissance architecture. The distance between the columns is almost the same as their height, thus creating the appearance of a series of squares crowned by hemispheres. In the pendentives between the arches are eight glazed terracotta *tondi* by Andrea della Robbia. The *vault* and the *lunettes* were frescoed by Poccetti. On the far left is the square window with a grating where, until 1875, the abandoned babies were deposited.

Interior. We first enter the airy and spacious Men's Cloister, designed by Francesco della Luna and completed by Stefano di Jacopo Rosselli. Above is the Art Gallery, housing Domenico Ghirlandaio's masterpiece the *Adoration of the Magi*. Other works of interest are the *Coronation of the Virgin*, by Maestro della Madonna Strauss, a rare little altarpiece of the 14th or 15th century; a *Madonna and Child*, by Sandro Botticelli; and a glazed *terracotta* of the same subject, by Luca della Robbia.

The gallery also has a collection of detached frescoes (of particular note, those by Lorenzo Monaco and Alessandro Allori) that were taken from various Florentine buildings. These can only be seen on request.

CHURCH OF SANTISSIMA ANNUNZIATA

During the epoch of Countess Mathilda, the monastery originated as a small oratory, built as an ex-voto to the Madonna after a siege by the German emperor Henry IV. It was enlarged in 1250 and five remaining Gothic windows can be seen on Via Battisti. It was completely renovated between 1444 and 1481 by Michelozzo. Leon Battista Alberti collaborated on the building and in 1470 he altered the large circular tribune, crowning it with a dome. The façade was made during the Renaissance with only one central arch. The arches to each side forming a portico were added in the early 17th century.

Cloister of the Votive Offerings. We enter this cloister by the central doorway. Known as the 'Chiostrino dei Voti,' for centuries all manner of votive offerings were collected here, from clothing to armour, flags and wax statues. These were

removed on the order of Pietro Leopoldo in 1780.

Around the walls of the cloister is what amounts to a synthesis of Florentine painting between the 15th and 16th centuries: the *Assumption* (1517), by Rosso Fiorentino and the *Visitation* (1514-1516), by Jacopo Pontormo represent the beginnings of Mannerism, while the classical Renaissance tradition is still seen in the *Marriage of the Virgin* (1513), by Franciabigio, and in the *Birth of Mary* (1514) and the *Arrival of the Magi* (1511), by Andrea del Sarto. The cycle continues with Alessio Baldinovetti's *Nativity* (1460) and the six *Miracles of St Filippo Benizzi,* the first (1476) by Cosimo Rosselli, the others (1509-1510) by Andrea del Sarto. A splendid marble *bas-relief* by Michelozzo is on the wall to the right.

Interior. Pilaster strips along the walls of the single nave frame the entrances to the various chapels. The decoration of the interior, carried out in the 17th and 18th centuries, is entirely baroque.

Immediately on the left is a small marble temple (1447-1461), containing many ex-voto, with a richly decorated silver altar, and an *Annunciation,* believed to be miraculous.

Continuing along the left side of the nave we come to the second and third chapels, decorated with beautiful *frescoes* (1454-1456) by Andrea del Castagno; in the fifth chapel is an *Assumption of the Virgin,* by Pietro Perugino; in the chapel of the Crucifix, at the end of the left wing of the transept, is a terracotta *St John the Baptist,* by Michelozzo.

The presbytery consists of a large rotonda made by Michelozzo, surrounded by nine chapels containing important paintings: in the third on the left is a *panel painting* by Perugino, and in the fourth, a *Resurrection,* by Bronzino. Giambologna turned the fifth into a personal memorial chapel, filling it with works by himself and his pupils.

In the first chapel on the right side of the church is a *Madonna in Glory,* by Jacopo da Empoli, and the ceiling in the third chapel was decorated by Volterrano.

Cloister of the Dead. From the left transept, (ask the sacristan for permission), we enter the Chiostro dei Morti. Part of the 15th-century rebuilding, it was later frescoed with a cycle of scenes relating to the *Order of the Servants of Mary.* Above the entrance to the church is Andrea del Sarto's masterpiece, the *Madonna del Sacco* (1525).

Leaving the church, we turn left onto Via Gino Capponi. On the nearest corner of the second street to the right – Via Giuseppe Giusti – is the house of Andrea del Sarto, *restructured by Federico Zuccari in 1578 and later acquired by him. Zuccari, the artist who completed Vasari's frescoes inside Brunelleschi's dome (☛*

The Orator
*(Etruscan-Roman
art, 1st century B.C.).*

city,' and this principle is clearly evident in this impressive structure, designed to overlook both the Giardino dei Semplici in front and the park behind. The façade has a sculptural quality with original and striking interpretations of Renaissance architectural design.

On the opposite side of the street, on the corner of Via Micheli, is the 17th-century Palazzo Velluti Zani di San Clemente, *built by the Marquis of Guadagni to a design by Gherardo Silvani.*

Returning along the street to the piazza, we pass under the arch on the left of the Spedale degli Innocenti and enter Via della Colonna. The name of this street refers to a large column which supported the roof of a 'tiratoio' (a yard where pieces of material were stretched and dried) which the Wool Guild once owned here.

Behind a long railing on the left we can see items displayed in the garden of the Archaeological Museum at no. 38.

ARCHAEOLOGICAL MUSEUM

p. 26), built a highly original house and studio for himself slightly further ahead (Via Giusti, no. 43) where he made use of the vogue for the non finito *technique, interpreted in late-mannerist style, seen in the barely outlined architectural elements.*

Continuing along the right side of Via Gino Capponi, we come to the long and lofty façade of Palazzo Capponi, *built in 1705 to a design by Carlo Fontana — the 'maestro' of Filippo Juvarra who worked mainly in Rome. All his works were based on the theory of 'bringing the countryside into the*

The Museo Archeologico of Florence houses the most im-

Portrait of a young woman, Greek art. Right, the Etruscan sarcophagus of Larthia Seanti (3rd century B.C.).

portant collection of Etruscan artifacts in Italy, and the second most important Egyptian collection (after Turin). Located in this building since 1879, the museum is sadly still under restoration from the severe damage caused by the flood of 1966.

The museum is based on two important collections: the Etruscan, created by the Medici and Lorraine Grand Dukes; and the rare and valuable Egyptian items discovered by the Franco-Tuscan expedition (1828-1829) led by Ippolito Rosellini and Jean-François Champollion.

The rooms dedicated to the Etruscan, Greek and Roman Antiquarium are on the first floor. Among the numerous Etruscan funerary sculptures are a marble *sarcophagus of the Amazons*, from Tarquinia; and an alabaster *sarcophagus of the obese Etruscan* from Chiusi. There is also an interesting collection of domestic items, including several small mirrors from the Etruscan period, and Greek and Roman bronzes. The most important statues in

the collection are: the *Idolino*, found in Pesaro in 1530 (depicting an athletic youth, this is a copy, made during the Augustan period, of a statue from the 5th century BC); *Minerva* (a Roman copy of a statue of Praxiteles); the *Orator* (an Etruscan-Roman piece from the 1st century BC); and the *Three-headed Chimera* (5th-4th century BC) also known as the Arezzo Chimera, after the city where it was discovered in 1533. It was restored by Benvenuto Cellini.

In the remaining rooms on the first floor is the Egyptian collection, presently arranged in eight chronological groups, dating from pre-history to the end of the New Kingdom. Some of the most important items are a tombstone from Saqqara, statues and portraits from the 18th Dynasty, various papyri, and the wooden funerary chariot of Amenthope, in almost perfect condition.

The second floor houses an important collection of Attic ceramics, the most valuable item being the *François Vase*, a splendid crater discovered in 1844-1845 in a tomb near Chiusi, and now much restored. Dating the piece to 570 BC, the inscription reads: "Ergòtimos made me and Clitias designed me".

Leaving the Archaeological Museum, we continue a little further along Via della Colonna and then turn right on Via della Pergola. A plaque at no. 59 notes that this is the house where Celli-

Bas-relief of the goddess Maat.

Left, water jar with Aphrodite and Phaon.

Handle on the lid of an Etruscan urn: two warriors carrying the body of a fellow soldier.

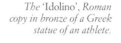

The 'Idolino', *Roman
copy in bronze of a Greek
statue of an athlete.*

'Mater Matuta',
*Roman goddess of
fertility.*

Below, the 'Arezzo
Chimera' *bronze
Etruscan statue dated
5th-4th century B.C.*

*Below right, the
rotonda of Santa
Maria degli Angeli,
designed by Filippo
Brunelleschi.*

ni *"made and cast the
Perseus". We then turn right
into Via degli Alfani, passing* Palazzo Giugni *(no. 48),
designed by Bartolomeo
Ammannati. On the left,
slightly further ahead, on
the corner of Via degli Alfani and Piazza Brunelleschi,
is the Rotonda of Santa
Maria degli Angeli.*

ROTONDA DI SANTA MARIA DEGLI ANGELI

The Rotonda is the unfin-
ished result of Filippo
Brunelleschi's reflections on
central planning. Octagonal
in design, it was begun in
1433, but work was inter-
rupted when it had reached a
height of 23 feet. The sixteen
external facets were achieved
by inserting a semicircu-
lar apse into each
corner. In 1936,
the Rotonda
was heavily re-
stored and the up-
per section clum-
sily "completed".
Today it houses
the Language
Department of
the University of
Florence.

*Continuing past
the Rotonda, we
cross Piazza Brunel-
leschi, then con-
tinue along
Via del Cas-
tellaccio.
This leads
into Via
de' Servi,*

*which will bring us back to
Piazza del Duomo. On the
corner of the two streets, at
no. 12, is* Palazzo Sforza Al-
meni, *built by Taddei between 1510 and 1520: the
'kneeling' windows, some of
the loveliest in the city, are
probably the work of Baccio
d'Agnolo or Bartolomeo
Ammannati.*

Palazzo Niccolini *(1548-
1550) at no. 15, is by Baccio d'Agnolo: the façade is
emphatically vertical and
has splendid graffiti decorations. On the corner of Via
Bufalini,* Palazzo Pasqui
*still has its solid 14th-centu-
ry arches on the ground floor
where, as is recorded by
plaques, Benedetto da Ma-
iano and Jacopo da Empoli
both had their workshops.*

The theatres

Zubin Mehta.

The first Florentine theatre was Roman: built at the time of the Roman Empire, its remains are now buried beneath Palazzo Vecchio and Palazzo Gondi. During the Middle Ages, miracle plays were performed in churches and on their paved forecourts, while the Renaissance witnessed the return of classical theatre. The first place specifically designed to house modern theatre with a stage and sets was, in fact, the Medici theatre, built on the first floor of the Uffizi. It opened on 16 February, 1586 with *L'amico fido* (The Faithful Friend) written by Giovanni de' Bardi, with scenery designed by Bernardo Buontalenti. From then on, the number of theatres gradually increased until, during the 1850's, there were fifteen, scattered throughout the entire city. Today only four remain. The *Verdi*, founded in 1854, hosts concerts, musicals, variety, operetta, ballet.

The *Niccolini* came into being around 1650 and the renovation work carried out in 1764 has, on the whole, remained unaltered to this day. Designed by Ferdinando Tacca and built with wood from the Camaldoli forests, the original *Pergola* theatre opened in 1657 with one of the first comic operas ever to be performed in Italy. It was replaced by a stone structure designed by Giulio Mannaioni (second half of the 18th century); this was completed in Neo-classical style between 1828 and 1837, when the wrought iron canopy at the entrance was also added. Today it is the most important Florentine theatre for dramatic performances (October to April).

The *Teatro Comunale*, originally known as the *Politeama Fiorentino*, first came into being in 1862 as an open-air amphitheatre, in one of the most prestigious new residential areas for the bourgeoisie. It was destroyed after only a year by a dreadful fire, though it was rapidly rebuilt and then roofed over. In 1933 it was entirely renovated; having suffered severe damage from bombs in 1944, it was finally modernized in 1958.

The theatre was given its present name and role in 1933 when it

Cross-section, Teatro della Pergola.

became the home of the 'Maggio Musicale Fiorentino,' the longest established Italian music festival and one of the most famous on the international level. Founded by conductor Vittorio Gui as a triannual event, it became annual in 1937 and has always sustained a precise artistic direction: highlighting the importance of lyric opera, with attention to its dramatic and visual aspects. It has therefore attracted important musicians and performers, from Gui himself to Furtwängler, from von Karajan to Muti, from Callas to Arturo Benedetti Michelangeli. Exceptional directors, artists and sculptors have also worked with the 'Maggio,' including Visconti, Reinaherdt, Wilson, de Chirico, Casorati, Cagli. The orchestra, choir and ballet company must also be considered vital to the success of the season, which runs from May to June.

Entrance to the Teatro Verdi.

4. **The Art of Power and the Power of Art**

Benvenuto Cellini's Perseus.

Republic of merchants, and of merchants turned princes, this area was the scene of long and bitter struggles between opposing factions — of fire, destruction and the rapidly changing fortunes of power and politics.

Our itinerary begins at Via de' Calzaioli, where the Guilds, the backbone of Florentine society, not only operated but also displayed their prestige in Orsanmichele. This is the area too, where Neri degli Abati, acting for the heads of the Neri faction, "set on fire the house of his relations in Orto San Michele, and burnt the entire core and heart and all the loveliest parts of the city of Florence," on 10 June 1304, as chronicled historian Giovanni Villani.

The echoes of other violent, historic events resound in Piazza della Signoria, built on top of the ruins of the houses of the Uberti family as a form of revenge on the defeated Ghibelline supporters. More than anything, however, this square represented power and was the stage for all the most important political events: here the Duke of Athens was expelled and Michele di Lando

tried to burn down the door of Palazzo Vecchio; Pier Capponi threatened the King and Savonarola was burned at the stake; the French planted a tree of liberty and the annexation of Tuscany to Piedmont was proclaimed. Now the seat of the city council, Palazzo Vecchio was built in the Middle Ages to represent republican freedom, only to become later the Renaissance residence of princes.

Sandro Botticelli, Madonna of the Magnificat.

The itinerary ends with visits to two formerly private residences. Palazzo Davanzati, built by wealthy cloth merchants, gradually fell into disuse, becoming little more than a ruin until it was bought in 1904 by antique dealer Elio Volpi. Palazzo Strozzi, on the other hand, has not suffered with the passing centuries, and was recently acquired by the city council. On the death of the last member of the family, Piero Strozzi, in 1907, it was ed that the American millionaire, Pierpont Morgan, wished to buy this historic Palazzo where the noble Strozzi family, resolute opponents of the Medici, had lived for four centuries.

Right, the impressive structure of Orsanmichele, both church and granary of the Florentine republic. Below, tripartite architectural feature on the ground floor. Centre page, panel portraying an apostle.

Although known as Via de' Calzaioli or 'street of the shoemakers,' it could have just as easily been dubbed that of the banner makers, doublet makers, cheese makers, flask makers, or painters. The shops of all these trades were to be found along this street which, linking the Cathedral and Palazzo Vecchio, has always been one of the most important commercial streets in the city. Indeed, it had to be enlarged twice, firstly in 1389, from Piazza della Signoria to Via Condotta, and again in 1842, continuing to Piazza del Duomo.

On the second occasion, the buildings on the left were most affected: on the right, the Adimari Tower (no. 13) was shortened, but not demolished.

Interrupting the sequence of 19th-century buildings is Orsanmichele and opposite, the church of San Carlo dei Lombardi, *begun in 1349 by Neri di Fioravante and finished in 1404 by Simone Talenti. The name derives from the fact that it was assigned to the Lombard company of St Charles Borromeo. Inside are paintings of various periods, from the 14th to the 18th century, including a* St Charles Borromeo in Glory, *by Matteo Rosselli (1578-1650).*

In the final section of the street, the 14th-century project for its widening was clearly

Andrea del Verrocchio, Doubting Thomas.

consistently planned, as can be seen from the repeated architectural design of sturdy arches on the ground floor, supported by co-lumns, and the windows crowned with rounded arches on the upper floors, such as on the Casa della Compagnia di Orsanmichele *(no. 23, 25 and 27r),* Palazzo Cavalcanti *(no. 11, 13, 15 and 17r), and* Palazzo dell'Arte dei Mercanti *(no. 15r).*

ORSANMICHELE

The origins and complex history of this unusual building are linked to the grain supplies of the Florentine Republic. In fact, Vasari relates that in 1284, Arnolfo di Cambio built a loggia "made of bricks, with a flat roof" to be used as a grain market on the site of San Michele in Orto, a church demolished around 1238.

The loggia was destroyed by fire in 1304, and was rebuilt and enlarged between 1337 and 1349, by Neri di Fioravante, Benci di Cione and Francesco Talenti. From 1367 to 1380, the same architects transformed the building into a palazzo, adding two floors and closing the arches on the ground floor, which was no longer used for business, but for religious functions instead, becoming the church of the Guilds. Grain was no longer sold here, but was stored on the upper floors

until 1569, when Cosimo moved the archive for legal documents there and had Buontalenti build the connecting arch to the Palazzo of the Wool Guild.

Exterior. The original structure of the loggia, formed by rounded arches resting on ten pilasters, is still clearly visible on the ground floor, and has not been affected by the delicate addition of the late-Gothic decoration.

The unusual character of the whole building is further emphasized by the extraordinary series of tabernacles around all four sides. Each contains the patron saint of a Guild, and together these form a rich anthology of 15th-century Florentine sculpture, with brief incursions into the

Panel portraying an apostle. Above, Stone workers, *relief by Nanni di Banco.*

4. The art of power and the power of art

Giambologna, bronze statue of Cosimo I. *Below left,* Neptune *by Ammannati and the Signoria tower by Arnolfo di Cambio.*

Orsanmichele, interior with the tabernacle by Andrea Orcagna. In the centre is a panel with the Madonna *by Bernardo Daddi.*

16th century, as well as being an obvious display of pride by the powerful corporations of the republican city.

Starting from the front of the church on Via de' Calzaioli, from the left: the Calimala (cloth merchants) represented by the statue of *St John the Baptist* (1412-1416), by Lorenzo Ghiberti; the Court of Commerce with the *Incredulity of St Thomas* (1467-1483), by Andrea Verrocchio; the Judges and Notaries Guild with *St Luke*, a bronze statue by Giambologna. On Via Orsanmichele: the Butchers Guild with *St Peter* (1408-1413), by Donatello; the Tanners with *St Philip* (c. 1415), by Nanni di Banco; the Wood and Stone-carvers with *Four Crowned Saints*, by Nanni di Banco; the Gunsmiths with *St George*, a bronze copy of Donatello's masterpiece in marble, conserved in the Bargello. On Via dell'Arte della Lana where the entrance is, opposite the palazzo of the same name (☛ p. 156): the Bankers and Moneychangers Guild with *St Matthew* (1419-1422), a bron-ze by Lorenzo Ghiberti; the Wool Guild with *St Steven* (1428), a bronze by Ghiberti; the Blacksmiths with *St Eligius* in marble, and a bas-relief by Nanni di Banco. In Via de' Lamberti: the Flax-makers Guild with *St Mark* (a copy of Donatello's original dated 1411-1413); the Furriers with *St Jacob* and a bas-relief with the *Beheading of the Saint*, attributed to Niccolò di Piero Lamberti; Physicians

and Pharmacists with the marble group *Virgin of the Rose* (1400), attributed to Pietro di Giovanni Tedesco; the Silk and Goldsmiths with the bronze statue of *St John the Evangelist* (1515), by Baccio da Montelupo.

Above the loggia are two orderly rows of mullioned windows, defined by the normal cornice along the string course as well as by the cornice originally at the springer of the arches.

Interior. Clearly reflecting its original function as a market, the interior is rectangular in form and the two columns do not really succeed in creating the effect of two aisles leading to a single, clear focal point. More obvious reminders of the original use can also be seen in the overflowing bushel carved in the cornice of a small door in the corner pilaster between Via Orsanmichele and Via dell'Arte della Lana, and in the outlets in the two central pilasters on the north side, for the grain sent down from the upper floors.

The 14th-century frescoes

QVI
DOVE CON I SVOI
CONTRATELLI FRA DOMENICO
BVONVICINI E FRA SILVESTRO
MARVFFI IL XXIII MAGGIO
DEL MCCCCXCVIII PER INIQVA
SENTENZA FV IMPICCATO ED ARSO
FRA GIROLAMO SAVONAROLA
DOPO QVATTRO SECOLI
FV COLLOCATA QVESTA
MEMORIA

A marble plaque near the centre of the piazza commemorates the spot where Girolamo Savonarola was burned at the stake.

in the vault are well-preserved (*Scenes from the Old and New Testaments*) and the stained glass windows with *Stories and Miracles of the Virgin* are most attractive.

At the end of the left aisle is a marble sculpture of *Virgin and Child with St Anna* (c. 1526), by Francesco da Sangallo. The tabernacle (1349-1359) by Andrea Orcagna dominates the right aisle. This richly decorated Gothic masterpiece contains an image of the *Virgin* (1347), attributed to Bernardo Daddi: the eight hexagonal bas-relief panels depict *Scenes from the Life of the Virgin.* On the back is a relief sculpture, also by Orcagna, of the *Assumption of the Virgin* (1359).

PIAZZA SIGNORIA

Here "in the past were the houses of the Uberti, rebels against Florence, and Ghibellines; and they made a piazza over their houses, so that they could never be rebuilt," wrote Villani. The area therefore was not the result of urban planning, but rather the dramatic outcome of political events. It was, in fact, the destruction of the Ghibelline houses and towers that determined the piazza's unusual shape, forming an octagon which has evolved into a unique open air museum.

At the end of Via delle Farine is the bronze equestri-

an monument to *Cosimo I* (1594-1598), by Giambologna. To the left of the front of Palazzo Vecchio is the *Neptune Fountain* (1563-1575), with the rather unpopular marble statue of the sea god by Bartolomeo Ammannati and helpers, one of whom was Giambologna. Of greater merit are the lively bronze figures of sea nymphs and satyrs around the fountain. Embedded in the pavement slightly in front of the fountain is a circular plaque indicating the spot where Fra' Girolamo Savonarola was burned at the stake on 23 May 1498.

On the steps in front of the Palazzo is a series of statues, almost all copies and all having some symbolic significance. Starting from the left is the *Marzocco* (a bronze copy of Donatello's original stone sculpture, now in the Bargello); next, a bronze group of *Judith and Holofernes* (a recent copy of Donatello's original, now housed inside Palazzo Vecchio, in the Sala dei Gigli); then the *David* (a marble copy of Michelangelo's masterpiece, now in the Academy Gallery); a marble group of *Hercules and Cacus* (1534), by Baccio Bandinelli.

The Marzocco, a sitting lion, is the symbol of Florence. Judith

The Cafè Rivoire on the corner of Palazzo Laweyson is one of Florence's most elegant meeting places. Below, bars and restaurants in Piazza Signoria.

Left, bronze figure of a Nereid on Neptune's fountain. Opposite page, below, view of the left side of Piazza della Signoria.

The palazzo of the Court of Commerce and the coats of arms of the Guilds, sculpted on the façade.

The 16th-century Palazzo Uguccioni may have been designed by Raphael. Below, the raised ashlars of the doorway with a bust of Cosimo I.

represents the Florentine Republic defeating tyranny. The David has a double meaning — as a symbol of the victory of republican liberty over the power of the Medici, but also of the ability of the small Florentine state to oppose the power of its external enemies. Hercules and Cacus, on the other hand, represent the victory of the Medici over their internal enemies.

Although the piazza is dominated by both Palazzo Vecchio and the Loggia della Signoria, we should not forget the various 'minor' buildings around the rest of the square.

Immediately opposite Palazzo Vecchio is the huge, bulky *Palazzo Laweyson*. Built in 1871, it is an unimaginative reinterpretation of a Renaissance building with, however, the addition of an extra floor (a departure from the classical model), and the use of cast iron in the cornice.

On the north side of the square, at no. 5, is the *Palazzo della Cassa di Risparmio*, housing the 'Alberto della Ragione' collection of contemporary art. Displayed in twenty-one rooms are works by all the major 20th-century Italian artists, including Corrado Cagli, Filippo De Pisis, Franco Gentilini, Ottone Rosai, Mino Maccari, Giorgio De Chirico, Giorgio Morandi, Carlo Carrà, Marino Marini. These will eventually be better displayed and arranged in the projected Museum of Contemporary Art.

At no. 7, just beyond Via delle Farine, is the late-Re-

naissance *Palazzo Uguccioni*. Begun in 1549, the building is similar in style to the contemporary architecture of Raphael and Bramante in Rome. The quality and distinctiveness of the structure are such that Mariotto di Zanobi Folfi, carpenter as well as architect, was probably responsible only for the construction, and not for the design, which popular opinion somewhat controversially attributes to Raphael, Michelangelo or even Antonio da Sangallo. The heavy rustication on the ground floor is deeply undercut, creating a marked *chiaroscuro* effect. Above are two floors with the feature, unusual for Florence, of Ionic and Corinthian half-columns on either side of windows with triangular and curved timpani, and small balconies.

On the east side of the square are the harmonious 14th-century *Palazzo della Condotta* (no. 9) and the *Court of Commerce* (no. 10), with the blocks of *pietra forte* left exposed on the façade. Originally these two buildings were separate, with a small alleyway between; the three small rectangular windows indicate where they were joined. Lastly, beneath the cornice of the first floor is a frieze with the coats of arms of the twenty-one Guilds and the lily, symbol of Florence.

PALAZZO VECCHIO

"And so that the palace would not be built on the land of the

Palazzo Vecchio seen from Palazzo Laweyson. The tower, 94 metres high, and the entrance, are assymetric to the façade.

and military architecture. The latter is clearly visible in the defensive nature of the narrow openings on the ground floor and the jutting, crenellated gallery supported on brackets, enclosing the two ramparts for sentries, one covered, the other open and protected by the crenellations.

The central section, with its fine cornice beneath two rows of trefoiled mullioned windows, enclosed in rounded arches, represents the 'civil' element. The only ful note in the entire structure is found in the nine painted coats of arms between the brackets of the gallery.

Just as the whole palazzo is 'offset,' so the doorway and the tower are also asymmetrical. Completed in 1310, the 308 ft tower was built on top of an earlier one, known as the 'Vacca,' which had belonged to the Foraboschi family and now became incorporated into the building. The tower widens towards the top to repeat the motif of the jutting gallery, though here it is finished with pointed crenellations.

Arnolfo's structure was enlarged by successive additions, which can clearly be seen on the left side beyond the entrance to the Sala d'Arme, where temporary exhibitions are held. The rough and rather botched joints, resulting from the creation of the Salone dei Cinquecento inside, were made in 1495 and the final, more skillful addition by Buontalenti, ex-

The addition of the 'Salone dei Cinquecento' is clearly visible from Via de' Gondi. Below, seen from Via Vacchereccia.

The first courtyard (1453). Designed by Michelozzo, it was decorated by Vasari in 1565 for the wedding of prince Francesco de' Medici.

Uberti, those who were making it set it off to a corner," in other words, slightly askance. In fact, rather than use the "cursed ground" of the defeated Ghibellines, the builders preferred to demolish a nave of the neighboring church of San Piero a Scheraggio.

This completely illogical choice, determined by political interests, became a victorious challenge to the creative ability of Arnolfo di Cambio. Making use of the asymmetrical aspect and the offset position, he succeeded in creating, between 1299 and 1314, one of the greatest monuments of Florentine civil architecture. Conceived as the residence of the *Priori* or the *Signoria* – the highest civic administrative body – the Palazzo became the Medici court from 1540 to 1565, only becoming the 'old' (vecchio) palace when the Grand Dukes moved to Palazzo Pitti. The Italian parliament sat here during Florence's brief spell as capital of Italy (1865-1871). Today it houses the city council.

Exterior. With its solid façade of rusticated *pietra forte*, Arnolfo's rectangular design succeeds in combining civil

The 'Salone dei Cinquecento' (right) seen from the gallery. Built by Antonio da Sangallo in 1495, the ceiling and walls were decorated by Vasari and his pupils. Below, Hercules and Antaeus, marble sculpture by Vincenzo de' Rossi.

tending down to Via dei Leoni, was carried out at the end of the 16th century.

First courtyard. The visit begins in the first courtyard (1453), where Michelozzo applied the innovative features used in Palazzo Medici to Arnolfo's medieval scheme. This was further modified by the rich decoration added by Vasari in 1565, on the occasion of the marriage of Francesco de' Medici to Joanna of Austria. As part of his design, the fountain in the centre with Verrocchio's *Putto and Dolphin* was built (now a copy; the original is located on Juno's terrace, inside), and the walls were painted with views of cities of the Austrian Empire.

Salone dei Cinquecento. Before entering the second courtyard (known as that of the *dogana*, or Customs), Vasari's double staircase (1560-1563) leads to the first floor and the Hall of the 500, a vast chamber (174 ft long, 72 ft wide, 58 ft high) where opposing political factions met. It was built in 1495 by Antonio da Sangallo for meetings of the People's Great Assembly, consisting of 500 citizens, created in September of the previous year, after the Medici had been expelled from Florence. From

1540 onwards, after the restoration of the Medici, Cosimo I used it for public audiences and receptions to demonstrate his uncontested power. Baccio Bandinelli was commissioned to install a raised tribune for the ducal throne and statues of illustrious members of the Medici family. The coffered ceiling in carved wood was consequently raised by almost 23 feet (1563-1565) and decorated by Vasari and helpers, who were also responsible for the frescoes around the walls eulogizing Cosimo's victorious enterprises.

Around the walls of the room is a series of important sculptures. To the left of the entrance is a model in plaster of *Florence defeating Pisa*, by Giambologna. The six marble statues of the *Labourss of Hercules* are by Vincenzo de' Rossi (1525-1587). In the middle of the far wall is a marble group representing *Victory* (1533-1534), sculpted by Michelangelo for the tomb of Pope Julius II, but unused and later presented to Cosimo by the artist's nephew.

Francesco's Study. To the right of the entrance is Francesco's *studiolo*, a 'Wunderkammer' created in a small, windowless space where the Grand Duke con-

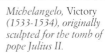

Michelangelo, Victory *(1533-1534), originally sculpted for the tomb of pope Julius II.*

cealed his collections of coins, glass, semi-precious stones and other rarities, inside painted cupboards. In the middle of the ceiling are frescoes of *Nature* and *Prometheus*, surrounded by the *Four Elements* (air, water, earth and fire). Represented in the corners are *The Four Temperaments* (phlegm, blood, bile and choler). According to ancient Greek medicine, the differing proportions of these 'humors' in the body determined an individual's physical constitution and character.

Completed in 1579, the treasures kept inside this gem of mannerist art were later transferred to Palazzo Pitti, and only at the beginning of the 20th century was the study reconstructed and partially restored. The interior may be viewed from the entrance as, for reasons of safety and conservation, the study can only be visited with special permission.

Sala di Leone x. Opposite the study is the entrance to the Quarters of Pope Leo x, begun by Giovanni Battista del Tasso and completed by Vasari. Only the room known as the 'Sala di Leone x' may be visited. The frescoes, by Vasari and assistants, depict the life of this humanist Pope, son of Lorenzo the Magnificent.

Second floor. On the second floor, the Quartiere degli Elementi (1555-1558) consists of a series of rooms, chambers

and terraces. The Sala degli Elementi is decorated with allegories of pagan divinities, painted by Vasari and Cristofano Gherardi. The original of Verrocchio's *Putto and Dolphin* is on Juno's terrace — originally a loggia open on three sides but enclosed at the end of the 16th century by Ammannati.

Returning through these rooms we now reach the apartments of Eleonora de Toledo, wife of Cosimo I. Eleonora's chapel, built by Giovanni Battista del Tasso, is decorated with important *frescoes* (1540-1545) by Bronzino. Passing through several frescoed rooms we arrive at the Chapel of the Priors, designed by Baccio d'Agnolo (1511-1514) and decorated with *frescoes* by Ridolfo del Ghirlandaio. The Sala dell'Udienza (Reception Room) follows: the caisson *ceiling* is by Giuliano da Maiano and on

The study of grand duke Francesco (1579). A masterpiece of mannerist art, it was created to house his collection of rare and precious items, subsequently transferred to Palazzo Pitti.

Benedetto and Giuliano da Maiano, entrance to the 'Sala dei Gigli' (right) with the statue of Justice.

Donatello, Judith and Holofernes. *Palazzo Vecchio, 'Sala dei Gigli'.*

The noble profile of Perseus, *one of Benvenuto Cellini's masterpieces, recently moved to a restoration workshop, open to the public, in the Uffizi.*

the walls are late 16th-century *frescoes* by Francesco Salviati. The marble-framed doorway with a statue of *Justice,* by Benedetto and Giuliano da Maiano, leads to the Sala dei Gigli (or Lily Room). Decorating the ceiling and walls, the fleur-de-lys was the symbol of the French House of Anjou, allies of the Guelf faction. The room has a marble doorframe by the two da Maiano brothers, as well as a large fresco (1482-1485) by Domenico Ghirlandaio and the original bronze statue of *Judith and Holofernes* by Donatello. Next is the Cancelleria (Chancellery) where Machiavelli worked, and the Map Room housing a large *globe* and *maps* painted on the cupboards by Ignazio Danti and Stefano Buonsignori.

Mezzanine. Down a flight of stairs from the Sala dei Gigli, we reach the mezzanine (not always open): housed in three rooms here is the 'Loeser Collection' of 14th- to 16th-century *paintings and sculptures* of the Tuscan school. Displayed in the other rooms here, only open with special permission, are antique *musical instruments* from the Cherubini Conservatory.

Sala dei Dugento. Returning to the first floor we come to the antechamber which precedes the Sala dei Dugento (almost always closed as this is the council chamber), with a caisson ceiling by Benedetto and Giuliano da Maiano.

LOGGIA DELLA SIGNORIA

The Loggia is as open and as public as the political policy of the Florentine Republic, which ordered it built for meetings, ceremonies and public receptions. It was also known as 'Orcagna's Loggia', Orcagna being the nickname given to Andrea di Cione, to whom it was mistakenly attributed.

It was, rather, built by Benci di Cione and Simone Talenti, both of whom were head of the Cathedral Works between 1376 and 1382. Although Florentine Gothic was at its height at the time, the design is classical and dignified. The tall structure consists of three rounded arches resting on clustered pilasters with engraved capitals. The barrel-vaulted ceiling is crowned by a balustrade behind which is a large terrace. Originally the loggia was decorated only with the lions on either side of the entrance and the medallions between the arches with sculptures of the *Theological and Cardinal Virtues,* designed by Agnolo Gaddi.

On 5 May , 1532, when the last council of the *Signoria* ceded its power to Duke Alessandro, the Loggia ceased to have a ceremonial function and was temporarily used to house the Duke's

View of the 14th-century Loggia della Signoria, also referred to as the Loggia dei Lanzi (lancers) or the Orcagna Loggia.

bodyguard, made up of German mercenary lancers. The building consequently assumed a third name: the 'Loggia dei Lanzi'.

As time passed, the Loggia became a prestigious showcase for important and valuable sculptures, a tradition which had already begun in the early 16th century and continued until the second half of the 19th century. On the left is the *Abduction of Polyxena* (1866), a marble group by Pio Fedi. In the centre is *Menelaus Supporting the Corpse of Patroclus*, a Roman copy of a Greek statue from the 4th century BC. Discovered in Rome while excavating near Porta Portese, it was presented to Cosimo I by Pope Pius VI.

From 27 April , 1554 to 5 December , 1996, Benvenuto Cellini's renowned masterpiece, the bronze figure of *Perseus*, dominated the arch on the left. Cellini worked on the statue for almost ten years (1545-1554) partly due to the complexity of the technique required by the size and the difficult form of the statue. The distance of the head of Medusa from the body of Perseus posed a problem for casting the bronze. Now damaged by the effects of pollution, the sculpture has been moved into the Uffizi and is housed in one

of the thirteen rooms once occupied by the magistrature of the Guilds. An exhibition concerning the history of the statue and the complex work of restoration can be visited on the ground floor of the Uffizi, in the right wing looking from Palazzo Vecchio.

Under the arch on the right, the most spectacular work is the marble *Abduction of the Sabine Women* (1583), by Giambologna, considered to be the first sculpture designed to be seen from all sides and angles. Behind is another marble group by Giambologna, *Hercules and the Centaur* (1599).

Arranged along the wall at the back are six *Roman statues of matrons* brought from the Villa Medici in Rome. On the wall to the right is a Latin inscription (composed by the scholar Giovanni Lami) commemorating the adoption, in 1750, of the Gregorian calendar, in which the year begins on January 1; previously in Florence the year began on March 25, the day of the Incarnation of Christ.

UFFIZI PALACE

The Uffizi derives its name from the thirteen most important civic and administrative offices (*uffici*) which Grand Duke Cosimo I had housed here, conveniently close to Palazzo Vecchio, after the conquest of Siena. The layout of the complex, which would be imitated in bureaucratic ar-

The Loggia beautifully illuminated at night-time during the concert held in memory of the victims of the bomb in 1993.

Above, Cellini's Perseus. *Left, the* Rape of the Sabine Women *(1583) by Giambologna, possibly the first statue ever designed to be observed from any angle.*

The Uffizi seen from the Oltrarno side of the river. To the left is the portico along the Lungarno degli Archibusieri which houses the first section of the Vasari corridor.

A perspective revealing how the Uffizi harmonizes with Palazzo Vecchio, an important architectural aspect of the building.

Anna Maria Ludovica, Electress Palatine (here portrayed with her husband, William of Düsseldorf) bequeathed the immense and invaluable Medici collections to the city of Florence.

chitecture of other cities throughout Europe, was designed by Giorgio Vasari in 1560. He continued working on the building until his death, and it was then completed by Alfonso Parigi and Bernardo Buontalenti in 1580. The work presented serious challenges: "Never have I had to build anything so difficult, nor so dangerous, with its foundations in the river and finishing up almost in the air," wrote Vasari himself.

A model of mannerist architecture, the Uffizi consists of two parallel arms with porticoed galleries, joined at the end along the river Arno by a linking structure with three large arches. The palazzo is one of the most classic examples of 16th-century urban architecture. There was no attempt to harmonize with preexisting medieval elements: rather, by incorporating the Palazzo della Zecca on the right and the old church of San Piero Scheraggio on the left, an entirely new style was invented. Some columns of the old church (consecrated in 1068) are still visible, forming part of the wall of the Uffizi on Via della Ninna. Building was completed in 1565 when Vasari's Corridor was opened. Crossing the river above Ponte Vecchio, this safe and private passageway links the Uffizi to the Grand Dukes' residence, the Pitti Palace.

Over the arch at the end is a *statue of Cosimo I* (1585), by

Giambologna. The statues in the pilaster niches along the portico are 19th-century. The entrance to the Uffizi Gallery is on the left.

UFFIZI GALLERY

The initial nucleus of what may be considered the first ever modern museum was brought here in 1580. This original group of works, chosen by Francesco (1541-1587), son of Cosimo I, is displayed in the Tribune designed by Bernardo Buontalenti. Thus began the history of a museum which has existed for over 400 years.

The period during which the gallery belonged to the Medici family was ended by an act which established the museum as public dominion. Anna Maria Luisa, the Palatine Electress, on bequeathing her extraordinary and immense art collection, imposed the single condition that no item should ever be removed or taken outside the Grand Duchy, but kept entirely in Florence as "being for the ornamentation of the State, for the benefit of the people and as an inducement for the curiosity of foreigners". In the 18th century it was Pietro Leopoldo of Lorraine (1765-1790) who decided to re-organize the gallery in a manner more appropriate to the times. The collection therefore gradually began to lose its original characteristic of a

Andrea del Castagno, fictive portrait of Dante Alighieri.

'Wunderkammer,' where arms, majolica, por-celain and scientific instruments were collected, and began to be arranged more systematically, based on the precepts of contemporary rationalism. In the period from the Unification of Italy (1861) to the early decades of the 20th century, the transformation from general museum to art gallery was completed. At the same time an acquisitions policy increased representation from all the Italian schools of painting.

The history of the gallery in its present form begins with the return, after World War II, of the works hidden in 1940, as well as those removed by the German troops and later recovered near the Austrian border by the Allied troops. The present, generally chronological arrangement dates from the period of reorganization following these events.

Struck by a devastating mafia terrorist bomb in 1993, the museum responded by not only repairing the damaged works quite swiftly, but also by making proposals to extend the exhibition area.

The visit, taking in all forty-two rooms of the gallery, is quite breath-taking. The collection of masterpieces is almost unequaled (1,550 works on display), and requires time that is rarely possible given the frenzied pace of modern tourism. A possible alternative to such rushed museum visits was proposed by Umberto Eco, who suggested concen-trating on a single painting or object. It could indeed be interesting to use the museum as an encyclopedia, for consultation instead of for reading from beginning to end, choosing only a few works, a period or an artist to study.

Room 1. The visitor first enters a large room on the ground floor, where the remains of the Romanesque church of San Piero a Scheraggio (demolished by Vasari to build the Uffizi) were uncovered in 1971. Displayed here are frescoes of *Famous Men* (first half of the 15th century), by Andrea del Castagno. In the corridor to the Gallery is Sandro Botticelli's *Annunciation*.

Room 2. The arrangement of this room is similar to a Tuscan church and housed here are three large altarpieces comprehensively representing 13th- and 14th-century Italian painting: the *Maestà*, by Cimabue; the *Rucellai Madon-*

Duccio di Boninsegna, the Rucellai Madonna.

Cimabue, Virgin Enthroned.

Giotto, the Ognissanti Madonna.

Pietro Lorenzetti,
Virgin Enthroned.
Right, Simone
Martini,
Annunciation.

Giottino, Pietà.
Below, one of
Masaccio's
masterpieces:
Madonna and Child
with Saint Ann.

na, by Duccio di Boninsegna; the *Ognissanti Madonna* (c.1310), by Giotto. Cimabue's *Maestà* is dramatically solemn, while Duccio's *Madonna* is more plaintive. Giotto is the greatest exponent of the revolution which took place in Italian painting beginning in the mid-14th century. Compared to the doll-like, rigid images of the 13th century, his Madonna is vividly human.

Room 3. This room is dedicated to 14th-century Sienese painting, still based on the Byzantine tradition but considerably influenced by French Gothic. One of the most important artists of the period was Simone Martini, whose *Annunciation with Two Saints* (1333) is displayed here. The Saints on either side are by his brother-in-law, Lippo Memmi. The Virgin, like the female image created by his friend, Petrarch, was man's idea of perfection. Surrounded by light, the Madonna is seen here in a pose which lends a poetic feel to the work.

Also in this room are paintings by the brothers Pietro and Ambrogio Lorenzetti, who tried to synthesize the Florentine and Sienese cultures. Ambrogio's *Presentation at the Temple* (1342) has an acute perspective which takes us right inside the building. This is the beginning of an attempt to find a realistic representation of space.

Room 4. This room houses examples of Florentine art from the 14th century. The artists represented are pupils or followers of Giotto, such as Bernardo Daddi, Taddeo Gaddi, Nardo di Cione, Andrea Orcagna, Giottino and Giovanni da Milano (the foremost exponent of the school of Giotto in Lombardy).

Rooms 5-6. The works here represent International Gothic, a perfect example of which is the famous *Adoration of the Magi* (1423), by Gentile da Fabriano (c.1360-1427), commissioned by the rich and powerful banker Palla Strozzi. Studied, rich in detail and narrative elements, the spectacular scene seems almost to have been painted simply to impress the Florentine bourgeoisie. This is one of the major examples of late-Gothic in Italy which, at a time when the old feudal aristocracy was in decline, had become 'courtly art,' admired by the middle class.

Rivaling Gentile's painting is the *Adoration of the Magi,* by Lorenzo Monaco (c.1370-c.1425), which exalts the aesthetic aspect of the scene, in contrast to the worldly character of courtly fantasy.

Room 7. We now move to the early Renaissance and a complete transformation in the world of art, comparable to that of a century earlier with Giotto. Masaccio, whose own *Adoration of the Magi* (1426) is in Berlin, was one of the

most important artists of this period. Displayed here are his *Madonna and Child* and *Madonna and Child with St Ann* (c.1424), which was started by Masolino. Masaccio painted one of the angels holding back the curtain, as well as the Madonna alluding to Brunelleschi's dome, familiar as a living person.

The *Battle of San Romano* (c.1456) celebrates the victory of the Florentines over the Sienese in 1432. In this painting, Paolo Uccello plays with the 15th-century rules of perspective as they were applied in Florence. He does not use perspective to make an item appear more real, but only to place it in space. Commissioned by Cosimo the Elder, the piece originally consisted of three panels; the other two are in Paris (the Louvre) and in London (National Gallery).

Domenico Veneziano (c.1406-1461) developed the problem of the relationship between theoretical space and its practical organiza-tion, between perspective and light; the most important work here is the *Sacra Conversazione* painted by him some time after 1440.

The diptych of the *Dukes of Urbino* (c.1465) is by Piero della Francesca, an assistant to Domenico Veneziano in his youth. He painted Battista Sforza and Federico da Montefeltro in profile, applying measurement and proportion

Piero della Francesca, portraits of Federico da Montefeltro and his wife, Battista Sforza. *Below, Domenico Veneziano,* altar panel with Santa Lucia dei Màgnoli.

Paolo Ucello, the Battle of San Romano. *The work, commemorating a victory of the Florentines over Siena, was commissioned by Cosimo il Vecchio and consists of three panels: the other two are in the National Gallery, London and the Louvre.*

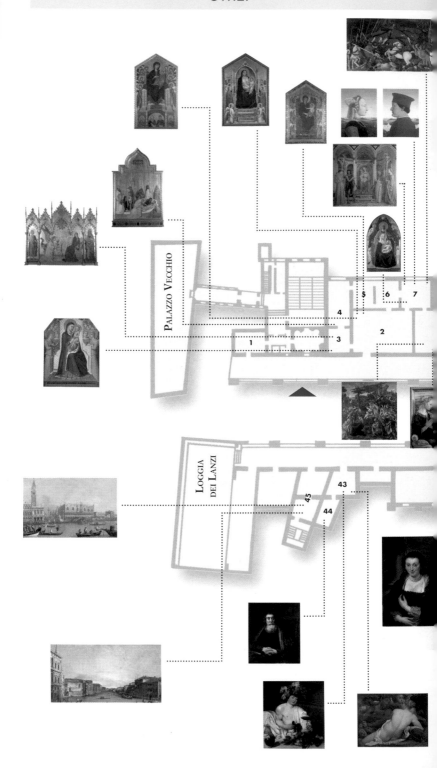

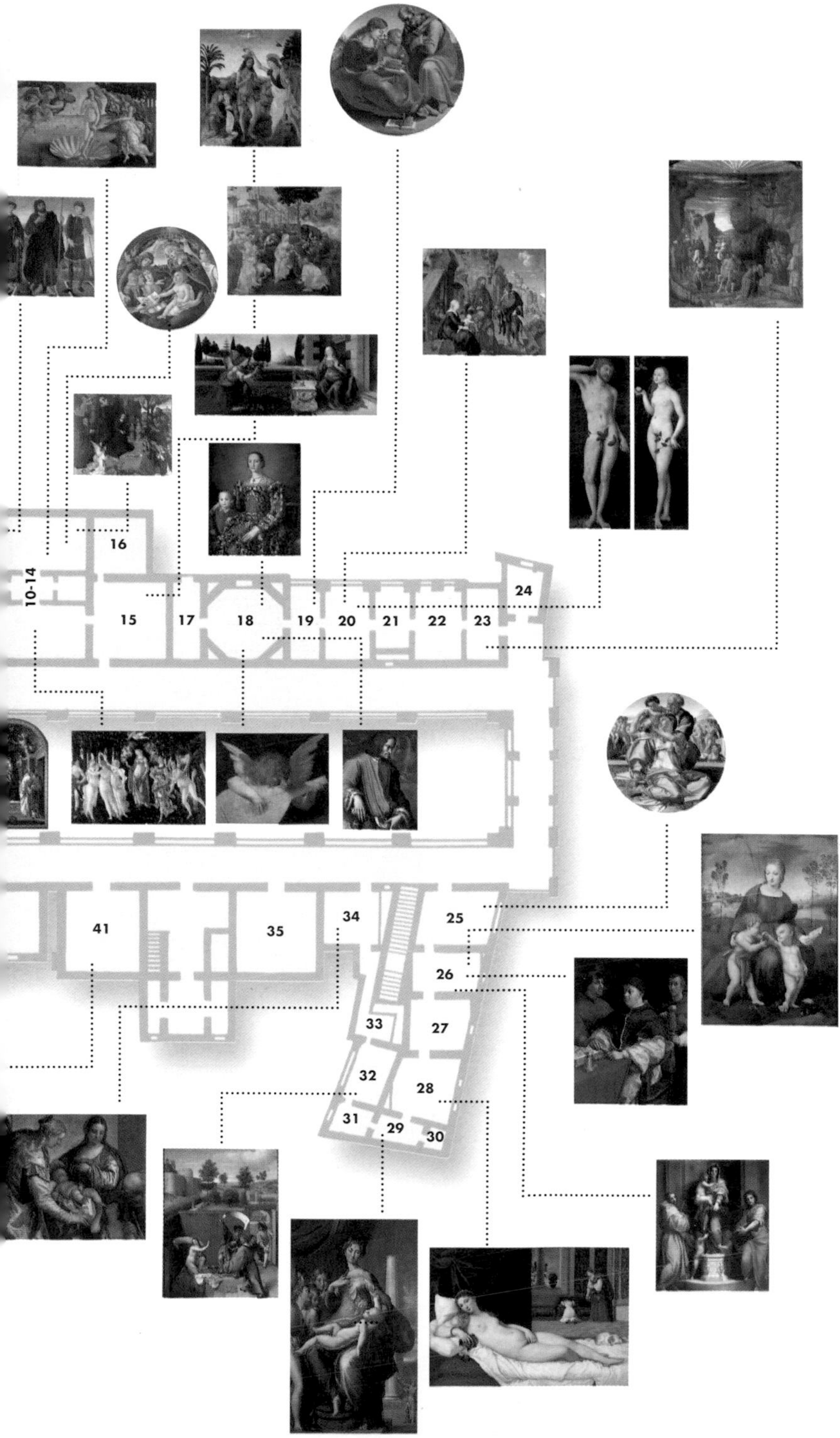

10-14

16

15 17 18 19 20 21 22 23 24

41   35   34   25

26

33   27

32   28

31   29 30

Filippo Lippi, Virgin and Child with Angels.

Filippo Lippi, Virgin and Child with Angels.

Top, Saints James, Vincent and Eustace, *by Piero and Antonio del Pollaiolo. Above, Filippino Lippi,* Madonna, *painted for the 'Sala degli Otto' in Palazzo Vecchio. Below, the* Adoration of the Magi, *by the same artist.*

to the details of the faces and the countryside with geometric perfection.

Fra' Giovanni da Fiesole, known as Fra' Angelico, the Dominican monk so admired by Masaccio, was supremely capable of rendering religious subjects with great humanity. Displayed here are his *Madonna and Child* and the *Coronation of the Virgin* (c.1435), both revealing the artist's sensibility to light which here takes on an almost unreal transparency and quality.

Room 8. Filippo Lippi, a follower of Masaccio's work and innovations, and his son Filippino Lippi, are represented in this room. Filippo tends to emphasize the relationship between human emotions and nature: from a technical point of view, the composition predominates over his use of colours and space. The *Madonna and Child with Angels* (c. 1460) is one of his

most admired works.

The *Madonna with Angels* (c. 1465), the *Adoration of the Magi* (1486) and the *Sacra Conversazione* are all by Filippino.

Room 9. Antonio del Pollaiolo was a painter, sculptor and goldsmith; the two small paintings of the *Feats of Hercules* were commissioned from him by Lorenzo the Magnificent about 1460. Here Pollaiolo turns his attention from the organization of space to the human body, no longer seen as a perfect form but representing physical strength and power. Also in this room are *Six Virtues* by Antonio's brother, Piero. The seventh allegory, *Strength*, is by the young Botticelli who, though still following his teacher's example, shows early signs of originality in the composition.

Rooms 10-14. These rooms house a fine collection of Sandro Botticelli's paintings. The latest of the great masters of the 15th century, Botticelli lived during the period of religious fanaticism instigated by Girolamo Savonarola. His concept of art recalls the innocence of the primitives and is controversially opposed to those who were, at the time, applying scientific principles through the study of perspective, proportion, classicism

Sandro Botticellli, the Birth of Venus. *Right,* the Madonna of the Magnificat, *also by Botticelli.*

and anatomy. Thus, in *Primavera* (c.1478) one of the most famous paintings in the Uffizi, perspective, light as a physical element, the reality of the setting, are factors of lesser importance; it is instead the linearity of composition, learned from Filippo Lippi, which is the principle feature. The *Primavera* may be interpreted on several levels: only an expert could understand the complex allegorical references, but we can all appreciate the beauty and grace of the figures.

Possibly inspired by Ovid's poems, the *Metamorphoses* and the *Fasti*, the *Birth of Venus* (1485) refers to Christian birth through the baptismal water. The figure of Venus represents natural beauty, her unadorned nudity a homage to purity and simplicity.

The *Portinari Tryptych* (1475), by Hugo van der Goes (1440-1482), is an excellent example of Flemish art, which stimulated much interest in late 15th-century Florentine artistic circles.

Domenico Ghirlandaio (1449-1494) was considerably influenced by this northern realism, as evident here in his ac-

claimed *Adoration of the Magi* (1487).

Room 15. This room represents the passage from 'antique' to 'modern'. The genius

of Leonardo da Vinci marks the opening of the new century. Although just seven years younger than Botticelli, and studying in the same school of Verrocchio, Leonardo's work is in clear contrast to the style of the *Primavera*. Indeed, it has been said that while Botticelli brings the 15th century to a close, Leonardo introduces the 16th. Botticelli wanted to go beyond the reality to grasp the concept, while Leonardo wanted to penetrate reality to reveal its secrets; he wanted practical experience of the matter.

An early work painted

Sandro Botticelli, Primavera *(1478), one of the artist's greatest works.*

Above, Hugo van der Goes, central section of the Portinari Tryptych. *Left, Leonardo da Vinci,* Annunciation.

Leonardo da Vinci, Adoration of the Magi *(top). Above, Andrea del Verrocchio, the* Baptism of Christ. *Some believe that the young Leonardo may also have worked on this painting.*

Above, Giorgio Vasari, portrait of Lorenzo il Magnifico, *based on contemporary paintings of Lorenzo de' Medici. Right, Agnolo Bronzino,* Eleonora di Toledo with her son, Giovanni, *a masterpiece of mannerist painting.*

while still in Verrocchio's workshop, the *Annunciation* (c. 1475) has an unusual dual composition. With his inspired symbolic interpretation, Leonardo seeks a new approach to the *Adoration of the Magi* (1482), one of the most frequent artistic subjects of the time. The manger has faded into the background, the Magi have become part of the crowd, and the phenomenon of the divine birth, perturbing both life and spirit, is in the foreground.

The panel painting of *Christ in the Garden* is by Pietro Vannucci, known as Perugino (1445-1524).

Room 16. Frescoed in 1589 by Ludovico Buti (c.1560-c.1603), the maps in this room depict the Grand Duchy of Tuscany.

Room 17. Scientific instruments were housed here at the time of the Medici. Displayed now are the Roman statue of the *Sleeping Her-*

maphrodite, and a group of *Amor and Psyche.*

Room 18. The oldest and first collection of the museum, representing an anthology of 16th-century artistic and philosophical precepts, was housed in this Tribune. The statues brought here by Cosimo III in the 1680's are particularly important: the *Medici Venus* (3rd century BC) is considered a masterpiece of classical sculpture.

The portrait of *Eleonora de Toledo with her son, Giovanni* (1545-1546) is by Agnolo Bronzino, one of the greatest exponents of Florentine mannerism. Eleonora, the first wife of Cosimo I, was found dressed in the same clothes in her tomb, and it is therefore thought that the portrait may have been made after her death.

There are several paintings by Raphael and his school in the Tribune, such as *St John in the Desert* (1518-1520), brought to the Uffizi in 1970 and restored in 1989.

Room 19. This room is dedicated to Pietro Vannucci, known as Perugino (c.1450-1523), Luca Signorelli (c.1450-1523) and other masters of the central Italian school.

Signorelli's works, among which the *Holy Family* and the *Madonna and Child*, clearly demonstrate the change from representational painting to conceptual art.

Rosso Fiorentino, Musician angel.

Room 20. Devoted to German painting between the 15th and 16th centuries. The moving *Portrait of the Artist's Father* (1490), by Albrecht Dürer, is part of the series begun by the artist with his famous self-portrait at thirteen years old (in Vienna). Also by Dürer is the *Adoration of the Magi* (1504), demonstrating a skillful combination of elements of Italian Renaissance painting with northern-Gothic expressivity.

The two splendid paintings of *Adam* and *Eve* are by Lucas Cranach the Elder (1472-1553).

Room 21. Dedicated to Venetian Renaissance painting, this room houses works by Giovanni Bellini and Giorgione.

Bellini's *Sacra Conversazione* (c.1485) has been described as mysterious and fascinating due to the obscurity of the subject (saints associated with pagan figures) and its comment on humanity.

Giorgione, more than others, represents the innovative movement in 16th-century Venetian painting, which no longer considers nature and history to be separate, incompatible elements. Both *Moses before Pharaoh* and the *Judgment of Solomon* are by this artist.

Room 22. Flemish and German artists, including Hans Holbein (1497/98-1543) — one of the greatest portrait painters of the 16th century.

Room 23. Works here are by Andrea Mantegna, the inspired innovator of northern Italian figurative art, and Antonio Allegri, known as Correggio.

Mantegna came from a classical background and had a sound knowledge of history and philosophy. He does not, however, eliminate nature from his historical subjects; indeed it becomes an integral part of history. In the *Madonna of the Quarry* (painted between 1466 and 1490), the Virgin appears mysteriously in a rural setting populated by shepherds, peasants and stone-masons.

The *Rest on the flight into Egypt* and the *Virgin and Child* are by Correggio who, like Mantegna, favours allegorical myths and is a forerunner of the baroque style of the next century.

Room 24. Restored in 1781 by the architect Zanobi dal Rosso, the room is known as the Miniatures Room, after the

Luca Signorelli, Holy Family.

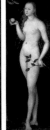

Above and left, two works by German artists: Adam and Eve, *by Lucas Cranach the Elder, and the* Adoration of the Magi, *by Albrecht Dürer. Below,* Epiphany, *by Andrea Mantegna.*

Michelangelo, the Doni Madonna *(1506-1508). The portrayal of the Holy Family is based on a powerful, almost sculptural concept of the forms.*

Above, Raphael, Pope Leo X with cardinals Giulio de' Medici and Luigi de' Rossi (1518). *Below left,* Madonna of the Harpies *(1517), by Andrea del Sarto, named after the figures decorating the sides of the base. Below right, Raphael, the* Madonna del Cardellino *(bullfinch) (1506).*

genre of works displayed here. Especially delightful are those by Giulio Clovio (1498-1578) and Bernardo Buontalenti (1531-1608).

Room 25. Paintings by Michelangelo and the Florentine school.

Displayed here is the *Doni Tondo* (c. 1504) by Michelangelo Buonarroti, described as the most modern mind of his day in all Europe. The work is named after Agnolo Doni, who commissioned it from the artist, probably on the occasion of his marriage to Maddalena Strozzi. Recently restored, the painting is the earliest confirmed as being by Michelangelo.

This image of the *Holy Family* is in sharp contrast to Leonardo's. Here, it is the symbolism, the concept that is important. According to one of the most probable interpretations, the Virgin and

St Joseph represent the Old Testament, while the Baby represents the future and the New Testament. In the background is the world, before the receiving of the Commandments. Here the generations are seen within the context of historical periods, while for Leonardo they are a natural progression.

Also in this room are works by Rosso Fiorentino (1495-1540) and Fra' Bartolomeo (1472-1517), who painted the *Apparition of the Virgin to St Bernard.*

Room 26. Works by Raphael and Andrea del Sarto.

Raphael succeeds in synthesizing the two opposing artistic concepts of Leonardo and Michelangelo in his *Madonna of the Goldfinch* (c.1506). Nature is interpreted as being divine in itself, and nothing else exists beyond it.

Described by Vasari as "the faultless painter," Andrea del Sarto hails a return to narrative painting. Named after the figures decorating the base of the pedestal, his *Madonna of the Harpies* is the expression of a complex research.

Room 27. This room introduces a further development in Florentine figurative art: Mannerism, represented here by Jacopo Carucci. Known as Pontormo, he was a most reserved and anxious character, described by Vasari as "destroying and doing again every day what he had done the day before, he racked his brains for ideas so hard that it was piteous". Pontormo looked to Michelangelo's achievements for inspiration, but also to developments from outside of Florence, including Dürer. His paintings reflect a particularly agonized struggle to reconcile the shifting role of art during his lifetime: the pursuit of rarefied beauty in contrast to art serving intellectual or spiritual purposes.

The *Supper at Emmaus* is one of his most important works. There is no additional historical interpretation in this painting; commissioned by the monks of the Certosa del Galluzzo, the realism of the scene is also repeated in a fresco there. The Gospel story is no longer simply visual, but can almost literally be read.

Other works displayed here are by Rosso Fiorentino (1495-1540), another innovative early 16th-century painter; and by Agnolo Allori, known as Bronzino (1503-1572), a pupil and friend of Pontormo.

Room 28. This room is dedicated to Titian Vecellio, perhaps the greatest 16th-century Venetian painter. Titian restored visual drama and the ability to communicate to Venetian art. His *Venus of Urbino* (1538) is one of the most beautiful representations of the female nude in the history of art. It fully demonstrates the passion for beauty and love of life, so much a part of his artistic expression. For the first time, art illustrates reality and human experience.

Room 29. This room is dedicated to Francesco Mazzola, known as Parmigianino. A pupil of Correggio, Parmigianino developed his own style of Mannerism. Portrayed in a gloomy landscape, his *Virgin of the Long Neck* (1534-1540) is extremely elegant, but haughty and distant: a far cry from Correggio's warm and amiable Madonnas.

Rooms 30-31. The artists here are Dosso Dossi (c.1489-1542), Ludovico Mazzolino (1480-1528) and Benvenuto

Lorenzo Lotto, Susannah and the Elders *(1517), a graceful composition showing the influence of Leonardo and Raphael. Below,* Madonna and Child with Angels *(1534-1540), a masterpiece by Parmigianino, also known as the* Madonna with the long neck.

Paolo Veronese, the Holy Family with Saint Barbara and Saint John, *a veritable masterpiece of light and tranquility.*

Above, Dosso Dossi, Witchcraft.

Below, Pieter Paul Rubens, Isabella Brandt. *In this portrayal of his first wife, the artist has succeeded in combining fragility and sensuality.*

Below right, Annibale Carracci, Venus with satyrs and cherubs.

Tisi, known as Garofalo (1480-1559), all representing the anti-classical school based in Ferrara. These artists from Emilia Romagna were influenced by the Venetian style of painting, and by Titian and Giorgione in particular.

Rich in bizarre and fantastic details (strange groups of men and women, magic ritual), Dossi's art was influenced by a contemporary masterpiece of Italian poetry: *Orlando Furioso*, by Ludovico Ariosto.

Room 32. Also dedicated to Northern Italian art, this room houses works by Lorenzo Lotto and Sebastiano Luciani, known as Sebastiano del Piombo.

Lorenzo Lotto, a cultured traditionalist opposed to the more fashionable Titian, was a religious artist whose style grasped the fervent imagination of the naive. In his *Holy Family with Saints* (1534), sanctity is found within the naturalness of the domestic scene. This is a typical motif often seen in German traditional painting, exemplified in the pose of the Virgin, leaning against the legs of St Ann.

Sebastiano del Piombo was a friend and disciple of Michelangelo. As an artist he felt intensely the conflict between an awareness of

nature and art as a cerebral act. The *Death of Adonis* is by Sebastiano.

Room 33. The 'Cinquecento' hall offers a panorama of 16th-century European painting, clearly influenced by the Protestant reform movement.

Room 34. Works by Paolo Caliari, known as Veronese (1528-1588), an acute observer of Venetian culture and society in the second half of the 16th century.

Veronese's painting is bright and luminous, enlivened by the intelligent use of colours evident in the *Holy Family with Sts Barbara and John.*

Room 35. While Veronese's art derives from nature, his friend and colleague Jacopo Robusti, known as Tintoretto (1518-1594), interpreted historical scenes with a strong moral sense and visionary style. The portraits seen in this room demonstrate this powerful tension.

Jacopo da Ponte, known as Bassano (c.1517-1592), is noted for his pleasing attention to detail, and the minor features found in his works. The painting of *Two Dogs and a Landscape* is a good example of the preferred subjects of this

Caravaggio, Bacchus. *The portrait appears secondary in importance to the magnificent still life.*

painter who invented a pastoral-religious style.

With his religious vision, Federico Barocci (1528-1612) actually anticipates the Catholic campaign, based on collective cult worship, against the Protestant Reform with its emphasis on the individual. The scenographic *Madonna del Popolo* is a work by him.

Room 41. On the other side of the staircase leading to the exit, this room houses works by Pieter Paul Rubens (1577-1640), Anthony Van Dyck (1599-1641) and Justus Sustermans (1597-1681).

Rubens, who also worked at the court of the Gonzaga in Mantua, is responsible for the two paintings of *Henry IV at the Battle of Ivry* (1627-1630) and *Henry IV's Triumphal Entrance into Paris.* Similarities may be seen with Leonardo's *Battle of Anghiari* in this powerful and dramatic battle-scene.

Room 42. Gaspare Paoletti (1727-1813) designed this room, known as "Niobe's," to house the works transferred from Villa Medici in Rome in 1775. The group of *Niobe and her Children* is a copy of an original Greek statue from the 2nd century BC.

Room 43. Displayed here are examples of 17th-century Italian art. First is Annibale Carracci (1560-1609)

who, along with his cousins, Agostino (1557-1602) and Ludovico (1555-1619), founded the Accademia degli Incamminati in Bologna.

The Bologna school broke away from the conventions of Mannerism, returning to a more natural style of art intended to appeal to the emotions and encourage devotion. Annibale concentrates on sentiment and the power of the imagination and in his *Bacchus,* naturalism and classicism combine to produce a highly sensual result.

Another great artist of the day was Michelangelo Merisi, known as Caravaggio (1570-1610). Caravaggio's reaction to late Mannerism was to achieve a startling realism, rather than to seek beauty. In contrast therefore to Annibale Carracci's naturalism, we find a form of realism which reflected the religious teachings of St Charles Borromeo – Archbishop of Milan and a contemporary of Caravaggio – based on the acceptance of reality. The paintings displayed (the *Bacchus,* the *Sacrifice of Isaac,* the *Medusa*) are all early works by the artist.

This selection from the 17th century is completed by works of Giovan Francesco Barbieri (known as Guercino), Salvator Rosa, Mattia Preti, Giulio Carpioni and Claude Lorrain

Caravaggio, Medusa, *tournament shield presented to Francesco I de' Medici by cardinal del Monte (the artist's patron).*

Below, by the same artist, the Sacrifice of Isaac.

— a French artist who lived in Italy for many years.

Room 44. Examples of Flemish and Dutch paintings. As well as works by Jan Steen, Gabriel Metsu, Hendrick Pot, Jacob von Ruysdael and Paul Brill, there are three masterpieces by Rembrandt van Rijn here: two *Self portraits*, and the *Portrait of an Old Man.*

Room 45. Dedicated to the 18th century, the greatest Italian, French and Spanish artists are here represented by Giambattista Tiepolo, Giovanni Antonio Canal (known as Canaletto), Jean-Baptiste-Siméon Chardin and Francisco Goya.

With Tiepolo, one of the richest periods of Venetian painting came to an end and new developments in Italian art began. The *Erection of an Emperor's Statue* (1734-1736) is one of his works.

Canaletto, a master of scenic painting and perspective which enhances reality without distorting it, is the author of *View of the Ducal Palace in Venice.*

The portraits of the *Countess of Chinchon* and *Maria Teresa of Vallabriga,* recently acquired by the museum, are by Goya.

Vasari Corridor. The museum continues in Vasari's Corridor, with another seven hundred paintings and the famous collection of *Artists' Self Portraits*, begun in 1675 by Leopoldo de' Medici, and still added to today. The corridor was built to a design by Giorgio Vasari and links Palazzo Pitti and Palazzo Vecchio, crossing over the top of Ponte Vecchio. It is only open at certain times of the year.

Returning to the Piazzale of the Uffizi, we turn right under the arch leading into the medieval street of Via Lambertesca. Under the arch is the Porta delle Suppliche *(Gate of Clemency) with a most unusual tympanum, made by Buontalenti who split the classical design in two and then turned the two halves back to front. Further ahead on the left are the houses of the Pulci family, now the offices of the* Accademia dei Gergòfili, *the oldest academy of agricultural sciences in Europe, now restored after the damage caused by the terrorist bomb in 1993.*

We now turn right onto the narrow little Chiasso de' Baroncelli, beginning a tour of the medieval streets of Florence which continues, turning left onto Chiasso del Buco, recently restored and reopened, and ending in Piazza de' Salterelli. From here we continue along Via Vacchereccia to the left; crossing

The Palazzi dei Pulci in Via Lambertesca after the bomb of 1993 (left) and as they are today (right).

over Via Por Santa Maria and passing by the Mercato Nuovo (Straw Market, ☛ p. 156), we turn left Via Porta Rossa as far as Piazza Davanzati. At no. 13 is Palazzo Davanzati.

PALAZZO DAVANZATI

To revive the original character of this merchant's residence, we should imagine the *pietra forte* of the façade covered with bright, cheerful colours, for lengths of wool and fabric were hung out of the windows of the upper floors to dry before being displayed for sale under the arches of the ground floor.

"A palace with three wool shops," is how Lorenzo di Giovanni di Gherardo Davizzi described the building in his declaration to the land register in 1469. Built by this family in the 14th century, the palace passed to the Bartolini family in 1516, and in 1578, to the Davanzati. After numerous other changes of ownership, the palace, at the time in an extremely poor state of repair, was bought by Elio Volpi, an antique dealer, in 1904. Volpi lovingly restored it, furnishing it richly and expertly in its own period style. However, subsequent financial problems obliged him to sell it to his American colleague, Benguiat. It was handed over to the State in 1950, and in 1956 it was designated as the 'Florentine House Museum,' exhibiting objects and works

of art from the Bargello and other museums in the city.

Façade. The abruptly vertical medieval façade is interrupted, yet also accentuated by the loggia above, added in the 16th century replacing a previous crenellated terrace. On the ground floor are three low, wide arches with pointed lintels. Each of the three floors above has five windows also with low arches. The functional 14th-century iron fixtures on the outside are extremely rare: the bars to close the shop doors on the ground floor, the lantern on the corner, the torch holders, the iron 'S' forms on the sills which held the rods for hanging out the wool.

Interior. In the internal courtyard are attractive octagonal columns (on the largest capital in the courtyard the faces of some members of the Davizzi family are carved) which support a narrow open staircase. This rises steeply, eventually becoming no more than ascending arches supported by corbels. The various rooms and spaces on each floor are linked by a stone gallery

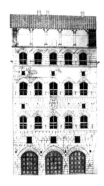

Palazzo Davanzati, the façade and the coat of arms of the family.

The room frescoed with Stories of the Mistress of Vergi.

Room with four-poster bed and cradle. Right, the 'Parrot Room'.

(originally made of wood, like the surviving one on the third floor), emphasizing the feeling of a genuine family residence, evident in the arrangement of the rooms in the house.

Domestic family life in the 14th century has been faithfully and charmingly reconstructed not only by the rich and accurate furnishings (tables, chests, cupboards, beds, crockery), but especially by the series of precious, brightly painted wall decorations, imitating the tapestries and hangings which once covered the walls. Particularly attractive are the *Sala dei Pappagalli* (parrots) and the *Sala dei Pavoni* (peacocks), on the first floor and, on the second, the bedroom with *frescoes* relating the medieval legend of the Châtelaine of Vergi.

Leaving the palace we continue left along Via Porta Rossa, turning right onto Via Monalda which brings us into Piazza Strozzi.

The Florentine Mansion

The evolution of the Florentine mansion reflects the city's history, providing a visual record of the various eras. The oldest still surviving are the towers, or tower-houses, built during the 11th century by feudal families who had moved into the town from the surrounding countryside. Their main purpose was defensive: a group of families forming a political faction would agree to build a defensive tower, which all could reach from the upper floors of their houses without having to go out into the streets. In the year 1200 there were 165 towers altogether, some as tall as 250 feet. In 1250, the council of the 'Primo Popolo' decided to eliminate this dangerous resource of the old feudal nobility, and ordered that all towers should be 'truncated' - lowered to a height of no more than 80 feet. From the end of the 13th century and throughout the 14th, the tower-houses gradually began to lose their original function, often becoming the family residences of the city's merchant bourgeoisie. Having been lowered in the mid-13th century, the houses now began to extend horizontally, although maintaining certain aspects of fortified buildings. *Palazzo Spini Feroni* (☛ p. 184), impressively dominating the entrance to the city from the Santa Trìnita bridge, and its contemporary, *Palazzo Peruzzi*, built on the ruins of the Roman amphitheatre (☛ p.152), both date from this period. Among the few surviving 14th-century examples are *Palazzo Davanzati* (☛ p. 119) and *Palazzo Frescobaldi* (☛ p.181). During the 15th century, the mansion lost its military

14th-century wooden chest. Left, room with bedstead of carved walnut.

Palazzo Strozzi

Filippo Strozzi wanted to make a "building which would be renowned throughout Italy and beyond". Thus on 6 August , 1489, as he wrote in his *Memoirs*, "as the sun was setting, in the name of God and as a good beginning for me and my descendants [...] I cast the first stone of the foundations".

Like his father Matteo before him, Filippo had been forced by the Medici to live a long period in exile. The building of his palace was therefore an expression of his desire to remain in Florence, and also gave him an opportunity to rival, not politically but artistically, his most powerful

View of Palazzo Strozzi from Via Strozzi. Note the unfinished section of the cornice designed by Cronaca.

function altogether, and assumed a new political and cultural significance. The house began, in fact, to represent the prestige of the family who commissioned it. In this sense, construction became a 'public event,' creating a hierarchical urban organization. *Palazzo Rucellai* (☞ p. 209) and *Palazzo Antinori* (☞ p. 187) were built during this period. With the birth of the Principality during the 16th century, the civic role of the palazzo ceased to exist: it was no longer directed to the public, but rather to the princely court. The courtiers of Cosimo and Francesco I turned their residences into symbols of distinction, manifestations of their originality and wealth. This period produced grand Mannerist buildings such as *Palazzo Ramirez di Montalvo* (1568, designed by Ammanati for a Spanish nobleman in the service of Eleonora de Toledo, wife of Cosimo I (☞ p. 228) and *Palazzo Nonfinito* 1593 and thereafter), designed by Buontalenti for Alessandro Strozzi (☞ p. 126). These particular characteristics became even more evident in the 17th century, when the city's trade and businesses entered a period of irreversible crisis and the wealthiest families directed their investments towards property. The grandiose Baroque palace (such as Palazzo Corsini ☞ p. 208) now not only had the function of representing the family's importance, but also of distancing it from the city.

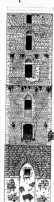

Opposite page, the Pagliazza tower (archaic term meaning 'straw pallet') used as a prison in the Middle Ages (☞ p. 153). Above, the tower of 'Dante's House' (a modern reconstruction which has copied the 14th-century 'truncation'). Right, example of a tower-house.

Above, the coat of arms of the Strozzi family. Right, 19th-century drawing of Palazzo Strozzi. Below, one of the attractive mullioned windows of the façade.

Below, view of the spacious courtyard designed by Cronaca.

opponents. When Filippo died on 15 May , 1491, however, the work had "scarcely reached the doorbells" on the ground floor. The first floor was completed in 1495, and on 12 July , 1500, the corbels of the cornice on the side towards today's Piazza della Repubblica were put in place. In 1504 "this palazzo of the Strozzi was finished and Lorenzo, Filippo's son, took his bride there and had a most beautiful wedding, with a wonderful display," as Luca Landucci, who had a pharmacist's shop on the Canto dei Tornabuoni, noted in his diary. Much was still to be done however, and many interruptions occurred until, with the death of Filippo the Younger in 1538, work came to a definitive halt, leaving the southern side and half of the cornice incomplete.

The design, based on Michelozzo's Palazzo Medici, was drawn up by Benedetto da Maiano, but Cronaca (Simone del Pollaiolo) also made a considerable contribution.

Façade. The basic, and quite majestic, concept was that of a perfect cube, made by repeating the same design as the façade on three sides, all with blocks which were not heavily rusticated, but were elegantly finished with vertical chiseling, gradually becoming lighter towards the top. On the ground floor level are a 'street bench,' a wide doorway

and small rectangular windows. The upper floors are defined by cornices and have mullioned windows with rounded, segmented arches. Crowning the structure is Cronaca's deeply jutting cornice with a traditional, classical decoration (ovuli, dentils and beads) but more showily realized than on other buildings. The handsome iron fitments (torch holders, rings for tethering horses, the corner lanterns) are all by Caparra.

Courtyard. Cronaca also designed the courtyard, clearly basing it on the concept of an 'optic pyramid,' one of the fundamental rules of perspective during the Renaissance. The two loggias on the ground and second floor are similar to those in Palazzo Medici, while the design of the first floor, with large and cruciform windows, is clearly 16th-century.

Interior. An important exhibition area, the palace also houses one of Florence's most prestigious cultural institutions, the *Gabinetto Scientifico Letterario*, founded in 1819 by Giovan Pietro Vieusseux. The Gabinetto has a library of over 500,000 volumes, the original nucleus of which was the circulating library opened by Vieusseux in 1840.

At the end of our visit to Palazzo Strozzi, we cross Via Strozzi and Piazza della Repubblica (☞ p.192) to return to Piazza del Duomo.

The Lorraine family in Tuscany

When Gian Gastone de' Medici died heirless in 1737, the future of Tuscany was no longer to be decided in Florence but in Paris or Vienna, dictated by the dynastic interests of the European sovereigns. Tuscany was assigned to Francesco Stefano, husband of the empress Maria Teresa of Austria, in exchange for the region of Lorraine which, under pressure from the French Bourbon family, had been assigned to Stanislao Leczynski, the ex-king of Poland and father-in-law of Louis XV. So that Tuscany would not pass by succession to Austrian rule, the Florentine nobles obtained an agreement that on the death of Francesco Stefano, the crown would pass to the second son of the ruling family. The Prince Consort arrived in Florence in 1737, but returned almost immediately to Vienna leaving the government in the hands of a regency which remained in charge until 1765, when Pietro Leopoldo, the second son of Francesco Stefano and Maria Teresa, arrived in Tuscany. The young man brought to Florence the ideas for reform which had inspired his education in Vienna. He came to the throne at the height of a severe famine which almost succeeded in ruining the already unstable finances of the state. Pietro Leopoldo immediately set about implementing a programmed of reforms aimed at improving agriculture which, according to his physiocratic ideals, was the basis of all wealth. In barely twenty years, Tuscany found itself so entirely reformed that it was held up as a model throughout Europe. The grain trade, until now a state monopoly, was liberalized; incentives for the sale and utilization of state property were created; the local administrative structure and tax system were reformed.

In 1790, on the death of his brother, Giuseppe II, Pietro Leopoldo left Tuscany to assume the imperial crown and Tuscany thus passed to his second son, Ferdinando III. Wars against revolutionary France were raging throughout Europe at the time and although the new sovereign followed a policy of strict neutrality, he was unable to avoid Tuscany's involvement in the conflict. Between 1799 and 1801 opposing armies passed through the state several times until, with the treaty of Lunéville, it was taken from Ferdinando and assigned to Lodovico of Bourbon-Parma. On his death in 1803 the crown passed to his son, Carlo Lodovico, under the regency of his mother, Marie Louise of Bourbon. But it is a time of rapid change: in 1808, Tuscany was annexed to the French Empire, and then separated from it again in 1809, when Princess Elisa Baciocchi, Napoleon's sister, was granted the title of Grand Duchess. In 1814, with the defeat of the French Emperor, Ferdinando III was able to return briefly to Florence, until, that is, Napoleon escaped from Elba. The following year, however, the French were defeated at Waterloo and the Congress of Vienna (1815) sanctioned Ferdinando's definitive return. He was succeeded on his death (1824) by his son, Leopoldo II, who ruled until 1859, when revolutionary movements forced him to leave Tuscany. The following year, a referendum approved the union of the old Grand Duchy with the Kingdom of Italy.

5. **In Dante's Footsteps**

17th-century astrolabe. Science Museum.

Distant echoes of Roman, medieval, Renaissance and baroque Florence intermingle along one of the most varied itineraries possible in the city. The central axis is formed by Via del Proconsolo, where the earliest walls, made of great red blocks of stone, were built in the 1st century BC, later rebuilt in 1078 during the reign of the *gran Contessa* Matilda. Inside the walls, one finds the extraordinary, yet often neglected, Pagliazza Tower, built over ancient Roman baths — the most striking indication of the city's Roman origins. 'Outside' the walls, in the most medieval part of the city, the curving form of Piazza Peruzzi reveals that it was built over an amphitheatre dating from the days of Hadrian. In Via del Proconsolo, the Badia and the Bargello represent two very different but equally important aspects of the Middle Ages, while the geometrical lines of Renaissance architecture are also to be seen in Palazzo Pazzi, and the nearby Palazzo Gondi in Piazza San Firenze. A dense network of streets, lanes and lofty towers was supplanted by the florid baroque monastery which was built in this piazza, although the medieval urban structure still continues on the right as far as the Arno.

Like Via del Proconsolo, Via de' Benci, indicating the position of the first ring of city walls, also denotes a change of periods and activities. Beyond lay a marshy area surrounded by groups of labourers' houses, which attracted the Franciscan monks to settle here and to found Santa Croce. The density and number of Renaissance palaces in this area provides social and economic evidence of the increasing expansion 'outside the walls'.

Marble plaque on the façade of Palazzo San Firenze.

Borgo Santa Croce is lined with such buildings, as is Via de' Benci where, moreover, the Horne Museum, housed in a small palace once belonging to the Corsi family, is a happy reminder of English enthusiasm for Florentine culture. Should you wish to accompany the visit to this area with a literary and social account of the lifestyle here not so very long ago, you may be guided by the novels of a 20th-century Florentine author, Vasco Pratolini. His *Tale of Poor Lovers* takes place entirely in Via del Corno, between Via de' Neri and Borgo de' Greci, and *Il Quartiere* described in the novel of the same title is none other than that of Santa Croce. The author was brought up in Via de' Magazzini, behind the Badia: "the street emerged from a background of rusticated stone, passed straight beneath me, curved slightly further ahead, disappearing from view, and led into the open space of Piazza della Signoria; a street of silence amidst the clamour all around".

Domenico Beccafumi, the Holy Family, *Horne Museum.*

The itinerary starts in Via del Proconsolo. The Proconsolo was the head of the Judges and Notaries Guild: his palace was on the corner of Via Pandolfini (now no. 6, as is indicated by a plaque). Via del Proconsolo traces the eastern side of the old Roman walls and the 'Porta Principalis Dextra,' later known as St Peter's Gate, was at the level of Via del Corso. The surname of Dante's Beatrice, Portinari, derives from the fact that they owned several properties close to this gate.

The little church of Santa Maria in Campo is an enclave of Fiesole in the heart of Florence. It was given to the Bishop of Fiesole by Pope Gregory IV in 1228, when he was forced to move to Florence after the destruction of his city. Taking Via del Proconsolo from Piazza del Duomo, the church is just a few yards ahead, in a little piazza on the left.

Also on the left of the street are Palazzo Non Finito (no. 12) and Palazzo Pazzi (no. 10).

PALAZZO NON FINITO

The bats and shells sculpted by Buontalenti in the tympani of the ground floor windows, hint at the skulls and masks now displayed in the showcases of the Museum of Anthropology which is housed here. Work was begun on the palazzo in 1593 for Alessandro Strozzi; in 1814 it was handed over to the Government of Tuscany and was used as the police headquarters of the Grand Duchy. From 1865 to 1871 the State Council sat here, and subsequently it became the administrative headquarters of the Post and Telegraph Office.

The original design was by Buontalenti, who worked on the building for at least seven years, completing the ground floor. He was succeeded by various other architects, including Vincenzo Scamozzi from Vicenza and Giovanni Battista Caccini, but the mezzanine above the first floor and one entire side of the courtyard still remained unfinished (*non finito*).

The building is, on the whole, mannerist in style, but there is a considerable difference between the front and the inner courtyard. Buontalenti's lively imagination is clearly evident in the highly sculpted appearance of both façades. The heavy rustication creates deep shadows and the richly decorated windows jut out imposingly. In contrast, Cigoli's courtyard and Santi di Tito's staircase seem almost to be a reinterpretation of Tuscan Renaissance sobriety. They represent the more tranquil and rational attitude of a period when design was more important than grandeur.

The Museo Nazionale di Antropologia ed Etnologia has been housed here since 1924. **National Museum of Anthropology and Ethnology.** The museum was founded in 1869

by Paolo Mantegazza, who had been appointed by Florence University as the first-ever Professor of Anthropology in Italy.

Drawn from many diverse cultures, the various items exhibited in the twenty-five rooms not only take us on a veritable 'trip around the world' but at the same time constitute an interesting history of science itself. Indeed, the exhibits range from those which belonged to the Medici collections, to some which were brought back from the third expedition of Captain Cook, to material collected by Paolo Graziosi among the Kafirs of Pakistan and donated to the museum in 1960. Some of the most fascinating exhibits are: a cloak of feathers made by Brazilian natives, a Tahitian priest's robe, costumes of the

5. In Dante's Footsteps

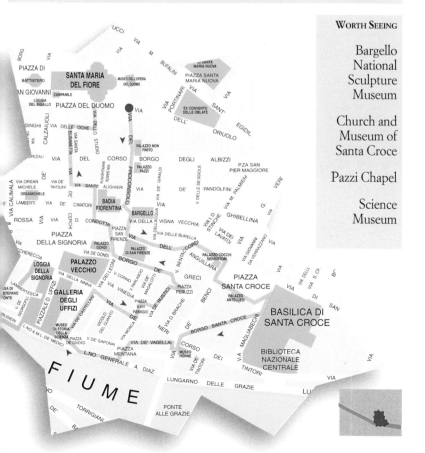

Benedetto Buglioni,
Virgin and Child *in
glazed terracotta. The
work decorates the
entrance to the Badia
Fiorentina.*

*Above, the Renaissance
Palazzo Pazzi (15th-
century) designed by
Giuliano da Maiano.
Also known as the
'Conspiracy Palace',
because of its connection
with the anti-Medici plot
of 1478. The decoration
on the mullioned
windows reproduces the
emblem of the family -
vines and ships with
billowing sails. Below,
the 'Chiostro degli
Aranci' (oranges) in the
Badia Fiorentina, frescoed
with* Scenes from the
Life of Saint Benedict
*attributed to Giovanni di
Consalvo (15th century).*

Japanese Ainu tribe, and a splendid war canoe from the Solomon Islands, decorated with mother-of-pearl.

PALAZZO PAZZI

The Pazzi family began the building in 1458 but lived here only for a few years. Their involvement in the plot against the Medici cost Jacopo and Francesco their lives, and the remaining members of the family had their possessions confiscated. The palazzo therefore passed first to the Cibò, an aristocratic family from Massa, and then to the Strozzi.

This perfect example of a Florentine Renaissance mansion was designed by Giuliano da Maiano, one of Brunelleschi's most brilliant and successful followers. The façade, divided horizontally into three by narrow, dentillated cornices, is notable for the innovative use of plaster above the ground floor rustication and the series of small circular windows on the third floor, a feature derived from Brunelleschi, not found in any

other contemporary building. The frames around the windows are richly decorated (vines and ships with unfurled sails symbolizing the mercantile wealth of the family), as are the capitals in the elegant courtyard with nine arches.

Continuing along Via del Proconsolo, on the right, immediately after the junction with the narrow Via Dante Alighieri, we come to the Badia Fiorentina.

BADIA FIORENTINA

Willa, mother of Ugo, the Margrave of Tuscany, founded the Badia with an act dated 31 May , 978. The orientation of the original church and of the later alteration carried out by Arnolfo di Cambio, was the opposite of today's. The apse, still visible in the structure, was on Via del Proconsolo, while the remains of the façade can be seen from a cloister which is entered from Piazza San Martino. The hexagonal bell tower, with its pointed spire, was built in 1330 on the circular base of one which was destroyed in 1307 as a punishment to the monks. According to Villani, they had refused to pay their taxes and "closed the doors in the face of the official tax collector and his retinue, and began ringing the bells". Benedetto da Rovezzano carried out various alterations before 1511, including the doorway on Via del Proconsolo (the present one is a 19th-century copy) and the re-arrange-

Filippino Lippi, altar panel in the Badìa Fiorentina portraying Saint Bernard's Vision of the Madonna.

ment of the atrium. Between 1628 and 1631, Matteo Segaloni completely modified the original plan, turning the interior into a perfect Greek cross with a south-north orientation, and renewing the medieval fixtures and decoration in mannerist, rather than baroque, style.

Interior. On the left wall is the *Apparition of the Virgin to St Bernard,* a masterpiece by Filippino Lippi; in the left wing of the transept is the *tomb of the Margrave Ugo,* by Mino da Fiesole, who also made the marble altar frontal with the *Virgin with Sts Leonard and Lawrence,* located on the wall nearest to the entrance, as well as the *tomb of Bernardo Giugni,* on the next wall.

From the presbytery we reach the Chiostro degli Aranci (Orange Tree Cloister), with two stories, built between 1432 and 1438 by Bernardo Rossellino. The upper loggia has two mullioned windows in white and green marble, possibly original elements of the earliest church, and is decorated with a fresco cycle of *Scenes from the Life of St Benedict,* most probably the work of Giovanni di Consalvo. This is one of the loveliest and most unusual artistic records of early Renaissance Florence: the Portuguese artist lived and worked during one of the liveliest artistic periods and drew eclectically on his knowledge of the works of Fra' Angelico, Masaccio, Domenico Veneziano, Filippo Lippi and Paolo Uccello.

On the opposite side of Via del Proconsolo, at the junction with Via Ghibellina, is the Palazzo del Bargello.

PALAZZO DEL BARGELLO

The Bargello is the oldest Florentine civic building and the only one which Dante would have seen almost completed. As the seat of power and justice for many centuries, it is the object of many popular tales and legends. It was, in fact, the headquarters of the *Capitano del Popolo* (chief magistrate) and then, after the battle of Montaperti, of the *Podestà,* and lastly, after 1574, of the head of police — the *Bargello.* One of its functions during this time was as a prison, and capital punishments took place in the courtyard. Those who were condemned to death passed their last night in the chapel, and their bodies were hung from the windows after execution. Those who were condemned, yet who had managed to flee the city, were hanged in effigy on the wall facing Via della Vigna Vecchia.

A watercolour painting of the Badìa Fiorentina in the Rustici codex, 1447-1453.

Above right, a view of the Bargello from Piazza San Firenze. Left, the courtyard of the palazzo where executions took place. On the walls are the coats of arms of the Chief Magistrates. The majestic stairway was designed by Neri di Fioravanti.

Above, the Saint Paul's cannon by Cosimo Cenni, named after the head of the saint decorating the breech. Below, Tino da Camaino, Madonna and Child. Right, the Pitti Tondo by Michelangelo.

In 1782, on the abolition of the death penalty, Pietro Leopoldo had the gibbet and instruments of torture put on display in the courtyard as a symbolic gesture. Restoration of the palace was begun in 1857 by Leopoldo II, the last Grand Duke of Tuscany, and the prisons were transferred to the Murate, on Lungarno Pecori Giraldi.

Built over a period dating from the mid-13th to the mid-14th century, two distinct phases are discernible in this immense building. The 13th-century core consisted of a narrower and lower block than the present structure, with smooth stonework and only a few openings in the wall; in the 14th century the walls were raised using rougher blocks of stone, but the mullioned windows are more elegant.

The entrance is from a doorway with a low arch, leading into the 'Volognana' tower, 187 feet high and possibly pre-dating the original structure.

Around three sides of the large courtyard is a portico with octagonal pilasters supporting slightly curved arches. In the centre is a well and on the fourth side, heavily decorated with coats of arms in stone and glazed

terracotta, is a *stairway* (1345), designed by Neri Fioravante and enhanced by an attractive *gateway* (1503), by Giuliano di Francesco da Sangallo.

Bargello National Museum. The Museo Nazionale del Bargello opened in 1865 and the exhibits begin in this courtyard.

Beneath the portico are important *marble sculptures* by Ammannati, Giambologna and Tribolo, as well as *St Paul's cannon*, named for the bust of the saint which decorates the breech.

The Sala del Trecento is on the eastern side of the courtyard: among the works displayed in this room are a *Virgin and Child*, by Tino da Camaino, and the group of *Three Acolytes*, by Arnolfo di Cambio. Through the entrance beneath the stairs we

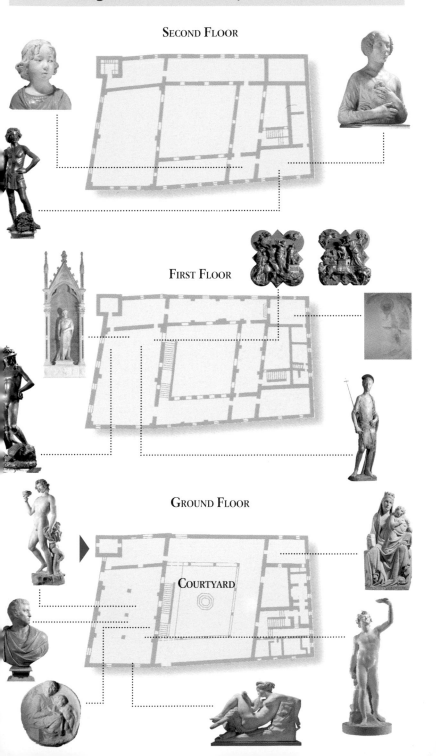

Bargello National Sculpture Museum

SECOND FLOOR

FIRST FLOOR

GROUND FLOOR

COURTYARD

come to the room dedicated to Michelangelo. Works include: the un-finished *Pitti Tondo*; the *Bacchus*, an early work (1496-1497); *Brutus*, the only bust ever sculpted by the artist. Also in this room are excellent pieces by Cellini, Giambo-logna and Jacopo Sansovino, as well as works by Tribolo, Ammannati and Ban-dinelli.

The stairway leads us to the first floor loggia with clustered pilasters and painted vaults. Arranged here is a series of bronze animals, including the famous *Turkey* which Giambo-logna made for the grotto of the Medici villa at Castello.

Michelangelo, Brutus, *personifying the republican virtues. Right,* Donatello, *Saint George. Now replaced by a copy, the statue decorated the façade of Orsanmichele until quite recently. Right, the loggia on the first floor houses many works by Giambologna. Far right,* Bacchus, *an early work by Michelangelo. Below,* Leda and the Swan *by Bartolomeo Ammannati.*

From the loggia we enter the spacious General Council Hall, designed by Neri di Fioravanti. The arches which

Left, Andrea del Verrocchio, Bust of a Lady Holding Flowers. *Below, Andrea della Robbia,* Bust of a Young Boy.

form this bright, well-lit space are based on the pre-Renaissance proportions of height to width (2:1). Dedicated to the works of Donatello, the chamber houses his famous *St George* (1416), brought from Orsanmichele; and the two *Davids*, one an early marble piece (1408-1409), the other his renowned bronze figure (c.1440). As well as other works by Donatello, the room includes the original *panels* which Ghiberti and Brunell-eschi prepared in 1401 for the competition for the North Door of the Baptistery, and sculptures by Michelozzo, Luca della Robbia, Desiderio da Settignano and Agostino di Duccio.

Various private collections are housed in the other first floor rooms: Arabian art is in the Islamic room; minor arts in the Carrand room; in the Avori room is a collection of 265 ivories; in the Sala delle Maioliche are china and pottery from the 15th to 18th centuries; the Bruzichelli room houses some 16th-century furniture. Frescoed on the far wall in the Chapel of St Mary Magdalen is *Paradise* (c.1340), including a portrait of a youthful Dante low down on the right.

Displayed in two rooms on the second floor are works by Giovanni and Andrea della Robbia, while the Bronzetti room houses the most impor-

tant collection of bronzes in Italy. Especially lovely are Benvenuto Cellini's *Hercules and Anteus* and *Ganymede*, by Giambologna. In the centre of the Verrocchio room is his bronze *David* (c.1470); also by him are the *Woman with a bouquet* and *Bust of Piero di Lorenzo de' Medici.* Various other late 15th-century works here include the *busts* by Antonio del Pollaiuolo, Francesco Laurana and Benedetto da Rovezzano.

The last room is dedicated to antique weaponry with some splendid items from various periods, belonging to the Medici, Carrand and Ressmann collections.

Leaving the Bargello, we follow the side of the building along Via del Proconsolo. Immediately after the junction with Via della Vigna Vecchia is Piazza San Firenze. On the left, with a wide set of steps leading up, is Palazzo San Firenze.

The Sacrifice of Isaac *represented by the two great artists who worked on the baptistery doors, Lorenzo Ghiberti (top) and Filippo Brunelleschi (above). Below, Andrea del Verrocchio,* David.

Interior of the church of Saint Philip Neri in Palazzo San Firenze. Both the splendid coffered ceiling and the allegorical sculptures of Charity *and* Purity *are by Giovacchino Fortini.*

PALAZZO AND CHURCH OF SAN FIRENZE

Palazzo San Firenze was not originally planned as we see it today. Totally demolishing an area of tightly packed medieval houses and lanes, a large monastery was to be built here for the order of St Philip Neri by Pietro da Cortona, shortly after 1640. Economic problems arose however, and Pier Francesco Silvani took over in 1645, beginning work on only the left section of the building (the church). The façade was completed by Ferdinando Ruggieri in 1715. In 1772, Zanobi del Rosso demolished a pre-existing church on the right and built the oratory there, duplicating the design of the left side. He then linked the two lateral sections to the central body (the convent), built between 1745 and 1749, with an imposing cornice. The final result is a fairly restrained late-baroque style, very different from the typically emphatic designs of Piero da Cortona.

The interior consists of a single, two-story hall with pilasters which frame spaces intended to house a regular series of altars, doors and ovals sculpted in high relief. San Firenze also houses several treasures of 17th- and 18th-century Florentine art: particularly gracious are the statues of *Charity* and *Purity*, by Giovacchino Fortini and the *Deposition*, by Alessandro Gherardini.

Just opposite Palazzo San Firenze, on the corner of Via de' Gondi with its lofty buildings leading into Piazza della Signoria, is the impressive Palazzo Gondi.

PALAZZO GONDI

Designed and built by Giuliano da Sangallo, the palace was started in 1489 but was not finished until 1874, when Giuseppe Poggi added a third door, a seventh window and the entire side on Via de' Gondi. The additions are barely visible due to the quality of the stone and construction, and in particular to the generally harmonious design.

Giuliano Gondi had long lived and worked outside Florence and when, in his old age, he decided to return, he wanted to build a residence which would rival those of the other wealthy families of the city. Giuliano da San Gallo, who was at the height of his career at the time, drew inspiration both from the already existing Palazzo Medici and from Palazzo Strozzi, then under construction, adding however, his own personal style. Here

Palazzo Gondi was built by Giuliano da Sangallo in the 15th century and altered by Giuseppe Poggi in the 19th century. The building, like many other important city residences, is surrounded by a stone bench on the street.

too, in fact, the rusticated stonework diminishes towards the top in the classic manner, but he somehow obtains an unusual result: the blocks on the ground floor create a pronounced *chiaroscuro* effect, while the decorative design of the other two floors is, instead quite subtle (note the repetition of the cross between the windows which, unlike Michelozzo's model, have single lights). The loggia on the roof is not set back as in other houses, but becomes a panoramic viewpoint which blends perfectly with the rest of the façade.

From Piazza San Firenze we take Via dell'Anguillara on the left of the church. At no. 14 is the Palazzo di Baldaccio d'Anghiari, *a medieval building ex-*

tensively altered in the 16th century; at no. 23, Palazzo Baccelli *with its sharply jutting profile, is 17th-century; the majestic* Palazzo Ginori *(no. 19-21) was built in 1775; the carefully restored building at no. 17 is typically 14th-century.*

At the end of Via dell'Anguillara we turn left into Via Torta, which takes its name from the curve which follows the original perimeter of the Roman amphitheatre; this leads us into Piazza Santa Croce.

PIAZZA SANTA CROCE

"This piazza is quite beautiful, with houses surrounding it like some lovely theatre set". So stated one of the first guides to Florence, continuing, "it is altogether well-proportioned and every year at Carnival time it is fenced off so that the young men can play the game of football to the best of their ability". The square was built as a twin to Santa Maria Novella, and was intended to hold the crowds of faithful who gathered there to listen to the sermons of the first Franciscan monks. Later, miracle plays were performed here, though these were again replaced by the tournaments and jousts of young noblemen (such as those of 1381, held for the wedding of Luchino Visconti) and in particular those

Two views of the square and church of Santa Croce. Above, the façade and bell tower seen from on high. Above left, a view of the piazza from the side of Via dell'Anguillara; on the far right is the dome of the Pazzi chapel. Below left, an imposing statue of Dante Alighieri *placed on the left in front of the church in 1968 (in 1865, it was erected in the centre of the piazza;*
☛ *photo on p. 213).*

Customs and festivals -2-

have been an integral part of the city's history. Many have been forgotten, while others have been dusted off and reinstated. One of the latter was the 'game of football,' evidently already well-established in the 16th century although it is difficult to tell when or how it originated. Though little or no proof exists, reference is inevitably made to older, quite violent games such as the Greek *spheromachia*, and the Roman *arpasto*. The earliest documentation dates from the beginning of the 15th century, and consists of some lines of poetry describing a match played in Piazza Santo Spirito. Historian Luca Landucci also related that on January 10, 1490, "the Arno froze so hard that football was played on it"; but it was during carnival time that football games were most frequently mentioned. Special events (usually illustrious weddings) also provided further opportunities and at least once an away game was even organized. It took place in Lyon where the resident Florentines, in honour of Henry III, "arranged a football match entirely of Florentine nobility," for

Historical football

"The ball flew high and did not hurt or harm anyone". The ball was actually a cannon-ball, fired across Piazza Santa Croce where a large crowd of spectators was following a battle over another ball made of "heavy, round leather / which held a gust of wind prisoner" as it was described by the 16th-century poet, Gabriello Chiabrera. The date was 17 February, 1530: the artillery of Charles V's besieging army was bombarding the city from the surrounding hills (☛ p.65), but the Florentines "not wishing to abandon an ancient tradition and also to show their utter contempt for the enemy, were playing a game of football".

The 'festival of Flora', taking place from 28 April to 3 May, is probably linked to the foundation of the city and accounts for the origin of its name. Many other festivals, both lay and religious,

"neither craftsmen, nor servants, nor commoners, but only honoured soldiers, gentlemen, noblemen and princes" were entitled to play in the most prestigious games. Eventually, probably due to strong competition from other games and forms of football, the tradition faded in popularity and finally ended altogether in January 1739 with a final game played in honour of the arrival of Francesco II and Maria Theresa of Austria in Florence. At the turn of the century, there were sporadic attempts to resurrect it, but it was not until 1930 – the fourth centenary of that historic match played under siege – that the tradition was definitively re-established, now be-

ing held as part of the celebrations for St John's Day, in June. New rules of play and arrangement of the teams were also decided. Each district of the city had a team (the blues of Santa Croce; the whites of Santo Spirito; the reds of Santa Maria Novella; the greens of San Giovanni) with twenty-seven players, divided into rear shooters, front shooters, foulers and wingers. A parade in historic costume is also held, during which the emblems of the four districts and of the Arts and Crafts Guilds, as well as sixteen flags representing the main magistratures and most important civic offices of 16th-century Florence, are carried through the streets. The style and colours of the costumes worn have been copied from drawings by Lorenzo Lotto and Andrea del Sarto.

rious images of the turesque procession which takes place before the game of storic football'. The articipants march to sound of flutes and the beat of drums. hough the tradition vas reintroduced as recently as 1930, many Florentines follow the football games with an nthusiasm reflected in the energy of the me. Above, and on left are two action-packed scenes in a match between the reds (Santa Maria Novella) and the ites (Santo Spirito).

Top of page, a detail of the Carnival of Florence *by Giovanni Signorini. Palazzo Pitti, Gallery of Modern Art. Two details date the picture fairly precisely: the bell tower which was built in 1847, and the unfinished façade; work on the decoration began in 1853. Above, a view of the façade of Palazzo Antellesi. Built by Giulio Parigi between 1619 and 1620, two separate properties belonging to the same family were elegantly combined into one. The frescoes were painted in record time by various artists, under the direction of Giovanni da San Giovanni.*

organized in Lorenzo the Magnificent's day, as recorded in the works of Luigi Pulci and Agnolo Poliziano. These gave way in turn to football games, evidence of which is seen in the marble plaque set into the façade of Palazzo Antellesi, indicating the half way line of the field. (☞ p. 136)

Complementing, or perhaps even affirming its theatrical aspect, two of the palazzi on the square seem almost to have been designed as if they were the wings or the backdrop of a stage set: at no. 1 is *Palazzo Cocchi-Serristori* and at no. 20-22 is *Palazzo Antellesi.*

PALAZZO COCCHI-SERRISTORI

The design of the façade, created by Giuliano da Sangallo between 1480 and 1490, could have derived from the amphitheatres of imperial Rome. The Florentine architect had visited Rome as a young man and had admired the ruins of the Colosseum, so much better preserved than the amphitheatre of Hadrian's day near Santa Croce. Clearly this gave him the idea of adding to the scenic nature of the piazza by introducing arches, entablatures and pilasters directly copied from the Roman buildings where dramatic performances were held. The six capitals of the pilasters with the motif of a radiant sun, represented by a youthful face sur-

rounded by leaves, are a reminder instead of the hermetic symbolism found in the Neoplatonic, humanist circles which Sangallo frequented. The palace was actually created by restructuring several houses belonging to the Peruzzi family, transforming the *pietra forte* blocks of the ground floor into load-bearing pillars.

PALAZZO ANTELLESI

Thirteen artists worked for twenty days (fifteen days in May, 1619 and five in May, 1620) to paint the façade of this building with allegories, putti and festoons. These hastily-painted decorations were part of the annual celebrations held in June for St John the Baptist, patron saint of Florence. The names of the artists, including Passignano, Matteo Rosselli, Giovanni da San Giovanni, Ottavio Vannini and Fabrizio Boschi, are to be seen in a scroll held by the third cherub from the church in the band beneath the first floor windows. These masters from the Drawing Academy were organized and directed by Niccolò dell'Antella, who had become owner of the earlier buildings through marriage. These had only recently been united into a single, entirely projecting façade using the typically Florentine and rather spectacular architectural feature of stone corbels or brackets. These be-

The austere interior of the church of Santa Croce which, over the centuries, has become a temple to Italian genius.

come closer, as do the windows, towards the central focus of the church, creating a clever effect of perspective.

CHURCH OF SANTA CROCE

Historian Giovanni Villani recorded that, "In the year of Our Lord 1294, on the day of the Holy Cross in May, the great new church of the Florentine Friars Minor of the Holy Cross was founded". His information is, however, contradicted by a slab in a corner pilaster between the right nave and the transept, where we read, "This church was founded on 3 May, 1295".

The design may almost certainly be attributed to Arnolfo di Cambio, who built this enormous cathedral over an earlier church, mentioned for the first time in 1228. While aspects of the grandiose French Gothic style are evident, they are modified by the more traditional local Romanesque. Work on the church continued for a long time and it was finally consecrated in 1443. Vasari made considerable alterations in the 16th century, whitewashing the frescoed walls and placing large altars against them. Finally, Gaetano Baccani's bell tower was built in 1847, and between 1853-1863 the façade was decorated in marble by Niccolò Matas. In 1865, the statue of Dante was placed in the centre of the piazza, then moved to the left side of the church steps in 1968.

With the triangular tympani along the sides of the church and the apse crowned with pinnacles, it is almost only possible to appreciate the distinctive exterior from a distance.

Interior. The church's T-shaped plan evokes the Egyptian cross, with three aisles separated by imposing octagonal pillars supporting wide, ogival arches. The roof of the central aisle has painted wooden beams and the extensive transept is enhanced by numerous chapels which open off it.

Today, it requires some imagination to picture the original appearance of this Franciscan church. It was, in fact, once entirely painted with frescoes representing scenes from the Book of Revelation and the Lives of the Saints. The paintings around the walls of the church constituted a real 'Pauper's Bible,' continuing the principal of religious teaching which the Franciscans practiced in their preaching in the square outside. This educative, cultural aspect evolved into the tradition, still quite evident and characteristic of this church, of burying famous personalities and scholars here.

Right aisle and transept. The overall theme guiding the vari-

The transept of the church seen from the side of the sacristy.

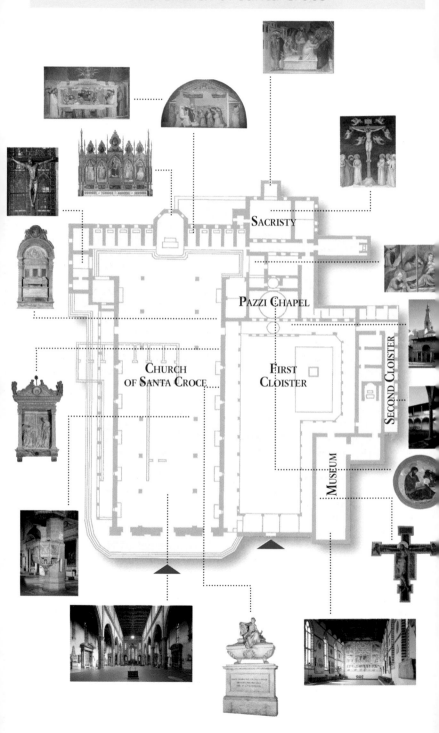

The Church of Santa Croce

SACRISTY

PAZZI CHAPEL

SECOND CLOISTER

CHURCH
OF SANTA CROCE

FIRST
CLOISTER

MUSEUM

Language and literature

The question of the importance of Florentine in the development of a national language has given rise to lively debate over many centuries. Leaving the various arguments aside however, Florentine speech is easily recognizable due to a particular phonetic feature caused by the aspiration of several intervocal consonants (c, t, p, d). While some attribute the resulting pronunciation to a distant Etruscan linguistic substratum, the origins are, instead, much more recent; in fact, the earliest written evidence dates from the 16th century. Moreover, Dante, an acute observer and scholar of the 'vernacular' makes no mention of the phenomenon. Dante (1265-1321) is generally recognised as the father of the Italian language and to him we owe the process by which everyday language was refined and formulated to become acceptable as a literary form too. The fame of the *Divine Comedy* and the public readings of it which were held in Florence and other cities of Italy contributed considerably to the diffusion of the new idiom. During the 14th century Francesco Petrarch and Giovanni Boccaccio, both in quite different ways, helped to improve the image of the vernacular, Petrarch with his refined Tuscan equally at ease with Latin terms and receptive to the influence of French and other languages, Boccaccio favouring his own contemporary Florentine. Their works, the *Canzoniere* and the *Decameron* both rapidly gained international renown. During the 15th century, at the height of the humanist revival, a return to the study of the Greek and Latin classics helped to enrich the vocabulary and develop a more formal elegance. During the 16th century, when a modulated and graceful style came into fashion, Italian became the language of culture in the most important foreign courts. In the same century heated and frequently polemical debate took place concerning the language and especially the evident superiority of written Florentine over other Italian dialects. Niccolò Machiavelli and Francesco Guicciardini were both enthusiastic upholders of this supremacy. Pietro Bembo, in his *Prose della volgar lingua* confirmed the superiority of written Tuscan vernacular which refused both sophistication and banality, and compiled the first Italian grammar. Gian Giorgio Trìssino of Vicenza tried to resolve the problems of pronunciation for non-Tuscans in an original, though quite unsuccessful, proposal to reform the alphabet. In 1582, in the splendid Medici villa of Castello near Florence, the Accademia della Crusca came into being for the purpose of promoting the Florentine 'language'. It tended instead, to dwell on minor aspects of provincial vernacular, giving rise to the scornful term 'cruscante', indicating a person who tried to perpetuate forms and expressions which had become obsolete and even ridulous. To its merit, however, the Accademia published the first dictionary of the Italian language (1612). Today this venerable institution has become a modern centre for research into aspects of linguistic evolution. The last great exponent of Florentine as the national language was Alessandro Manzoni (1785-1873), who, in revising his novel *The Betrothed*, came to "rinse it in the waters of the Arno" in an attempt to revitalize the links between spoken and written language which, during the 19th century with the development of a kind of 'lingua franca' comprehensible to all, had become increasingly weakened. Today the standardization of language resulting from the media and mass communications is the last phase in this process, favoured by the city's diminished political and economic importance compared to the decisional and influential centres, in particular Rome and Milan.

The 15th-century stone pulpit by Benedetto da Maiano: the bas-relief panels portray Scenes from the Life of Saint Francis. *Above right, the* tomb of Niccolò Machiavelli, *an 18th-century monument by Innocenzo Spinazzi. Below, Bernardo Rossellino,* Monument to Leonardo Bruni. *Below right, Taddeo Gaddi,* Crucifixion, *Sacristy of Santa Croce.*

ous artists (amongst whom, Santi di Tito, Vasari and Cigoli) who worked on the six side chapels is that of the *Passion*. Between the first and second chapels is the *tomb of Michelangelo* (1564), by Vasari, and on the pilaster opposite is a marble relief of the *Madonna and Child* (1478), by Antonio Rossellino. Between the second and third altars is the *Monument to Dante Alighieri* (1829), followed by the neoclassical *monument to Vittorio Alfieri* (1810), by Antonio Canova. On the third pillar on the right is a *pulpit*, a late masterpiece by Benedetto da Maiano, with five panels representing *Scenes from the Life of St Francis*. Beyond the fourth altar is the *tomb of Niccolò Machiavelli* (1787), and beyond the fifth an *Annunciation* in *pietra serena* by Donatello, one of the finest of the early Florentine Renaissance. Next is Bernardo Rossellino's *monument to Leonardo Bruni* (1444-1445) — a model for funerary monuments ever since. The series of tombs ends with those of *Gioacchino Rossini* (1900) and *Ugo Foscolo* (1939).

Continuing around the right wing of the transept we come to the large Castellani Chapel, where the tertiary Franciscan order – of which Dante was a member – met. The *frescoes* (1385) are by Agnolo Gaddi and assistants. From here we enter the Baroncelli chapel with frescoes by Taddeo Gaddi (*Scenes from the Life of the Virgin,* 1332-1338), who also

designed the stained glass windows. There is some debate over the attribution of the polyptych on the altar, believed to be either by Gaddi or by his teacher, Giotto.

Passing through a doorway by Michelozzo we come to a corridor and then turn left into the large 14th-century sacristy. On the right wall are *frescoes* by Niccolò Gerini, Spinello Aretino and Taddeo Gaddi (the *Crucifixion*); the inlayed 15th-century *cupboards* are by Giovanni di Michele; displayed in the glass cases are precious reliquaries, missals and vestments from various epochs. At the far end is the Rinuccini Chapel, closed off by the original wrought iron railings (1371), decorated inside with *frescoes* (1363-1366) by Giovanni da

Donatello,
Annunciation
(1435).

Milano. The corridor leads to the Medici Chapel, a fine example of classic Renaissance architecture by Michelozzo. There is a splendid glazed terracotta *altarpiece* (1480), by Andrea della Robbia.

Returning to the church we now come to the chapels along the back of the transept. There are five on the left and five on the right of the main chapel, each founded by one of the noble families living in the neighbourhood. In the Peruzzi Chapel, fourth on the right, are S*tories from the Life of St John the Evangelist* (right wall) and S*tories from the Life of St John the Baptist* (left wall) by Giotto, who also painted the famous *Scenes from the Life of St Francis* (1320-1325) in the Bardi Chapel beside. "In Giotto's art we are aware of one of the greatest creative forces ever seen in painting. Everything is design and architecture, there is not a single line which is not essential and which does not contribute to creating a superior level of reality" (André Barret).

In the main chapel, the most Gothic structure in the church, are frescoes (c.1380) by Agnolo Gaddi illustrating the *Legend of the True Cross*, inspired by Jacopo da Varagine's *Golden Legend*. On the main altar is a polyptych by Niccolò Gerini and Giovanni del Biondo representing the *Virgin and Child Enthroned with Saints.*

Continuing to the left of the Main Chapel, in the fourth (Pulci-Beraldi) are *frescoes* by Bernardo Daddi and a beautiful *altar-frontal* in glazed terracotta, partly oil-painted by Giovanni della Robbia. The fifth chapel (Bardi di Vernio) is decorated with *frescoes* (c.1340), by Giotto's most original pupil, Maso di Banco.

Taddeo Gaddi, Nativity *(detail).* Baroncelli Chapel.

Giovanni da Milano, The Resurrection of Lazzarus. *Rinuccini Chapel.*

Giotto, The Death of Saint Francis. *Bardi Chapel.*

Above, Giotto, Saint Francis Giving the Rule of the Order. *Bardi Chapel. Right, Donatello,* Crucifixion.

The graceful second cloister, probably designed by Brunelleschi and built in 1453 by Rossellino (opposite page, above, a medallion in one of the spandrels). Below, the Santa Croce polyptych *by Niccolò Gerini and Giovanni del Biondo.*

Continuing along the left side of the transept, the chapel enclosed by railings (1335) is also of the Bardi family. Inside is a wooden *Crucifix* (1411), by Donatello. Last is the Machiavelli Chapel with the neo-Renaissance *tomb of the Countess Sofia Zamoyska* (1837-1844), by Lorenzo Bartolini.

Left aisle. This side too has a series of funerary monuments: *Luigi Cherubini, Leon Battista Alberti* (by Lorenzo Bartolini,

1840-1850), *Carlo Marsuppini* (a masterpiece by Desiderio da Settignano), *Galileo* and his pupil, *Vincenzo Viviani.*

The cloisters on the right side of the church not only house further works of art, but are in themselves architectural gems.
In the centre of the first, 14th-century cloister is a bronze *by Henry Moore and a figure of* God the Father Seated, *by Baccio Bandinelli. On the far side is the Pazzi Chapel.*

PAZZI CHAPEL

As does the dome of Santa Maria del Fiore, the Cappella de' Pazzi reveals similarities between the work of Brunelleschi and Arnolfo di Cambio. Here, however, Brunelleschi's rationality does not perfect Arnolfo's work, but simply complements his architectural concepts.

The chapel was financed by Andrea de' Pazzi and was used as a chapter house, with a chapel behind the altar where this merchant family could bury its dead. Work began in 1429 and was personally followed by Brunelleschi, who saw the interior completed in 1444, though he never saw the dome which was only erected in 1459.

Façade. This light and open façade is the only one to have been left to us by Brunelleschi, and even this does not entirely correspond with his original design. Six Corinthian columns

white walls. In particular, the spandrels contain terracottas (*Four Evangelists*) made by Luca della Robbia to a design by Brunelleschi, coloured not only with white and blue, but also with green, brown, light pink and yellow.

From the first cloister we reach the 14th-century former refectory, where we begin our visit to the Museo dell'Opera di Santa Croce.

SANTA CROCE MUSEUM

The most outstanding piece in the imposing former refectory is Cimabue's renowned *Crucifix*, immediately on the right. Completed prior to 1271, it was the most tragic and famous victim of the 1966 flood.

On the far wall is a large fresco depicting the *Last Supper*, by Taddeo Gaddi (dated 1333, the year of another disastrous flood). The first painting of this subject in Florence, it consequently became the model to decorate later monastic refectories (☞ p.146). Four *Stories from the Bible* and the *Tree of Life*, also by Gaddi, follow.

Six panels on the walls to the sides are all that remain of a large *fresco* by Andrea Orcagna, one of the finest pieces of 14th-century Florentine painting. On the left is Donatello's bronze statue of *St Louis of*

support an attic floor, decorated with a series of pilaster strips and with a large arch rising in the centre. On the frieze of the architrave are *cherubs' heads* engraved by Desiderio da Settignano; in the vault of the portico are *tondi* and small *rosettes* in glazed terracotta by Luca della Robbia, who also made the figure of *St Andrew* above the door, the attractively decorated panels of which are by Giuliano da Maiano.

Interior. The extremely simple interior repeats the elements of design seen in the Old Sacristy in San Lorenzo; in particular, the basic measurement of twenty *braccia* (arm's length, the equivalent of 23 inches) which is the diameter of the dome and of the sides of the central block which supports it within the otherwise mainly rectangular structure. Also familiar is the clever introduction of colour within the abstract forms created by the gray outline of the arches and pilasters on the

The Pazzi Chapel (above) with the only façade ever designed by Brunelleschi. Left, the ceiling of the dome in the portico, decorated with glazed terracotta tondos and rosettes by Luca della Robbia. Below, Saint Luke, one of the four tondos which decorate the spandrels in the ceiling of the chapel, also by Luca della Robbia.

Last Suppers

During the Renaissance, the larger monastic orders were among the most importan clients commissioning works of art for their churches, monasteries and all building belonging to the religious communities in general. The rooms and halls where th monks worked, prayed or ate together were decorated with images which re called the true faith, the foundation and history of their order and the spiritual val ues which they pursued. The didactic function of the paintings was an important el ement within the church from the earliest times: "Pictures are just as useful to an i literate person as writing is to the literate," wrote Pope Gregory in the 6th century Particular attention was given to the decoration of the refectories, or *cenacol* where the monks came together to eat. Dining at the same table while listening t readings from the scriptures had an important symbolic meaning, representing a vi tal aspect of life in the monastic community — a liturgical rite.

Given the importance of the *cenacoli* in the cultural and spiritual life of the monas teries, they were decorated with splendid frescoes, the favourite subject obviously be ing the Last Supper during which Christ initiated the sacrament of the Eucharist.

Santa Croce

The *Last Supper* (1333) in the large refectory of the basilica is one of Taddeo Gaddi's greatest works, and the prototype for all similar paintings thereafter. Judas is in the foreground, alone on the near side of the table behind which sit Christ and the Apostles. Next to Jesus, John the Evangelist – the youngest and also the most beloved of the Apostles – rests his head against of the Saviour. Above the *Last Supper* are other frescoes by Taddeo Gaddi: *St Benedict in Solitude, Christ dines in the House of the Pharisee, St Francis receives the Stigmata, Scenes from the Life of St Louis of Toulouse* and the large *Tree of the Cross.*

Sant'Apollonia

Painted by Andrea del Castagno when he returned from Venice, this *Last Supper* (1444) is set in a magnificent hall decorated with coloured marble. Above i are scenes from the Passion of Christ: the *Crucifixion,* the *Deposition* and the *Resurrection.* In fact the refectory constitutes a little museum dedicated entirely to Andrea del Castagno: in addition to the works already mentioned, a *Pietà* and a *Crucifix* by the artist are also displayed here.

[Entrance: via XXVII Aprile 1. ☛ T3/F3. Opening times 9-14; closed on Mondays].

San Salvi

In the refectory of the Vallombrosan monastery of San Salvi, this *Last Supper* was frescoed by Andrea del Sarto in 1526-1527. It risked destruction during the siege of 1529, but was saved thanks to an agreement between Charles v and the Florentines by which the attacking troops were to avoid military operations in the area surrounding the church. The former monastery buildings have been transformed into a small museum with works by Florentine artists of the 16th century (Raffaellino del Garbo, Giorgio Vasari, Ridolfo del Ghirlandaio, Pontormo, Bachiacca and Benedetto da Rovezzano).

[Entrance: via di San Salvi 16; ☛ T6/L5. Opening times 9-14; closed on Mondays].

Ognissanti

The scene in the refectory of the Franciscan monastery of Ognissanti was painted by Domenico Ghirlandaio. One of the greatest exponents of the Florentine high Renaissance style of painting, the artist set his *Last Supper* (1480) in an everyday, 15th-century interior, opening onto bright countryside. The fresco contains many symbolic references: the peacock in the window on the right, displaying its splendid tail feathers, signifies the immortality of the soul; the skylark on the left is the spirit of justice, capable of soaring to the heights. In the background are cypress trees, a symbol of death; and cherries and oranges, which represent the joy of Paradise.

Cimabue, Crucifix. *The work was seriously damaged by the flood waters in 1966.*

The large refectory in Santa Croce with frescoes by Taddeo Gaddi and Andrea Orcagna. Above, Taddeo Gaddi and Andrea Orcagna, the Last Supper *(detail). Below, the courtyard of Palazzo Spinelli with graffito decoration.*

Toulouse (1424), originally made for Orsanmichele.

Displayed in the other five rooms of the museum are various examples of 14th- and 15th-century art.

A *doorway* by Benedetto da Maiano leads us into the *second cloister* (1453): one of the most delightfully harmonious in all of Florence, its two-storied arcading is attributed to Bernardo Rossellino.

Leaving the museum, we turn left onto Via Magliabechi. Slightly further ahead, on the other side is Borgo Santa Croce, which leads to Via de' Benci.

Lying outside the 13th-century city walls, Borgo Santa Croce contains some of the finest examples of Renaissance architecture. On the left are Palazzo Gherardi *and* Palazzo

Mori-Ubaldini. *On the right is the impressive* Palazzo Spinelli, *built between 1460 and 1470 by the Spinelli family, important merchants in Santa Croce, who also paid for the furnishings of the sacristy in the church. The façade, splendidly decorated with graffito, has an elegant doorway and windows with rounded arches. The graffito is continued in the courtyard, two sides of which have a loggia. Note the sophisticated decoration of the capitals and bases, possibly designed by Bernardo Rossellino.*

The courtyard of the nearby Palazzo Serristori *is just as attractively decorated. Built at the end of the 15th and beginning of the 16th centuries, the courtyard has a portico around three sides, while the fourth has half vaults, thus creating a theatrical effect of enlarged space which may be attributed to Baccio d'Agnolo.*

The road ends with the sturdy Alberti Tower. *The loggia on the ground floor elegantly resolves the problem of the sharply abrupt junction with Via de' Benci.*

We now turn left towards the Arno. Just past the junction with Corso de' Tintori, on the left, is the Horne Palazzo and Museum.

PALAZZO HORNE (FORMERLY PALAZZO CORSI)

The building which houses the museum was created from the profits of Renaissan

The Alberti tower with its attractive loggia.

trade, and restored several centuries later by an enthusiastic English antiquarian.

In the late 15th century, Cronaca made this compact and elegant building from a small palace which had originally belonged to the Alberti family, and later became the property of a family of cloth merchants, the Corsi. At the end of the 19th century, it was bought by Herbert Percy Horne (1844-1916). An art historian and collector, friend of Dante Gabriele Rossetti and Oscar Wilde, he restored it between 1912 and 1914, subsequently leaving it to the Italian state. It has been a museum since 1922.

Above the level of the 'street bench,' graduated rustication was only used on the façade to decorate the doorway and corner. Only one side of the courtyard has arches; two others form a gallery, supporting the first floor loggia. The fourth side should be imagined as it once was, opening onto flower and vegetable gardens. The decoration of the capitals, bases and bands between the floors is of very high quality.

Horne Museum. The entire house is an excellent example of the aesthetic taste for placing art in an everyday context: it is an important arrangement of paintings and sculptures, but also of furniture, glass, chi-

na and bronze bas-reliefs. Displayed on the ground floor are collections of coins, seals, medals and ceramics.

On the first floor: in the small room to the right are works from the 14th to the 16th centuries, including a *Holy Family* by Domenico Beccafumi, the first work to be acquired by Horne. In the main room are: *Allegory of Music,* by Dosso Dossi; a much deteriorated fragment of a triptych depicting *Scenes from the Life of St Julian,* attributed to Masaccio; a *Deposition* and other scenes by Benozzolo Gozzoli; two *panels* by Bernardo Gaddi and a *triptych* by Piero Lorenzetti. Next is the room housing the most important work in the museum, a *St Stephen* attributed to Giotto.

On the second floor is an inlayed Tuscan *sacristy cupboard*, dated first half of the

Palazzo Horne, housing the Museum, seen from Via dei Benci. Centre page, the Holy Family *by the Sienese artist, Domenico Beccafumi (first half of the 16th century), one of the earliest items in the collection now housed in the late 19th-century palace built by Herbert Horne. Below, the first room on the first floor of the museum.*

*Giotto, (attrib.)
Saint Stephan.
Horne Museum.*

15th century; a late 16th-century walnut dresser; a diptych of the *Virgin and Child and Pietà*, by Simone Martini; part of a 15th-century *chest*, by Filippino Lippi; a *Virgin of the Candelabra*, in painted plasterwork by Antonio Rossellino.

In the late 16th century, the Camerata dei Bardi (Company of Bards) met in this palazzo. Led by Vincenzo Galileo (father of the renowned astronomer), this group of creative musicians invented the genre of melodrama.

Leaving the museum, on the other side of the street, at no. 5 is Palazzo Bardi.

Palazzo Bardi, meeting place of the 'Camerata', a group of musicians credited with the invention of melodrama. Below, the Science Museum, once the palace of the city judges, seen from the Arno. Right, microscope made by Giuseppe Campani in the 17th century.

PALAZZO BARDI

The prototype of the Renaissance palace, Palazzo Bardi was almost certainly designed by Brunelleschi around 1430, some fifteen years before Palazzo Medici and about twenty before Palazzo Pitti. Built for the Busini family, it was bought by the Bardi in 1483.

The structure's design is well-proportioned and restrained: the doorway is framed with smooth blocks and the first and second floors have eight windows each. The only decoration consists of two coats of arms of the Busini family at the sides, sculpted in stone. Brunelleschi's innovative style can be best seen in his method of treating the stonework decorated with graffito friezes and in the unusual form of the curved window frames.

Along the side of Palazzo Bardi is the narrow street known as Via de' Vagellai (named for the workers in charge of the vagelli, or cauldrons used for dying fabrics). At the end of the street we enter Piazza Mentana and cross over to Lungarno Diaz, which runs along the bank of the Arno. In the past, rafts of tree trunks were collected here, after having been sent downstream from the Casentino forests.

We continue along the Lungarno to Piazza dei Giudici, where we find the interesting Museum of the History of Science.

INSTITUTE AND MUSEUM OF THE HISTORY OF SCIENCE

Founded in 1930, the Istituto and Museo di Storia della Scienza is housed in one of the oldest buildings in the city: dating from before the 12th century, from 1574 to 1841 it was the seat of the city judges.

The collection consists of approximatel 5,000 original so

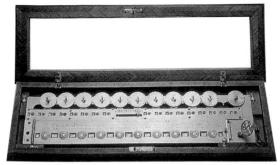

entific instruments, divided into two core groups: initiated by Cosimo the Elder, the Medici collection contains instruments and appliances, as well as superb examples of Renaissance mathematical tools (including Galileo's original instruments from his School and the Accademia del Cimento). The Lorraine collection consists of experimental and educational appliances and tools, dating from the creation of the Museum of Natural History and Physics, founded by Pietro Leopoldo (1775). This collection reflects the evolution of scientific research between the 18th and 19th centuries, and offers important insight into the 'new' disciplines such as chemistry, electricity, magnetics, pneumatics, surgery and gynaecology. In Room XI are some important telescopes made for the astronomical observatories at the Spècola and Arcetri.

The Institute and Museum have two libraries. The old library consists of the Lorraine collection of over 200 texts dating from 1475 to the end of the 19th century. The modern library is the most up-to-date on the subject in Italy, and contains approximately 6,000 specialist titles, 30,000 miscellaneous texts and various journals.

Having visited the History of Science Museum, we continue along Via dei Castellani on the left to the junction with Via de' Neri. On the corner here is the Loggia del Grano (*Grain Market*), *built to a design by Giulio Parigi in 1619, decorated by Chiarissimo Fancelli da Settignano with the fountain and a bust of Cosimo II in the keystone of the central arch. At the end of the last century, when it had ceased to serve its original function, it was elevated and used for theatre performances.*

Opposite, on the corner of Via de' Leoni, is the impressive Filipetri Tower. *Further ahead,* Palazzo da Diacceto (*at no. 33*) and Palazzo Soldani (*at no.*

23) still show clear signs of their medieval origins.

From Via de' Neri we turn onto Via San Remigio. A plaque on the corner shows the level reached by the Arno during the 1333 flood. Further on is the little church of San Remigio, a Gothic renovation of an earlier building founded in the 11th century. Inside, the church is divided into three aisles by octagonal pillars. Fragments of 14th-century frescoes are on the walls.

Leaving the church, we take Via Vinegia to the right and then turn left into Via dei Rustici, leading into Piazza Peruzzi.

PIAZZA PERUZZI

This secluded piazza is a reminder of Roman and medieval Florence. Its curving side corresponds to what was once a section of a large Roman amphitheatre (early 2nd century AD). The seating area measured 371 by 291 feet, and the internal arena, 210 by 131 feet. The path around the perimeter is still easily recognizable from nearby Via Bentaccordi and Via Torta, while at no. 7 in Piazza Peruzzi, the rounded sandstone arches of the ground floor are perhaps part of the original structure.

During the Middle Ages, the entire piazza was the private courtyard of the Peruzzi family: owners seen on their coat of arms were holders of a considerable fortune made first as cloth merchants and later as bankers and moneylenders. During the 13th and 14th centuries, the various properties of the family in this area were rebuilt and arranged in and around this courtyard, forming a veritable enclave, the confines of which were indicated by stone coats of arms (of the original fourteen, thirteen can still be seen, such as those on the façade of Palazzo Cocchi-Serristori). The style of the buildings is particularly evident on Via de' Benci: on the ground floor are the rusticated barrel-vaulted shops and warehouses and the rectangular windows of the stores above.

From the piazza we briefly follow Via Bentaccordi, and then turn right to Borgo de' Greci, continuing into Piazza San Firenze. From here we take Via Condotta turning right into Via de' Magazzini. At the end is the picturesque little Piazza San Martino.

PIAZZA SAN MARTINO

The square and the entire surrounding area are rich with reminders of Dante. Dante was, in fact, born in the building now housing a trattoria established at the beginning of the 16th century by the artist Mariotto Albertinelli, who quite simply swapped paintbrushes for kitchen pans.

Piazza Peruzzi seen from the arch in Via de' Benci (top). Above, a view of the church of San Remigio, founded in the 11th century. Below, Borgo de' Greci: the street was given this name in the second half of the 15th century when a group of Byzantine intellectuals took up residence here after fleeing from Constantinople when the city was conquered by the Turks (1453).

Immediately beside it is the controversial 20th-century reconstruction of the so-called 'Dante's House'. Exhibitions of painting are held on the ground floor, while a museum documenting Dante's Florence is located on the floors above.

At the end of the narrow Via Santa Margherita (the street from which one enters Dante's House) one finds the *church* of the same name. This is one of the oldest in Florence, and was once financed by the Portinari family. This is not, however, the true 'Church of Dante': the remains of the Romanesque façade can be seen on Via del Canto alla Quarcònia, and in 1480 the *Bonòmini Oratory* (the façade of which is on Piazza San Martino) was built on the area of the original apse. The interior is decorated with a series of frescoes relating *Scenes from the Life of St Martin*, the *Seven Works of Charity* and two *Scenes of Daily Life*. Attribution is rather uncertain, although they are generally considered to be by the school of Ghirlandaio. These paintings provide one of the liveliest and most interesting descriptions of everyday life in Florence at the end of the 15th century.

Opposite is the *Castagna Tower*, which was the first seat of democratic government in the city: here, in 1282, the Priors of the Guilds convened for the first time. Next door, entering through the Prefecture, we come into a cloister with a statue of *Margrave Ugo of Tuscany*. From here we can also make out the traces of the original façade of the Badia Fiorentina.

From Piazza San Martino we turn left into Via Dante Alighieri, and continue to Piazza dei Cerchi. Turning right along Via de' Cerchi and crossing the Corso, we come to Via Santa Elisabetta.

This street actually follows the direction of the Byzantine walls and brings us into a small piazza where we find the majestic Ghiberti Tower-House, *and the recently restored* Pagliazza Tower. *Due to its semi-cylindrical shape, the latter was long believed to be Byzantine. It was, rather, built on the exedra of some Roman baths, as is explained in a small museum inside the tower.*

Continuing along Via Santa Elisabetta, we reach the junction with Via delle Oche. From here, by turning either left (Via del Campanile) or right (Via dello Studio) we return to Piazza del Duomo.

The Compagnia dei Buonòmini (Company of Goodfellows) was established to help the very poor. Top, the façade of the little oratory in Piazza San Martino which belonged to the company. Above left, the interior with frescoes by followers of Ghirlandaio. Above, the opening where alms were left; the plaque above it promises "two thousand and eight years of indulgence" to benefactors.

The 'false' home of Dante (left) which dates from the early 20th century. Beside, the entrance to the real house, today the 'Trattoria Pennello', so called because it was first opened by a painter.

6. **The Oltrarno**

In 1537, Duke Alessandro – the last descendant of Cosimo the Elder, founder of the Medici dynasty – was assassinated by his cousin, Lorenzino (immortalized in the 19th century by the play *Lorenzaccio*, by Alfred de Musset). To succeed him, the Florentine nobility chose Cosimo, the eighteen-year-old son of Giovanni dalle Bande Nere, a soldier from a minor branch of the family. The young duke immediately showed his mettle by defeating the republican army, led by Filippo Strozzi, at Montemurlo, as they marched on the city. In 1539, Cosimo married Eleonora de Toledo, daughter of the Viceroy of Naples. In 1540, they moved from Palazzo Medici on Via Larga to Palazzo Vecchio, and in 1549, Eleonora bought Palazzo Pitti. When Siena was defeated in 1555 after a lengthy siege, an enlarged, regional state came into being with Cosimo as its Grand Duke, a title which Pope Paul V conceded to him in 1569.

The rise of Cosimo I and the creation of the Grand Duchy opened a new chapter in the history of the city. Just as in the 14th century Arnolfo di Cambio and Giotto, and Brunelleschi in the 15th, had shaped the city, giving form and order to the haphazard early medieval urban growth, so Cosimo and his successors reorganized the city to correspond to the new requirements of the princely court around which the life of the city now revolved. "His policies made Florence into a capital which was a formally and politically controllable entity. Thus the internal structure of the city had to adequately represent royal power and the greatness of the state" (G. Fanelli).

Our itinerary therefore covers a part of the city which, although it preserves some signs of its ancient history, was greatly altered from the end of the 16th century onwards by the urban initiatives of the Tuscan Grand Dukes, starting with Palazzo Pitti which became their residence.

Opposite page, statue of Victory *by Vincenzo Consani (1866). Above, hippopotamus, Museo della Spècola. Below, detail of Buontalenti's Grotto.*

View of the 'New' Market, or the Loggia del Porcellino (Boar). Above, the circle on the pavement in the centre of the loggia where merchants guilty of fraudulent bankruptcy were pilloried and ridiculed. Below, the palace of the Wool Guild. Below right, the Porcellino (1612), a bronze boar by Pietro Tacca, copy of a Greek marble statue now in the Uffizi. It is said that whoever throws a coin into the fountain will return to Florence.

Starting from Piazza del Duomo, we take Via Roma and cross Piazza della Repubblica (☞ p. 156) Via Calimala. The street is named after the Calimala – or Cloth Merchants – Guild, one of the most powerful of the seven major guilds in medieval Florence. From the end of the 14th century onwards, their headquarters were established nearby, in a palazzo on Via Calimaruzza which still bears their coat of arms on the façade.

In Roman times, Via Calimala and Via Roma formed the north-south axis of the city, crossing the east-west axis in Piazza della Repubblica (where the Forum covered an area approximately a quarter of the size of today's piazza). The southern city gate was located at the end of Via Calimala, near the Loggia del Mercato Nuovo. This led to the bridge over the Arno, where the roads linking Florence to Rome (the Cassia), southern Tuscany (the Volterrana) and the sea (the Pisana) converged. Given its strategic position, the area became the commercial centre of the city during the Middle Ages, the base for all the major guilds and the most important Florentine businesses.

Just beyond Piazza della Repubblica, on the block between Via di Orsanmichele and Via de' Lamberti, is the 16th-century Palazzo dell'Arte della Lana (Wool Guild) *which, unfortunately, was clumsily and inappropriately 'restored' at the beginning of the 20th century.*

At the end of Via Calimala is the loggia of the Mercato Nuovo (Straw Market), also known as the Loggia del Porcellino.

LOGGIA DEL MERCATO NUOVO

In 1421, no less than seventy-two banks and money lenders were located around this square, making it the financial heart of the city. In times of conflict, the city's war chariot was housed in the middle of the piazza.

The loggia, where commerce in silk and gold took place, was built during Cosimo I's time between 1547 and 1551, to a plan by Battista del Tasso. In the 19th century, straw hats, for many centuries traditionally hand-crafted in this area of the city, were sold in the market. Still today, brightly-coloured stalls sell Florentine arts and crafts.

On the pavement in the centre of the loggia is a marble plaque indicating the place where merchants con-

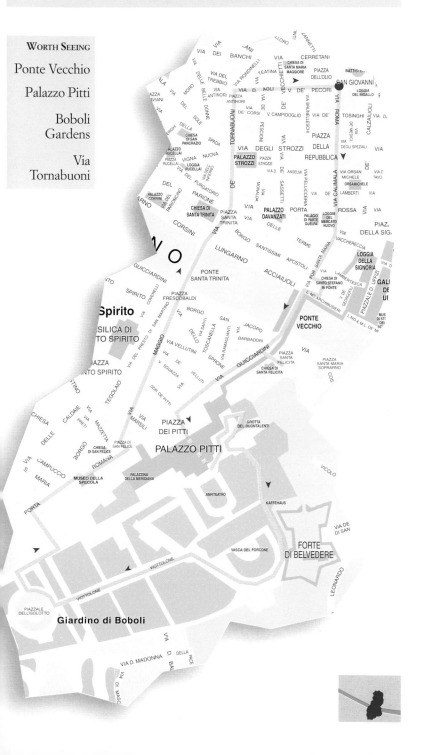

6. The Oltrarno

WORTH SEEING

Ponte Vecchio

Palazzo Pitti

Boboli Gardens

Via Tornabuoni

The Amidei tower is one of the few medieval buildings in Via Por Santa Maria to have survived the German bombs which destroyed this once major and picturesque street of the old city centre. Below, the Romanesque façade of the deconsecrated church of Santo Stefano al Ponte seen from Via Por Santa Maria. An interesting little museum of religious art is attached to the church.

demned for fraudulent bankruptcy were pilloried. On the south side of the market is a bronze statue of a boar known as the *Porcellino* (1612), by Pietro Tacca.

On the right side of the square, coming from Via Calimala, is the Palagio di Parte Guelfa.

PALAGIO DI PARTE GUELFA

This building was the headquarters of the Guelph magistrates, responsible for the care and maintenance of the city walls, fortresses and public buildings, as well as for the administration of the confiscated wealth and property of exiled Ghibellines. Built in the early 1300's, it was enlarged by Brunelleschi a century later and altered by Vasari at the end of the 16th century. Its present appearance is the result of restoration carried out in the 1920's. It houses a library, and various cultural events are held in its elegant chambers.

Following the left side of the loggia, the continuation of Via Calimala is Via Por Santa Maria ('Por' is an abbreviation of Porta — the city gate). This was one of the most important streets in medieval Florence, and from the end of the 14th century the silk trade was concentrated here. The headquarters of the Guild were located in nearby Via del Capaccio.

In 1944, the retreating German army mined all the bridges along the Arno. Only Ponte Vecchio escaped destruction but, in order to prevent the passage of allied tanks and transport, the neighbouring streets were bombed, completely reducing the buildings to rubble. Thus almost all that remains of the medieval street is the Baldovinetti tower (*no. 4r*) on the corner of Borgo Santi Apostoli, and on the right, closer to Ponte Vecchio, the Amidei tower (*no. 9r*).

On the left, just before the bridge in a small piazza, is the deconsecrated church of Santo Stefano al Ponte.

SANTO STEFANO AL PONTE

Records of the church date back to the 12th century; between the 13th and 14th centuries it was rebuilt with a single nave.

The lower part of the façade, with its green and white marble doorway and, on either side, doors with mullions above, is the original Romanesque structure. The Gothic section is a 13th/14th-century alteration.

The interior, redesigned during the 17th century in baroque style, houses 16th and 17th century *paintings* by Tuscan artists. During the 19th

The doorway of Santo Stefano al Ponte decorated in green and white marble - a characteristic feature of Florentine Romanesque and Gothic architecture.

century, the unusual *stairway*, designed in 1574 by Bernardo Buontalenti for the church of Santa Trìnita, was placed here leading up to the presbytery. The *altar* (1591) in coloured marble is by Giambologna.

Beside the church is a recently-opened museum of religious art.

Museum of Sacred Art. Entrance to the Museo di Arte Sacra is from a door to the right of the façade. The museum houses religious works of art from churches no longer administered by the diocese of Florence. Exhibits include a fine collection of *gold and silverware* and *church vestments*; works by the Maestro della Madonna Strauss (active in the late-14th and early-15th centuries); the Maestro of the Horne Triptych (first half of the 14th century); Giovanni del Biondo (second half of the 14th century); Masolino da Panicale (1383-1447); and Paolo Uccello (1397-1475).

Dated between 1295 and 1300, the *Virgin Enthroned* by Giotto was seriously damaged by the bomb which exploded on 27 May, 1993 in Via dei Gergòfili, and was restored by the Opificio delle Pietre Dure.

The 14th-century wooden sculpture of the *Lamentation for the Dead Christ*, fortuitously retrieved from a charcoal kiln, is most moving. The 15th-century wooden statue of *Mary Magdalen* and the painted terracotta *crib*, attributed to Santi di Buglione (1494-1576), are both charming pieces.

PONTE VECCHIO

The "old bridge" is, in fact, the oldest bridge in the city, and the only medieval one to have survived destruction during World War II.

A bridge has existed in this part of Florence from early Roman times. Originally slightly further upstream, it was frequently swept away by

Giotto, Virgin and Child*, Museum of Santo Stefano al Ponte.*

Three views of Ponte Vecchio, the oldest bridge in the city and the only one to have survived destruction during the second World War.

The shops on Ponte Vecchio seen from behind (right). Only a few fortunate people actually live in this unique setting. An intriguing yet noisy place for a home, especially on busy days.

Top, a view of the Vasari Corridor where it runs along the portico of Lungarno Archibusieri and then across the bridge. Above, the portico where there were once shops and houses, similar to those on the bridge. Right, the Manelli tower, one of the four which once stood at the corners of the bridge. Centre page, a grotesque sculpture at the corner of the bridge with the Lungarno Archibusieri.

the river in full spate until the present one was built in 1345.

Even when it was first built, Ponte Vecchio was lined with houses and shops, rented out to butchers and greengrocers by the Wool Guild who were responsible for its administration. At the end of the 16th century, Grand Duke Ferdinando I decided to house gold and silversmiths there instead, and even today the bridge is famed for its jewelery shops.

The Vasari Corridor, built in 1565 by Giorgio Vasari to link the Uffizi and Palazzo Pitti, runs above the shops on the side nearest the Gallery. On the Oltrarno side, the corridor deviates around the Mannelli tower as the owners refused Cosimo I permission to cross through it.

At the end of the bridge we can still clearly see the three ancient roads which converged here. To the right was the Via Pisana, now corresponding to Borgo San Jacopo (☛ p. 182); to the left was the Via Cassia, now Via de' Bardi; in the middle is Via Guicciardini, which follows the old Via Volterrana. This widens slightly, just after the bridge, into the piazza of the church of Santa Felìcita.

CHURCH OF SANTA FELÌCITA

The origins of the church of Santa Felìcita (4th century) date as far back as the establishment of Christianity in Florence. In fact, from the 3rd century onwards a Christian community existed in this area, gradually growing with the steady arrival of populations from Greece, the Far East and Rome. These groups formed a second, Christian, centre in the city, on the south side of the Arno, quite separate from the Roman town on

The 18th-century façade of the church of Sanaà Felicità. The present building replaced a Romanesque church, itself built over an early Christian temple.

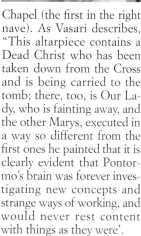

A detail of Jacopo Pontormo's magnificent Deposition, one of the masterpieces of Florentine Mannerism. Below, an Angel in a fresco by the same artist.

Tondos of saints Luke and Matthew.

the other side of the river. "For at least a couple of centuries (roughly from 250 to 450), pagan Florence and Christian Florence lived relatively autonomously from each other" (M. Adriani).

The present church is Romanesque in origin, though it was frequently modified throughout the centuries. It finally underwent complete renovation by Ferdinando Ruggeri between 1736 and 1739. **Interior.** Santa Felicita contains one of the greatest works of mannerist art: Pontormo's *Deposition,* the large altar panel in the Barbadori

Chapel (the first in the right nave). As Vasari describes, "This altarpiece contains a Dead Christ who has been taken down from the Cross and is being carried to the tomb; there, too, is Our Lady, who is fainting away, and the other Marys, executed in a way so different from the first ones he painted that it is clearly evident that Pontormo's brain was forever investigating new concepts and strange ways of working, and would never rest content with things as they were'.

Designed by Brunelleschi around 1420, the Barbadori Chapel was painted with *frescoes* (1525-1528), by Pontormo and his pupil, Agnolo Bronzino. As well as the altarpiece, Pontormo painted the splendid *Annunciation* and three of the *Four Evangelists* which decorate the spandrels in the vault.

At the end of the right transept is an excellent *St Ann with St Joachim,* attributed to Michele di Ridolfo del Ghirlandaio (1503-1577). In the sacristy and the chapter house are 14th- and 15th-century works by Taddeo Gaddi, Niccolò di Pietro Gerini, Pacino di Bonaguida and Neri di Bicci.

Giusto Utens, Pitti Palace and the Boboli Gardens. *Museo di Firenze Com'era. Painted in the 17th century, the palace is shown as it was designed by Brunelleschi. Below, the rusticated stonework of the façade.*

Below, Francesco de' Cecchi (18th century), Palazzo Pitti, *Biblioteca Marucelliana. The palace is seen here with the two wings added but the rondò on either side have not yet been built. Opposite page below, an unusual view of the courtyard.*

Leaving the church, we walk along Via Guicciardini towards Palazzo Pitti. This street, like Via Por Santa Maria, suffered considerable damage during the last war. Despite this, however, some important old buildings survived, such as Palazzo Franceschi *(at no. 11-13), by Anton Maria Ferri (1651-1716) and, on the corner of Piazza Pitti,* Palazzo Guicciardini-Benizzi, *where the famous historian, Francesco Guicciardini, was born in 1482. The present appearance of the palace dates from 1620, when it was renovated by Gherardo Silvani.*

At the end of Via Guicciardini is the extensive area of Piazza Pitti, completely dominated by the majestic palazzo. With its façade measuring 673 feet, it is the largest mansion in Florence.

PALAZZO PITTI

Merchant, banker and enemy of the Medici, Luca Pitti commissioned Brunelleschi to design a palace for him in 1440. This was the period when the most eminent families of the city competed with each other to transform their residences

into symbols of power representing their role in the life of the city. Work began only after Brunelleschi's death, however, around 1458, under the direction of Luca Fancelli.

The Pitti wanted to build a palace which would be much more impressive than the Medici residence on Via Larga begun in 1444 (now Palazzo Medici-Riccardi). To ensure its grandeur, they even ordered that the windows should be as big as the doors of their rivals' mansion. This foolish competition left the Pitti doubly defeated: not only did they see the Medici triumph politically, but they also found themselves in financial difficulties. Thus, almost a century later (1549), the building was bought by Eleonora de Toledo, wife of Cosimo I, and became the ducal residence.

The Medici immediately set about creating the Boboli Gardens and enlarging the palace which, in Brunelleschi's original plan, consisted only of the seven central windows of today's palace. Bartolomeo Ammannati worked on the spacious internal courtyard from 1558 onwards, and beginning in 1618, Giulio and Alfonso Parigi extended the front of the palazzo to its present dimensions. Work continued during the 18th and 19th centuries, culminating with the addition of the two rondeaux at the sides: the one on the right (1764) was made by Giuseppe Ruggieri, and the one on the left (1839) by Pasquale Poccianti.

Although generally conforming to the original style, the modifications do little to enhance the linear severity of Brunelleschi's design, characterized by rustication that diminishes progressively towards the top of the structure. The separation of the three floors is accentuated by floor-markers identical to the main cornice, each one supporting a small balcony. The windows on the ground floor – framed, like all of the others, by radiating arches – are staggered in respect to those on the floors above.

Palazzo Pitti was the residence of the Tuscan Grand Dukes – first the Medici, then the Lorraine – from 1549 until 1859, when Leopoldo II of Lorraine left Tuscany which, in 1860, voted to become part of the Kingdom of Italy. During the period when Florence was capital of Italy (1865-1871), it was the royal palace of Vittorio Emanuele II, and subsequently remained the Florentine residence of the ruling family.

The various dynasties which lived in the palace created quite astonishing collections of art, furnishings and decorative items, now exhibited in

the museums and monumental apartments.

The central doorway opens onto a majestic, porticoed courtyard, for which Ammannati adopted the classical superimposition of the Doric, Ionic and Corinthian orders, reiterating the motif of graduated rustication. On the right is the stairway leading up to the Palatine Gallery on the first floor. Tickets for the Palatine Gallery, Gallery of Modern Art, Silver Museum, Boboli gardens, and Costume Gallery are all sold at the ticket office on the right, just beyond the stairway.

PALATINE GALLERY

The Galleria Palatina was created by the Lorraine Grand Dukes at the end of the 18th and beginning of the 19th centuries, turning what had once been the private quarters of the Medici dukes and duchesses into reception rooms. The museum was opened to the public by Leopoldo II in 1828. As well

Palazzo Pitti seen from Piazza San Felice (above). Left, detail of a demi-column in the courtyard. Ammannati reinterpreted classical models (in this case Doric) in a manneristic style using completely novel elements and details such as the rusticated rings of the column, harmonising with the façade.

The crowned lion between the brackets of the window provides the only decorative element on the façade.

Antonio Canova, Venus Italica, Palatine Gallery, in the Sala di Venere.

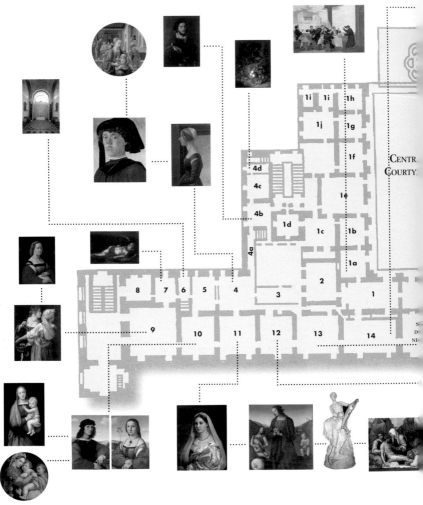

as works acquired by the Lorraine, the gallery houses various items from the Medici collection left to the city of Florence in 1745 by the last Medici, Anna Maria Ludovica.

The collection consists mainly of 16th- and 17th-century works of art. It represents a panorama of Florentine paintings from the period of the Renaissance to Mannerism (Botticelli, Andrea del Sarto, Fra' Bartolomeo, Rosso Fiorentino, Pontormo, Bronzino) as well as Italian art (eleven paintings by Raphael and thirteen by Titian), and European art (Rubens, Van Dyck, Murillo and others).

The works, in magnificent period frames, are intentionally arranged throughout in a purely decorative manner, as an example of the princely collections which all European courts created during the 17th and 18th centuries.

1. Sala Castagnoli. Beyond

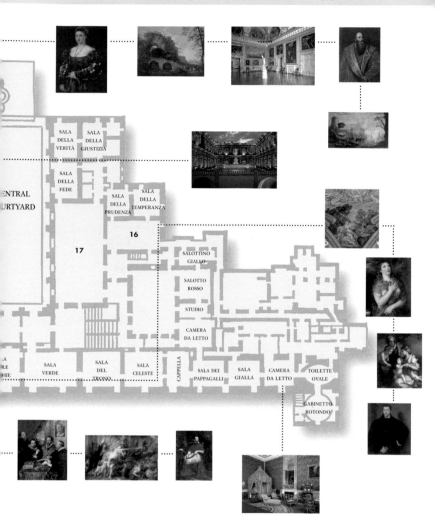

the entrance hall known as the Gallery of Statues, the tour begins with the room named after Giuseppe Castagnoli (1754-1834), who frescoed the ceiling with *Apollo* and the *Signs of the Zodiac.* In the centre of the room is the beautiful *Table of the Muses,* one of the most famous items produced by the Opificio delle Pietre Dure: the top (1837-1851) was made to a design by Giovan Battista Giorgi, while the bronze base (1851) is the work of Giovanni Dupré. Around the walls are *medallions* of members of the Medici and Lorraine families.

1a. Sala delle Allegorie. The Allegory Room is entered from a side door in the Sala Castagnoli: this is the first room of the apartments where the grand duchesses once lived. Decorated with frescoes by Baldassarre Franceschini, known as Volterrano (1611-1689), the paintings include the *Trick of the Parish Priest*

Sandro Botticelli, Portrait of a Young Man Wearing *Mazzocchio.*

Sassetta, Madonna della Neve.

Baldassarre Franceschini, known as Il Volterrano (1611-1689), the Trick of the Parish Priest, Arlotto.

Arlotto, also by Volterrano; some delicate *genre paintings*, by Giovanni da San Giovanni; and a *Virgin and Child*, by Artemisia Gentileschi.

1b. Sala delle Arti. The Arts Room is decorated with 19th-century *frescoes* by Domenico Podestà. The room houses mainly 17th-century Florentine *altar panels* from the churches and monasteries which were closed in the 19th century.

1c. Sala dell'Arca. The Ark Room was frescoed in 1816 by Luigi Ademollo with *David brings the Ark to Jerusalem.* The door opposite the entrance leads to the Chapel of the Grand Duchess. The altar is 19th-century and has a 17th-century panel by the Neapolitan artist Giovan Battista Caracciolo representing the *Rest on the Flight into Egypt.*

1d. Sala delle Vetrine. This little corridor to the right contains a collection of small Dutch *paintings* of the 17th century, Italian *miniatures*, and *still lifes.*

1e. Sala di Ercole. The Her-cules Room is decorated with neo-classical frescoes by Pietro Benvenuti (1769-1844) representing the *Trials of Hercules.* Of particular note are the 18th-century Sèvres vase in the centre and the set of early 19th-century tables with porphyry tops decorated with semi-precious stone inlay.

1f. Sala d'Aurora. Named after the fresco *Aurora riding Pegasus*, by Gaspare Martellini (1785-1857).

1g. Sala di Berenice. Frescoed by Giuseppe Bezzuoli (1784-1855) with *Berenice abandoned by Titus.* The walls were decorated in the 19th century with a fine blue silk. Various 17th-century Tuscan paintings are displayed here.

1h. Sala di Psiche. Named for the fresco in the centre of the ceiling depicting the *Abduction of Psyche*, by Giuseppe Collignon (1776-1863). The room is dedicated to works painted by Salvator Rosa during his Florentine period (1640-1649).

1i. The Empress' Vestibule and Bathroom. These two elegant neo-classical rooms with period furnishings were made for Marie Louise of Hapsburg-Lorraine, Napoleon's wife, who never actually occupied them.

1j. Sala della Fama. Paintings by minor Dutch and Flemish artists are exhibited here.

2. Sala della Musica. Returning to the Casta-gnoli room, we now enter the Music Room, named after the neo-classical drum-shaped furniture around the walls. In the centre is a large *table* in malachite with a gilded bronze support, by Philippe Thomire (1751-1843).

3. Galleria del Poccetti. The gallery is named after Bernardino Poccetti, who was attributed with the *frescoes* on the ceiling. However, these are now recognized as being the work of Matteo Rosselli (1578-1650), or of his pupil, Filippo Tarchiani (1576-1645). Here too, is a splendid rectangular table (1716) made for Cosimo III, probably by Giovan Battista Foggini.

Important 16th- and 17th-century paintings exhibited here are by Domenico Fetti, Federico Barocci, Pontormo, Rubens and Giuseppe de Ribera (1783-1842).

4. Sala di Prometeo. Frescoed around 1830 by Giuseppe Collignon, the Prometheus Room houses an unusual collection of tondi (paintings which are circular in form). One such is the *Virgin and Child*, a major work by Filippo Lippi, datable to the mid-15th century. This is the oldest work in the Palatine Gallery.

Also displayed here are portraits by Botticelli: the *Portrait of a Young Woman* who has been identified as Simonetta Vespucci, Giuliano de' Medici's lover; and the *Portrait of a Young Man in a Mazzocchio* (a typical Florentine headdress of the 14th and 15th centuries).

Next are Tuscan and Flo-

rentine mannerist works of art: the *Adoration of the Magi* (1523) and the *11,000 Martyrs* (1530), both by Pontormo; the tondo of the *Holy Family* is by Domenico Beccafumi (1486-1551). Also in this room is the renowned painting of the *Young Bacchus*, by Guido Reni (1575-1642).

4a. Corridoio delle Colonne. Entered from a side door in the Sala di Prometeo, the Corridor of Columns houses small paintings of the Dutch school dating from the 17th and 18th centuries.

4b. Sala della Giustizia. The name of the Justice Room derives from the subject of the *frescoes* on the ceiling by Antonio Fedi (1771-1843). Displayed are 16th-century works of art from Venice and the Veneto region, including Titian's *Portrait of Mosti* (c.1530) and the *Portrait of a Gentle-*

Filippo Lippi, Virgin and Child.

Sandro Botticelli, Portrait of a Young Woman.

Titian, Portrait of a Young Man.

The Sala di Saturno
(Saturn Room)

*Above, Napoleon's
Bathroom. Right,*
Still Life *by Rachel
Ruysch.*

Caravaggio, Sleeping
Cupid.

*Below, Artemisia
Gentileschi,* Judith
and Holofernes.
Right, Raphael, La
Gràvida.

man, by Paolo Veronese, as well as various portraits by Jacopo Tintoretto.

4c. Sala di Flora. 16th-century Florentine works, including two *Stories of Joseph*, by Andrea del Sarto.

4d. Sala dei Putti. The last room before returning to the Sala di Prometeo. Among the Flemish and Dutch works displayed here are the *Three Graces* (1622), by Rubens and splendid *Still Lifes* (1715 and 1716), by Rachel Ruysch.

5. Sala di Ulisse. The Ulysses Room is decorated with *frescoes* by Gasparo Martellini, commissioned on the occasion of Ferdinando III of Lorraine's return to Florence after the Congress of Vienna (1815).

Among the paintings displayed here are the *Madonna dell'Impannata* (1513-1514), a work by Raphael executed during his period in Rome, and the *Death of Lucrezia*, an early master-

piece by Filippino Lippi (1457-1504).

6. Bagno di Napoleone. Reached from a small atrium which connects the Sala di Ulisse to the Sala dell'Educazione di Giove. Made in 1813 by Elisa Baciocchi for the imperial apartment, Napoleon's Bathroom still has its original neo-classical furnishings.

7. Sala dell'Educazione di Giove. At the time of the Medici, the Room of the Education of Jupiter was the main bedroom in the grand ducal apartments. The most important work here is Caravaggio's *Sleeping Cupid* (1608).

8. Sala della Stufa. The Stove Room is named after the clay pipes which heated the Grand Duke's room. The *Four Ages of Man* (1637) on the walls are Pietro da Cortona's masterpiece.

9. Sala dell'Iliade. The Iliad

Raphael, Madonna and Child with Saint John, *better known as the* Madonna della Seggiola.

Raphael, portraits of Agnolo and Maddalena Doni.

Room is entered by returning to the Sala dell'Educazione di Giove and turning right. This room was redecorated in neo-classical style between 1825 and 1829; in the centre is a statue of *Charity* by Lorenzo Bartolini (1777-1850).

Displayed here is another masterpiece by Raphael: *La Gràvida* (The Pregnant Lady, 1504-1508); and two important works by Andrea del Sarto: the *Assumption of the Virgin* (1526), known as the *Panciàtichi Madonna*, and the slightly earlier *Assunta Passerini.*

Caravaggio's influence can be seen in the two works by Artemisia Gentileschi in this room, *Judith and Holofernes* and *St Mary Magdalen.* Both were painted between 1614 and 1620, when Artemisia lived in Florence in the court of Cosimo II.

10. Sala di Saturno. The frescoes in the Saturn Room were designed by Pietro da Cortona and executed by Ciro Ferri. The room contains a wonderful sequence of major works by Raphael: portraits of *Maddalena* and *Agnolo Doni* (1506-1507); the *Madonna and Child*, known as the 'Madonna del Granduca' (1505-1506), bought in 1799 by Ferdinando III; the *Madonna and Child with Young St John* known as the 'Madonna della Seggiola' (Virgin of the Chair, 1514); the *Portrait of Cardinal Inghirami* (1516); the *Madonna del Baldacchino* (Virgin of the

Canopy) which the artist began in 1507 but left unfinished when he departed for Rome; the *Vision of Ezechiel* (1518).

On the wall opposite the window is a *Deposition* (1495), by Pietro Perugino, with a bright Umbrian landscape in the background.

Also in this room are two important works by Andrea del Sarto: the *Trinity's Dispute* (1517) and the *Annunciation* (1528). The *Salvator Mundi* (1516) by Fra' Bartolomeo is an equally impressive piece.

11. Sala di Giove. This is the throne room, decorated with *frescoes* and *stucco work* by

Raphael, Portrait of a Lady or, La Velata.

Bartolomeo della Porta, known as Fra' Bartolomeo, Deposition.

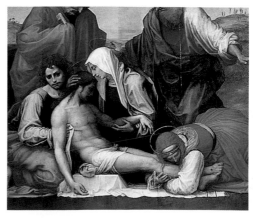

Peter Paul Rubens, the Consequences of War.

Pietro Perugino, Madonna and Child, *also known as the* Madonna del Sacco (Bolster).

Peter Paul Rubens, the Four Philosophers. *Right,* Victory, *by Vincenzo Consani (1866). Below, Anthony Van Dyck,* Portrait of Cardinal Bentivoglio.

Volterrano. Displayed here is one of Raphael's most lovely works – *La Velata* (Veiled Woman, 1516). Vasari tells us that the model for the portrait was actually the artist's lover, known as Fornarina, daughter of the Roman baker, Francesco Luti. Recent cleaning has restored the original, delicate shades of the work, revealing the subtle tones of white, the grey of the dress and the soft, radiant pink of the flesh.

The works displayed here include an *Annunciation* (c.1512) and *St John the Baptist* (1523), by Andrea del Sarto; the gentle *Madonna del Sacco*, by Perugino (1445/50-1523) and the *Holy Family* (1615), an important early work by Rubens.

The *Deposition* by Bartolomeo della Porta (1472-1517) is one of the most important Florentine paintings of the early 16th century. The artist, better known as Fra' Bartolomeo, became a monk in 1500 to abide to a vow made when, as a follower of Savonarola, he had been forced to take refuge from a crowd of irate Florentines in the monastery of San Marco. A supporter of Savonarola until the latter's arrest and execution in 1496, Fra' Bartolomeo burnt all of his early, profane paintings to ensure eternal salvation.

12. Sala di Marte. The ceiling of the Mars Room is frescoed with the *Triumph of the House of the Medici*, by Pietro da Cortona. On the right wall is *The Consequences of War* (1638), a masterpiece of Flemish painting by Pieter Paul Rubens. In this powerful allegory, the artist demonstrates his ability to "transmit an intense energy to everything" (E. Gombrich). The allegory is of Mars who, torn from the arms of Venus by Discord, tramples the Arts and Charity underfoot.

The *Four Philosophers* is also by Rubens. The painting actually represents (from left to right) the artist, his brother Philip, and the humanists Lipsius and Wouverius.

On the wall opposite are two delightful works by Murillo (1618-1682), both of the *Virgin and Child*; on the entrance wall is the *Portrait of Cardinal Bentivoglio* (the Pope's ambassador in France and the Low Countries), by Flemish artist Anthony Van Dyck (1599-1641).

13. Sala di Apollo. The frescoes decorating the Apollo Room were planned by Pietro da Cortona and carried out by his pupil, Ciro Ferri (1634-1689). In the middle of the right wall is a splendid altar panel of the *Madonna Enthroned with Saints* (1522), by Rosso

Sala di Apollo, detail of the decoration designed by Pietro da Cortona and carried out by Ciro Ferri.

Fiorentino, a masterpiece of early mannerist art. It was originally located in the Dei chapel in the church of Santo Spirito, and was enlarged to fit the frame upon being brought to the Pitti in the 17th century.

The two superb paintings by Andrea del Sarto displayed in this room, the *Holy Family* and the *Medici Holy Family,* dated a few years later, show quite clearly how far removed Rosso's mannerist style was from the work of his master.

There are also two important works by Titian here: *Mary Magdalen* (1531), and the *Portrait of an English Youth,* (c.1540). Ernest Gombrich wrote of this painting: "He seems to gaze at us with such an intense and soulful look that it is almost impossible to believe that these dreamy eyes are only a bit of coloured earth spread on a piece of canvas'.

14. Sala di Venere.

The Venus Room is decorated, as are the four previous rooms, with allegorical *frescoes* by Piero da Cortona (1596-1669). In the centre is one of the masterpieces of Italian neo-classical sculpture — the *Venus* by Antonio Canova (1757-1822), commissioned by Napoleon in 1810. The most important paintings displayed here are four works by Titian: spanning a period of approximately thirty-five years, they provide a good panorama of his artistic development.

The oldest work is the *Concert* (1510-1512), a masterpiece of early 16th-century Venetian painting. It was first bought by Cardinal Leopoldo de' Medici as a work by Giorgione, but is now accepted to be an early Titian. Perhaps the most famous is the *Portrait of a Lady,* better known as 'La Bella' (1536-1538): commissioned by the Duke of Urbino, it is the first recorded example of a portrait sold as a work of art, with no reference

Andrea del Sarto, the Holy Family.

Titian, Portrait of a English Youth. *Below left, Titian,* Mary Magdalen. *Below, the Sala di Venere (Venus Room).*

Salvator Rosa, Port at Sunset.

Salvator Rosa, Landscape with a Broken Bridge.

Titian, Portrait of Pietro Aretino. *The portrait was commissioned from Titian in 1545 by Aretino himself who then presented it to grand duke Cosimo I as a gift.*

Titian, Portrait of a Lady, *also known as* La Bella.

to the subject herself. Both the portrait of *Julius* II and the portrait of *Pietro Aretino* are dated 1545; the former is a copy of Raphael's painting dated 1511-1512.

Other works of note in this room are the *landscapes* by Salvator Rosa, a Neapolitan painter who worked at the Medici court from 1640 to 1649, and the *Peasants Returning from the Fields* by Pieter Paul Rubens (1577-1640), a wonderful rural scene in baroque style.

15. The Royal Apartments. First the Medici and then the Lorraine Grand Dukes lived in these rooms. When Florence was capital of Italy (1865-1871), they became the official residence of the king, Vittorio Emanuele II. They consist of a series of magnificently furnished and decorated rooms.

The first room – the so-called Sala delle Nicchie, or Niches – leads into the Sala Verde, frescoed by Giuseppe Castagnoli in the early 19th century. Here we find a large

17th-century ebony *cabinet, gilded bronzes, lapis lazuli* and *semi-precious stones.*

The Sala del Trono is completely decorated in red, with furniture dating from the Lorraine and Savoy periods. As well as 18th- and 19th-century Japanese and Chinese porcelain, is the throne of Vittorio Emanuele II under a large canopy.

In the Salone Celeste (or Blue Room, named for the colour of the material of the Lorraine period covering the walls) are a series of *portraits of the Medici,* by Justus Sustermans, as well as some magnificent 17th and 18th-century furniture.

The chapel – once the private alcove of Prince Ferdinando de' Medici – is decorated in late-baroque style with 17th-century white and gold plasterwork. Displayed here, in a magnificent frame of tortoiseshell, gilded bronze and semi-precious stones, is a *Virgin and Child,* by Carlo Dolci (1616-1686).

Named for the parrot motif on the Lorraine wall covering, the Sala dei Pappagalli leads into the apartments of Queen Margherita, wife of King Umberto I of Italy who succeeded Vittorio Emanuele II.

The first room, the Queen's drawing room or Sala Gialla (Yellow room — the colour of

Room prepared and arranged for an exhibition.

the brocade on the walls), was once Prince Ferdinando's game room. A beautiful neoclassical chandelier hangs from the ceiling.

Next are the queen's bedroom and the oval dressing room, originally created for Marie Louise of Lorraine and decorated with painted stucco work. The fireplace made of lilac marble is particularly elegant.

The last room is the circular drawing room where the queen entertained and conversed with the ladies of her court.

Returning to the Sala dei Pappagalli, we enter the quarters of Umberto I, consisting of four small rooms used by the king during his visits to Florence. The furnishings in the bedroom are 19th-century; the study has a silk wall covering and 18th-century furniture; the Red Room was furnished during the Lorraine period, and lastly the yellow 'salottino,' the king's antechamber, is decorated with 19th-century paintings.

16. Sala di Bona. Linked to the antechamber by a small corridor, the room was entirely frescoed in the early 17th century by Bernardino Poccetti. On the longer walls are the *Conquest of the City of Bona* (the ancient Ippona, in Africa), a triumph by the fleet of the Knights of St Stephen in 1607; and the *Conquest of Prevesa* (originally Nicopoli, in

The room of Queen Margherita.

Albania) by the Tuscan navy in 1605. On the shorter walls are *Grand Duke Ferdinando I welcomes Piccolomini, prisoner of the Turks* and a *View of the Port of Livorno.*

17. Sala Bianca. Adjacent to the Bona Room, the White Room was once the palace ballroom. It now houses temporary exhibitions with entrance from the atrium of the Palatine Gallery. Adjoining the ballroom is the suite reserved for visitors (dei Forestieri) consisting of the rooms of Prudenza (Prudence), Temperanza (Temperance), Verità (Truth), Giustizia (Justice) and Fede (Faith).

The second floor of the palace houses the Gallery of Modern Art.

GALLERY OF MODERN ART

The Galleria d'Arte Moderna was established in 1784 by Grand Duke Pietro Leopoldo of Hapsburg-Lorraine. It has been housed in Palazzo Pitti

Silvestro Lega, In the Artist's Studio.

Pietro Tenerani, Psyche Abandoned (1816-17).

since 1922, when the collections of modern art belonging to the Italian state and the city of Florence were brought together in rooms on the top floor of the palace vacated by the departure of the royal family. The collections were completely reorganized and given their present arrangement between 1972 and 1979.

The Gallery houses approximately 2,000 works, including some important sculptures. The collection not only provides a complete panorama of Italian art from the late 18th century to the 1920's, but also has some excellent works by non-Italian artists.

Rooms 1-12. Following the development of Italian figurative art chronologically, our visit begins with works by Pompeo Batoni (1708-1787), who was inspired by Correggio and Raphael. The fine range of paintings exhibited in these rooms covers the movements of Neo-classicism and Romanticism, dating from the second half of the 18th century and early 19th century until the period when Florence was capital of Italy. Among the major artists rep-

View of Room 9.

resented in these rooms are: Antonio Canova (1757-1822), Pietro Benvenuti (1769-1844), Luigi Sabatelli (1772-1850), Giuseppe Bezzuoli (1784-1855), Francesco Hayez (1791-1882), Lorenzo Bartolini (1777-1850) and lastly, Giovanni Dupré (1817-1882).

Room 13. Some portraits painted when Florence was capital are displayed here, including the *Self Portrait* of Giovanni Fattori and the *Signora Morrocchi* (1855-1860), by Antonio Puccinelli, two important works representing a new attention to nature.

Room 14. Housed here are landscapes dating from the mid-19th century. The artists belonged to the 'Staggia School,' the first school of landscape art in Tuscany, established in Staggia (near Siena) in 1854 by Serafino de' Tivoli, artist and collector from Livorno. In 1855, Serafino went to Paris where he was greatly influenced by the naturalism of the Barbizon school, based on the careful observation of nature as opposed to academic classicism. After 1856, the artist became one of the foremost members of the Florence-based Macchiaioli group, which met in the former Caffè Michelangelo on what is now Via Cavour.

Room 15. The works of Cristiano Banti (1824-1904) are housed in this room.

Rooms 16-18. Works by the

Stefano Ussi, Expulsion of the Duke of Athens.

most famous Macchiaioli painters including: Silvestro Lega (1826-1895), Telemaco Signorini (1835-1901), Federico Zandoméneghi (1841-1917) and Giovanni Fattori (1825-1908).

Rooms 19-20. These rooms are dedicated to the late 19th-century academy with works by Antonio Ciseri, Raffaello Sorbi, Stefano Ussi and Giuseppe Bellucci.

Rooms 21-22. Here one finds works celebrating the Risorgimento, painted during the fifty years following Italian unification. In Room 21 is Giovanni Fattori's famous *Charge of the Cavalry* (1873).

Rooms 23-24. Macchiaioli paintings belonging to the Ambron and city of Florence collections, including works by Telemaco Signorini, Giovanni Fattori, Vito d'Ancona and Vincenzo Cabianca.

Rooms 25-27. Represented here are Tuscan and Neapolitan post-Macchiaioli artists such as Egisto Ferroni, Niccolò Cannicci and Domenico Morelli.

Rooms 28-30. The last rooms are dedicated to the movements of Decadentism, Divisionism and Symbolism, and also contain some post-

Impressionist works by Tuscan artists including: Galileo Chini, Gaetano Previati, Medardo Rosso, Plinio Nomellini, Giovanni Costetti, Elizabeth Chaplin and Armando Spadini.

Returning back down the stairs, we re-enter Ammannati's courtyard; on the opposite side is the entrance to the Museo degli Argenti.

Museo degli Argenti

Housed in the summer quarters of the Medici court, the Museo degli Argenti exhibits items once belonging to the Medici and Lorraine dynasties. It thus provides extraordinary insight into the aesthetic tastes of 16th- and 17th-century princely courts.

Frescoed in the 17th century by Giovanni da San Giovanni and the Bolognese artists Michelangelo Colonna and Agostino Mitelli, the twenty-six rooms all have period furnishings. The exhibits include silverware, vases of carved ivory and rock crystal, amber, gems, cameos, Chinese and Japanese porcelain, enamels and jewelery. Once belonging to

Ottone Rosai, Tavern Scene.

Figurine of baroque pearls and enamel on a gold base.

Giovanni Fattori, the Palmieri Rotonda.

Gala carriage.

Pendent of baroque pearls, gold, and precious gems.

the Palatine Electress Anna Maria Ludovica de' Medici, the jewelery collection includes unusual little baroque animals of Flemish production, made from pearls, gems and gold. Also displayed is Ferdinando III's elegant travelling case, crafted by Parisian silversmiths.

Lorenzo the Magnificent's collection of *antique vases* is of particular importance: these rare Roman and medieval pieces were mounted on gilded silver stands in the 15th century.

As we leave the palace we may also visit the little Carriage Museum, housed in the rondeau on the right. At present the museum is only open two mornings a week and one may enter by showing an entrance ticket to any of the Pitti Galleries or to the Boboli Gardens.

CARRIAGE MUSEUM

The Museo delle Carrozze includes seven coaches (with their original harnesses) once belonging to the Lorraine and Savoy families; as well as two litters and a portable sedan-chair.

The coach decorated with gilded silver is especially beautiful, as are the three wooden sedans with painted and gilded carvings, commissioned from acclaimed Florentine craftsmen by Ferdinando III in 1815 on his re-

turn to Tuscany after the Congress of Vienna.

On the opposite side of Ammannati's courtyard, facing the entrance to the palace, is a fountain and grotto. To the right of the grotto is a carriage gateway, now serving as the entrance to the Boboli Gardens. The entrance ticket must be bought in advance from the ticket office on the right side of the courtyard.

In front of us at the top of the shallow flight of steps is the amphitheatre from where we begin our visit to the gardens. It is worth, however, first visiting the Meridiana Palace, which is to the right, following the parapet of the steps and then crossing the large terrace extending in front of the Palazzina.

MERIDIANA PALACE

Begun in 1776, the Palazzina della Meridiana was completed by Pasquale Poccianti between 1822 and 1840. Vittorio Emanuele II lived here when Florence was capital of Italy (1865-1871), and the beautiful silk wall coverings and furnishings date from that period.

Two important collections are housed here: the Galleria del Costume and the Donazione Contini Bonacossi.

Costume Gallery. Examples of costume and everyday dress from the 18th century to the 1920's are displayed in

The Meridiana Palace.

View of the Amphitheatre. Begun at the end of the 16th century, the work was completed by Alfonso Parigi after 1618.

thirteen rooms. Extremely well documented, the exhibits follow the evolution of female dress in particular.

Contini Bonacossi Collection. Destined to one day reside in the extended and enlarged Uffizi gallery, this fine collection of paintings was started by the Contini Bonacossi with the help and advice of famous art historian Roberto Longhi. It was donated to the state in 1974.

Permission is required from the Museums and Fine Arts Department to visit the collection which consists of Italian works of art from the 13th to the 18th centuries. Artists such as Cimabue, Duccio di Boninsegna, Andrea del Castagno, Sassetta, Giovanni Bellini, Bramantino, Paolo Veronese and Jacopo Tintoretto are represented, as well as the Spanish artists, El Greco, Velázquez and Zurbarán.

Having visited the Palazzina della Meridiana, we retrace our steps to the amphitheatre.

Boboli Gardens

Covering an area of some 49,000 square yards, the Bo-boli is one of the foremost examples of an italianate garden created

during the 16th and 17th centuries, unique for its harmonious combination of art and nature. Extending over the side of the hill which rises from the Pitti Palace to Fort Belvedere, and across to Porta Romana, one can enjoy delightful walks here in a natural setting which is, at the same time, a work of art.

Commissioned by Eleonora de Toledo, the wife of Cosimo I, it was created by Niccolò Tribolo who began work in 1550. Ammannati and Buontalenti took over the work after Tribolo's death, and were in turn succeeded in 1618 by Giulio and Alfonso Parigi, who established the present layout of the garden.

Amphitheatre. Begun in the late 16th century, and completed after 1618 by Alfonso Parigi. In the centre is an Egyptian obelisk, placed here during the 18th century. In front is a large Roman basin in grey granite, dating to the imperial age. The amphitheatre affords a wonderful view of the city and dominates the area behind the palace with the courtyard and the *Artichoke Fountain* (1642), by Francesco Susini.

Francesco Susini, the Artichoke Fountain *(1642).*

Woman's outdoor costume.

The Neptune Lake and Fountain (1565-1568) with a statue by Stoldo Lorenzi. Below, the 'Kaffeehaus'.

The wide avenue known as the 'Viottolone' which leads to the Isolotto designed by Giulio and Alfonso Parigi in 1618.

The Casino and Garden of the Cavaliere with the Monkey Fountain in the centre.

Buontalenti's Grotto. Continuing in the opposite direction to the Palazzina della Meridiana, we reach a wide drive leading to the rondeau on the left of the palace. In the area in front of the exit is the *Fountain of Bacchus* (1560), by Valerio Cioli, probably representing Morgante, Cosimo I's court jester.

On the same side as the Bacchus is a short path which leads to Buontalenti's Grotto (1583-1588), flanked by statues of *Ceres* and *Apollo* by Baccio Bandinelli. The interior consists of three chambers: in the first are copies of Michelangelo's *Prisoners* (the originals are now in the Academy); in the second, *Paris and Helen* (1560), a sculptural group by Vincenzo Rossi; the third is frescoed by Poccetti and houses Giambologna's *Venus* (1579-1587).

From the Neptune Fountain to the Kaffeehaus. Turning back we take the avenue, flanked by low hedges and adorned with Roman statues, which runs along the side of the amphitheatre (one can also meander up the hill through the maze of shady little alleys which lead to the upper level of the garden).

At the end of the avenue is a small lake with a statue of *Neptune* (1565-1568), by Stoldo Lorenzi, in the centre. An alleyway on the left leading away from the area of the fountain takes us to the Kaffeehaus, a domed pavilion in Rococo style, designed by Zanobi del Rosso in 1776. From the terrace we have a wonderful uninterrupted view of the city and the surrounding hills.

Towards the Piazzale dell'Isolotto. Taking the alley which climbs up around the back of the Kaffeehaus and borders Fort Belvedere above (☛ p. 243-247), we reach the highest level of the tiered steps around the Neptune Fountain. In the middle is the enormous statue of *Abundance*, begun in 1608 by Giambologna and completed by Pietro Tacca.

Taking the avenue on the right, we reach the Giardino del Cavaliere (Knight's Garden) with its 16th-17th-century Monkey Fountain, and the so-called *casino* or little house. Constructed around 1700 for Gian Gastone (the last Medici Grand Duke), it was subsequently remodeled by the Lorraine. The Porcelain Museum has been housed here since 1973. The collection includes Italian, French, German and Viennese pieces from Palazzo Pitti, formerly belonging to

various ruling families of Tuscany.

Turning back again, we walk down to the Prato dell'Uccellare. Here the wide avenue known as the Viottolone begins, descending towards the Piazzale dell'Isolotto, one of the most charming areas of the garden, created by Giulio and Alfonso Parigi beginning in 1618. The piazzale is surrounded by tall hedges of holm oak and boxwood, punctuated with stone and marble statues. In the centre is a large pool out of which rise statues of *Perseus* and *Andromeda*, by the school of Giambologna. On the island in the centre, amongst ornamental plants and lemon trees, is a copy of the *Oceanus Fountain* (1576), by Giambologna (the original is now in the Bargello).

From the Piazzale dell'Isolotto we turn left and reach the 'Annalena gate' which leads to Via Romana. With a modest deviation to the left, we reach Porta Romana, *a massive city gate built between 1328 and 1331 as part of the last circle of city walls.*

We now return back along the road towards the centre. At no. 17 is Palazzo Torrigiani *where the famous Spècola Museum is housed.*

THE SPÈCOLA MUSEUM

Inaugurated in 1775 as the Imperial and Regal Museum of Physics and Natural History, the Museo della Spècola was founded by Grand Duke Pietro Leopoldo, consolidating the valuable Medici scientific collections as well as books and instruments from the Accademia del Cimento. The palazzo was nicknamed the Spècola (from *specula* or observatory) when an astronomical observatory was created there.

As well as valuable zoological exhibits, the museum boasts a remarkable col-

Above, view of the Isolotto and the lake with statues of Perseus *and* Andromeda, *by the school of Giambologna. In the centre of the lake is a copy of the statue of Oceanus by Giambologna; the original is in the Bargello National Sculpture Museum. Above, Porta Romana. Below, hippopotamus, in the Museo della Spècola.*

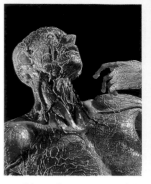

School of Clemente Susini, the
Lymphatic system *(right)*. Section and
route of the trigeminal nerve *(below)*.
Anatomical models in wax.

lection of *anatomical models in coloured wax.* These were almost all made in its historic laboratory, active from the mid-18th century when the art of ceroplastics flourished in Florence, becoming a veritable school, until 1895. Famous anato-mists such as Paolo Mascagni (1755-1815) and skilled wax modellers such as Clemente Susini (1754-1814) worked in the laboratories here. Also exhibited are some *allegorical scenes* by the wax modeller, Gaetano Zumbo (late 17th century). Based on the sombre themes of death and disease, these wax masterpieces are astonishing not only for their lifelike appearance and meticulous accuracy but also for the great care taken in their composition.

On the first floor is the *Galileo Tribune,* consisting of a vestibule and recess richly decorated with marble, frescoes and mosaics by Nicola Cianfanelli, Gasparo Martellini, Luigi Sabatelli and Giuseppe Bezzuoli. Leopoldo II commissioned it to be made in 1841 on the occasion of the Congress of Italian Scientists.

After visiting the Spècola Museum we continue along Via Romana in the direction of Piazza Pitti. On the left, at the junction of Via Mazzetta and Via Maggio, is the small Piazza San Felice. In the centre is a

Piazza San Felice. Cosimo I placed this marble column here in 1572. After removal, it was returned to the piazza in 1992.

marble column *erected by Cosimo I in 1572 and replaced here in 1992. The poetess Elizabeth Barrett Browning lived and died in the palazzo at no. 8, as recorded by a plaque on the façade.*

Also in this square is the church of San Felice, with its attractive Renaissance façade.

CHURCH OF SAN FELICE IN PIAZZA

The church of San Felice is mentioned in records for the first time in 1066, but the present building dates from the 14th century. The mid-15th-century façade is attributed to Michelozzo.

The church contains important works of art dating from the early 14th to the 18th centuries. In the first altar on the right is a fresco of the *Pietà*, by Niccolò Gerini; in the fifth is a terracotta *Pietà* (1500-1515), attributed to Giovanni della Robbia; in the sixth is a *Madonna of the Girdle with Saints* (1520), by Ridolfo del Ghirlandaio, a follower of Raphael; in the seventh, a *Madonna with Saints* (1430), attributed to Bicci di Lorenzo and Stefano d'Antonio. In the main chapel is a large wooden *Crucifix* by the school of Giotto, datable to the early 14th century; and two panels of *St John the Evangelist* and *St Mary Magdalen*, by the school of Botticelli.

On the altar of the chapel

Façade of the church of San Felice in Piazza.

Crucifix, *school of Giotto.*

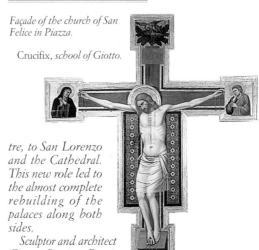

at the top of the left aisle is a polyptych with a *Virgin and Child* in the centre (1409-1413), which is attributed to Gherardo Starnina.

On the left side, in the seventh altar is *St Felix coming to the aid of St Maximus,* a fresco begun by Giovanni da San Giovanni and completed around 1636 by Volterrano. In the sixth altar is a triptych with *Sts Augustine, John the Baptist, Julian and Sigismund* (documented in 1467); in the fifth altar is a triptych by the school of Botticelli (late 15th-century) with *Sts Anthony Abbot, Rocco and Catherine of Alessandria.*

Leaving the church we continue along Via Maggio towards the Santa Trìnita bridge. 'Maggio' is a contraction of Maggiore (major): in fact, the importance of the street was greatly increased in the 16th century when Cosimo I chose it as the route for official processions from the Pitti Palace towards the cen-

tre, to San Lorenzo and the Cathedral. This new role led to the almost complete rebuilding of the palaces along both sides.

Sculptor and architect Giovan Battista Foggini (1652-1725) lived at no. 48; at no. 42 is the Palazzo della Commenda, *previously the Corsini palace, renovated at the end of the 17th century by Gherardo Silvani; at no. 28 is* Palazzo Peruzzi de' Medici, *also renovated by Silvani; opposite, at no. 13, is* Palazzo Zanchini, *designed in the 16th century by Santi di Tito. At no. 11 one finds* Palazzo Michelozzi, *altered during the second half of the 16th century, and no. 26 is the* Palazzo of Bianca Cappello, *the famous lover of Grand Duke Francesco, renovated between 1570 and 1574 by Bernardo Buontalenti. The façade is decorated with attractive grote-sques in* graffito (1579-1580), *by Bernardino Poccetti.*

Via Maggio ends at the narrow Piazza Frescobaldi, just before the Ponte a Santa Trìnita. On the left at no. 2 is the 14th-century Palazzo Frescobaldi, *restored in 1921.*

SANTA TRÌNITA BRIDGE

Originally built in wood in the mid-13th century, and later in stone, the Santa Trìnita bridge (pronounced with the

The attractive loggia with the Medici arms; below is a fountain decorated with a grotesque mask and a scrolled basin, a masterpiece by Bernardo Buontalenti. Below, the palace of Bianca Cappello. Left, Via Sguazza.

The medieval outskirts

Several Florentine streets which once lay on the edges of the historic town centre still bear the name *borgo*, or hamlet. These came into being after 1000 AD when, with the increase in population, settlements began to develop outside the walls, along the main routes of communication. These clusters of houses were enclosed within the enlarged ring of defensive walls which the city authorities began to build in 1173 (► p.66-67). In some of these, such as Borgo Santi Apostoli and Borgo San Jacopo many magnificent original medieval houses and structures still exist.

Borgo Santi Apostoli and the church of Santi Apostoli. On the right bank of the Arno, running parallel to the river, Borgo Santi Apostoli links Via Por Santa Maria to Piazza Santa Trìnita. The borgo hosts an almost uninterrupted series of mainly medieval buildings, which are, on the whole, intact and of an unusually high standard. The magnificent *Palazzo Acciaioli* (at no. 8) has a façade with three rows of windows crowned by rounded arches, and a tall *tower* on the side towards the Chiasso delle Misure. The *Casa Acciaioli* at no. 10 is a typical 16th-century residence, though the overhang on the side towards Chiasso Cornino and other features belonging to an older construction can clearly be identified. The *Casa Altoviti* (no. 12) has the typical 14th-century design of arches with heavy stonework between. The façade of the magnificent *Palazzo Borgherini* (no. 19), attributed to Baccio d'Agnolo, is almost entirely plastered, with rusticated stonework at the corners. On the left is the little Piazza del Limbo, dominated by the façade of the Santi Apostoli church. A plaque above the left door erroneously states that the church was founded on 6 April, 805 by Charlemagne, and consecrated by Bishop Turpino. It is instead a very fine example of Florentine Romanesque which may be dated to the late 11th century. The façade is of rough stone, rising in the centre to the height of the central nave, with a 16th-century doorway attributed to Benedetto da Rovezzano. The interior has three naves divided by columns of green marble from Prato with composite capitals and rounded arches. The roof has decorated, polychrome beams and the apse is semicircular. The side chapels were made during 15th- and 16th-century renovations. At the end of the left nave is a glazed terracotta *tabernacle* by Giovanni della Robbia, and beside is the *tomb of Oddo Altoviti* by Benedetto da Rovezzano (1474-c.1554).

The series of attractive houses and palaces continues to Piazza Santa Trìnita. Of particular note are the *Buondelmonti* and the *Salutati* palazzi (no. 22 and 29 respectively).

Borgo San Jacopo and the church of San Jacopo Soprarno. On the Ol-

ry Rossi Cerchi tower, is the *Bacchino fountain* with a statue attributed to Giambologna. Further ahead, at the junction with Via de' Ramaglianti (at no. 9), are the twin towers of the Ramaglianti and the Belfredelli; the Barbadori tower is at no. 54r. Just beyond the junction with the picturesque Via Toscanella – where a dense and historic network of craftsmen's and artist's workshops still survives – is the Marsili tower (no. 17); on the façade is a copy of a glazed terracotta *Annunciation* (the original is now housed inside). Further ahead is the *church of San Jacopo Soprarno*, dating from the 11th century but periodically renovated. The splendid portico and doorway in white and green marble (12th-13th century) was brought into the city from the church of San Donato in Scopeto, outside Porta Romana, which was destroyed during the siege of 1529. Now deconsecrated, the church's interior has three naves; damaged by the flood in 1966, subsequent restoration work has brought to light some Romanesque columns beneath the 18th-century dec-

Irarno side of the river, the Borgo leads from Ponte Vecchio to Piazza Frescobaldi and thus the Santa Trìnita bridge. First mentioned in 1182, it represents the beginning of the Via Pisana, the ancient road linking Florence and Pisa. The council began to protect this part of the city towards the end of the 12th century, probably erecting a fortified palisade which was then transformed into a defensive wall at the end of the 13th century. The tall towers on either side of the street are today reminders of their original defensive function. The first section of the street, nearest to Ponte Vecchio, suffered damage from the German mines in 1944. Facing the end of the bridge, set into the corner of the 13th-centu-

oration. The church has a number of interesting 17th- and 18th-century *paintings* of the Florentine school and a 15th-century wooden *crucifix*. Just beyond the church (at no. 1, 2 and 3r), the *Palazzo Frescobaldi* hosted Charles of Valois in 1301. On the corner with Via dello Sprone, beneath a small loggia bearing the Medici coat-of-arms, is the *Buontalenti fountain*, a little masterpiece of urban decoration from the second half of the 17th-century.

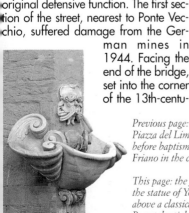

Previous page: centre, Borgo Santissimi Apostoli; left, a view of Piazza del Limbo, named for the cemetery for infants who died before baptism once located here; right, Nativity *by Maso di San Friano in the church of Santissimi Apostoli.*

This page: the façade of the church of San Jacopo Soprarno (top); the statue of Young Bacchus attributed to Giambologna stands above a classical marble basin (centre); fountain by Bernardo Buontalenti dated 16th century (left).

Detail of Palazzo Frescobaldi: the family arms are placed between the first and second floors on the façade. Projection supported by stone brackets on a building in Via Toscanella (below).

Giovan Battista Caccini, Summer, *one of the four statues at the corners of Ponte Santa Trìnita.*

View of the city with Ponte Santa Trìnita in the foreground (below).

accent on the first 'i' as it derives from the vulgar form of the Latin *Trìnitas*) was swept away by the disastrous flood of 1333. It was rebuilt and again destroyed in 1557. That year, as part of the plans to enhance the route leading from Palazzo Pitti along Via Maggio and Via Tornabuoni to the cathedral, Cosimo I commissioned Bartolomeo Ammannati to rebuild it. In 1608, the four statues symbolizing the four seasons were placed at the corners: on the left side are *Autumn*, by Giovan Battista Caccini and *Winter*, by Taddeo Landini; on the right are *Spring*, by Pietro Francavilla and *Summer*, by Giovan Battista Caccini.

Bombed by the Germans on August 4, 1944, it was rebuilt to Ammannati's design in 1952, under the guidance of the famous American art historian, Bernard Berenson.

On the other side of the bridge, dominated by the baroque façade of the church of Santa Trìnita, is the piazza of the same name. In the centre is the Column of Justice, *a Roman monolith brought here from the Baths of Caracalla; the statue of* Justice *on top was sculpted by Francesco del Tadda (1497-1585). Cosimo I had the column erected in 1554 to celebrate the victory against the Sienese at Marciano, a year before the city of Siena fell to Florence.*

The area was rebuilt in the form we see today under Cosimo I, mainly around the time of the defeat of Siena and the birth of the Grand Duchy in Tuscany. The palazzi around the square and the church of Santa Trìnita have, however, a much longer history.

Immediately on the right after the bridge is Palazzo Spini-Feroni, *with a crenellated roof. It was built in the 13th century as protection for the bridge itself. The city council sat here when Florence was capital (1865-1871), and in 1875 it was restored to its medieval structure. Following the side in front of the Column of Justice, we come to Borgo Santi Apostoli (☞ p. 182).*

Remaining in the piazza, at no. 1 is Palazzo Bartolini Salimbeni *(1520-1523), built to a design by Baccio d'Agnolo; at no. 2 is* Palazzo Buondelmonti, *built in the late 13th century and renovated in the 16th century, possibly also by Baccio d'Agnolo.*

Left, stone plaque recording the rebuilding of Ponte Santa Trìnita in 1569 by Bartolomeo Ammannati, commissioned by Cosimo I. Below, Taddeo Landini, Winter, twin of the statue on the opposite page.

CHURCH OF SANTA TRÌNITA

Founded in the second half of the 11th century, this was the first Vallombrosan church in Florence. Originally it lay outside the city walls and was only enclosed within the defensive circle when it was extended by the city authorities at the end of the 12th century (1172-1175). During the 14th century, the church was enlarged and renovated in Gothic style. Work was interrupted in 1348 by the devastating outbreak of plague, however, and was only completed in the early 15th century.

The present baroque façade (1593-1594) in *pietra forte* was designed by Bernardo Buontalenti.

Interior. The Gothic style interior has three naves divided by pilasters and pointed arches. Remnants of the old Romanesque structure can be seen on the inner façade. The church contains important works by three major artists of the early Florentine Renaissance: Luca della Robbia, Desiderio da Settignano and Domenico Ghirlandaio.

The visit begins in the right nave. In the third chapel is a *Madonna Enthroned with Child and Saints* on gold leaf background, by Neri di Bicci (1419-1491). On the left wall is a *Madonna Enthroned with Child and Saints* (1390-1395), by Spinello Aretino.

The fourth chapel is entirely 15th-century, including the

Below, Piazza Santa Trìnita with the column of Justice raised here in 1554 by Cosimo I. The statue of Justice was made by Francesco del Tadda.

The baroque façade of the church of Santa Trìnita designed in pietra forte by Bernardo Buontalenti.

wrought iron gate, and is decorated with an altar panel of the *Annunciation* and frescoed *Scenes from the Life of Mary* (1420-1425), by Lorenzo Monaco.

Just off the transept is the Sassetti Chapel, with Domenico Ghirlandaio's famous fresco cycle illustrating *Scenes from the Life of St Francis of Assisi* (1483-1486). The scenes are set in 15th-century Florence and various buildings and monuments are visi-

The Sassetti chapel decorated with Scenes from the Life of Saint Francis, Miracle of the Boy Brought Back to Life *by Domenico Ghirlandaio; the scene takes place in Piazza Santa Trìnita and the earlier Gothic façade of the church can be seen as well as Palazzo Spini on the left and the bridge before it collapsed in 1557.*

Centre, the Viviani coat of arms (designed by Giovan Battista Foggini) on Palazzo Viviani.

Below, the Sassetti chapel, Domenico Ghirlandaio Saint Francis Receives the Rule of the Order; *Palazzo Vecchio and the Signoria loggia can be seen in the background, while Lorenzo The Magnificent is portrayed in the right foreground.*

Right, Sassetti chapel, Domenico Ghirlandaio, Nativity.

ble (including the earlier Gothic façade of Santa Trìnita), as well as some contemporary figures (including Lorenzo the Magnificent, a friend and colleague to Sassetti). On the altar is an *Adoration of the Shepherds* (1484), by Domenico Ghirlandaio. In this work, the artist practically reproduces the shepherds of the *Portinari Tryptych*, by Van der Goes, now held in the Uffizi (☞ p. 111).

In the second chapel of the left transept, is the *tomb of Benozzo Federighi, Bishop of Fiesole* (1454), by Luca della Robbia. The marble monument is decorated with a band of glazed and painted terracotta tiles.

In the fifth chapel of the left nave is a wooden statue of *Mary Magdalen*, by Desiderio da Settignano. According to Vasari, it was completed by Benedetto da Maiano around 1455. In the fourth chapel is a fresco of *St John Gualberto forgiving his brother's murderer* (c.1440-1450), by Lorenzo di Bicci. Behind the altar is a lunette of *St John Enthroned, Saints and Blessed Vallombrosans* (1455) by Neri di Bicci. On the right, the panel depicting the *Annunciation* with *Adam and Eve expelled from Terrestrial Paradise* (1491), also by Neri. Historian Dino Compagni (1260-1323) is buried in the chapel.

VIA TORNABUONI

This is probably the most elegant street in the city centre. On the ground floors of these prestigious palaces, mostly built during the 16th and 17th centuries, are stylish and fashionable shops.

At no. 3, on the corner of Via del Parione, is the 16th-

The emblem of the Theatine Order above the entrance to the church of San Gaetano; the cross, on a triple mount, is flanked by allegorical figures of Hope *and* Poverty *by Balthasar Permoser, 1686-89.*

century *Palazzo Minerbetti.* At no. 5 is *Palazzo Strozzi del Poeta* which was the residence of the Florentine poet and literary figure, Giovan Battista Strozzi, at the beginning of the 17th century. A classic example of Florentine baro-que, the façade (1626) is by Gherardo Silvani. At no. 6 is the 17th-century *Palazzo Medici Tornabuoni,* created by joining and adding upper floors to two 14th-century houses. At no. 7 is the *Palazzo del Circolo dell'Unione,* probably built by Vasari to a design by Giambologna.

Crossing the junction with Via Strozzi, we come to *Palazzo Corsi* at no. 16 (today the Banca Commerciale) built by Michelozzo in the mid-15th century and renovated in 1736 by Ferdinando Ruggieri. At no. 15 is *Palazzo Viviani,* remodelled in 1695 by Giovan Battista Foggini. At no. 19 is *Palazzo Larderel,* built in 1580 to a late-Renaissance design by Giovanni Antonio Dosio.

baroque style by Matteo Nigetti (1604-1630). The façade, in pietra forte, *was designed by Gherardo Silvani and his son Pier Francesco, completed by the latter in 1683.*

From Piazza Antinori we return to the Cathedral along Via degli Agli (where Filippo Brunelleschi was born) and Via dei Pecori.

Palazzo Antinori, a typical example of a 15th-century Florentine residence, built between 1461-1469 to a design by Giuliano da Maiano.

Loggia modernized by Cigoli in 1608 and moved to the side of the church when work took place during the 19th century.

The interior of the church of San Gaetano, one of the few baroque interiors to have remained intact.

At the far end, Via Tornabuoni widens into Piazza Antinori. At no. 3 is the Palazzo Antinori (1461-1469), *a typical example of a 15th-century Florentine mansion, built to a design by Giuliano da Maiano.*

Opposite is the church of San Gaetano, *which was already documented in the mid-11th century. It was completely rebuilt in*

Religious architecture -2-

The Renaissance. When Filippo Brunelleschi designed the dome of Santa Maria del Fiore, he made no attempt to adapt the size and shape to the limitations of current building techniques. On the contrary, he met the challenge of covering the immense open space at the centre of the cathedral transept by developing new engineering methods which would enable him to put his design into practice. To achieve this, he made a careful study of Roman antiquities which provided him with the techniques and examples he needed. The Renaissance represented a reaction to the prevailing Gothic style and a return to classical principles, but with a fresh approach. A building was no longer the result merely of specific construction methods used by the master builders, but became instead the realization of an architectural plan based on the abstract principles of proportion and symmetry.

Sacrestia Vecchia, San Lorenzo

Completed by Brunelleschi some time before 1429, the Old Sacristy is a masterly example of the Renaissance concept of space. The sense of harmony is created by the strict proportional relationships between the various elements of the structure.

Church of San Felice

First mentioned in records in the 11th century, it was altered during the 14th century and again in the two successive centuries. Attributed to Michelozzo, the Renaissance façade (1452-1460) is one of the few remaining in Florence.

The façade of Santa Maria Novella

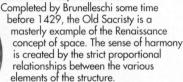

One of the masterpieces of Florentine Renaissance architecture, the façade was designed by Leon Battista Alberti and dates from the second half of the 15th century. The facing of green, white and black marble emphasizes the perfect proportions of the form and is a return to the patterns and colours of Tuscan Romanesque architecture. Along the lower part of the façade are six tombs with pointed arches and two smaller doors, part of the original Gothic façade which had been left unfinished.

San Lorenzo, interior

Originally the city's cathedral, the church was almost completely rebuilt during the first half of the 15th century to a design by Brunelleschi. It is divided into three naves by columns with Corinthian capitals supporting rounded arches.

Mannerist and Baroque. The harmony and proportion of the Renaissance tradition not only dominated the appearance and culture of the city during the 15th and 16th centuries, but also influenced the development of later styles and tastes. Consequently, little of the grandeur of Roman Baroque is to be found in Florence. Apart from rare exceptions, the architecture of Florentine 17th- and 18th-century churches could therefore be defined as 'post-mannerist' rather than Baroque.

Sacrestia Nuova, San Lorenzo

The New Sacristy was commissioned by Pope Leo X from Michelangelo in 1520, and finished by Giorgio Vasari and Bartolomeo Ammannati in the mid-16th century. The innovative style is recognized as the prototype for Mannerist architecture. Michelangelo gave the structure a giddying upward thrust, with tapering windows in the lunettes. The immense marble monuments introduce an element of powerful tension, entirely the opposite of the perfect harmony of Brunelleschi's Old Sacristy.

The façade of Santa Trinita

The *pietra forte* façade (1593-1594) is a late Mannerist work by Bernardo Buontalenti.

The façade of Ognissanti

Designed by Buontalenti's pupil Matteo Nigetti, the façade was added between 1637 and 1638.

Church of San Gaetano

Perhaps the most important Baroque building in the city. The façade, in pietra forte, was begun in 1604 by Matteo Nigetti and completed by Pier Francesco Silvani in 1639.

The chapel of Sant'Andrea Corsini, in Santa Maria del Carmine

Completed by Pier Francesco Silvani in the early-1680's, this is one of the most important examples of Roman Baroque in Florence.

7. **Renaisssance on the Banks of the Arno**

Leading from the cathedral to the Oltrarno, passing through some of the most elegant streets in the city, this itinerary could be described as that of Masaccio. Indeed, the great artist's frescoes in the Brancacci Chapel of the Carmine Church had an enormous impact on 15th-century Florentine painting, thus touching the very roots of Renaissance art.

As architect and sculptor, Masaccio had closely studied Brunelleschi and Donatello, but in the art of painting he was virtually unprecedented: as Vasari notes, "Certainly everything done before him can be described as artificial, whereas he produced work that is living, realistic and natural". Thus a visit to the Brancacci Chapel is an obligatory part of our tour of the city, and more than enough to justify a walk around the 'Other side' of the Arno. And yet, many other pleasant surprises await the visitor in this popular, working class area — not least of which the numerous the antique dealers' and

craftsmen's workshops that lend the Oltrarno its lively and colourful character.

The traditional skills and crafts carried on in the many workshops are a long-standing and important feature of this area, dating from the arrival in the city of the Benedictine Umiliati Friars. Specialists in making wool cloth, these monks came to Florence from Lombardy in 1206, summoned by Bishop Ardingo. Some forty years later, they built a monastery, church and workshops in the area now occupied by the Church of Ognissanti. The river Arno provided energy to drive the wheels, machinery and hammers which beat the raw wool until it became soft and supple. The establishment of the Florentine wool mill, on which the city's wealth was based during the 14th and 15th centuries, dates from this period. When the Carraia Bridge was first built in 1218, the friars rapidly extended their business and trade to the southern side of the river.

At this time too, the most important mendicant orders began to settle on the edges of the city, in the hamlets which formed just outside the city walls. In 1250, the St Augustine hermits came down from the hills of nearby Arcetri where they had been living, to found the monastery of Santo Spirito, in a sparsely-populated area then known as Casellina. Just a few years later, the Carmelite monks founded the Carmine Church on a site which still lay outside the city perimeter. Around these two religious communities, the most popular working class area of the city developed.

Marino Marini, Venus.

Below, the church of San Frediano in Cestello and Lungarno Soderini from Ponte alla Carraia, *by Emilio Burci, Uffizi, Department of Prints and Drawings.*

Opposite page, detail of a marble coat of arms with the fleur-de-lys, emblem of Florence.

Several views of Piazza della Repubblica. Right, the busy portico where the flower market is held on Thursday mornings. Below, detail of the Caffè Gilli.

From Piazza del Duomo, we take the elegant Via Roma to arrive at Piazza della Repubblica.

PIAZZA DELLA REPUBBLICA

This is the most modern piazza in the city centre. It was made between 1885 and 1895, when the city council decided to demolish the entire area around the old medieval market which had been built over the ruins of the Roman forum. Also in the square was the Loggia del Pesce (fish market, 1567), designed by Giorgio Vasari, later dismantled and reconstructed in Piazza dei Ciompi in 1951. In the same period the *Column of Abundance* was erected in the piazza, indicating the point where the two principal Roman roads crossed.

The square is famous for its cafés, especially the 'Giubbe Rosse' where writers and intellectuals met during the 1920's and '30's.

Passing under the triumphal arch built by Vincenzo Micheli in 1895, we walk along Via Strozzi with its famous boutiques: walking alongside Palazzo Strozzi (☞ p. 121), we reach Via Tor-nabuoni at the junction of Via della Vigna Nuova and Via della

The arch built by Vincenzo Micheli in 1895.

Below, Palazzo Larderel, formerly Giacomini, built in 1580, standing between Via della Vigna Nuova and Via della Spada.

Spada, where our itinerary continues.

Via della Spada veers abruptly to the right compared to the general axis of Via Strozzi. This deviation from the overall pattern of the streets represents part of the fascinating history of the city.

At the time of the foundation of Roman 'Florentia,' Via della Spada in fact represented the 'decumanus maximus'. This axis formed the basis for the division of land to the west of the city into lots which were awarded to veterans of Caesar's army.

enaissance on the Banks of the Arno

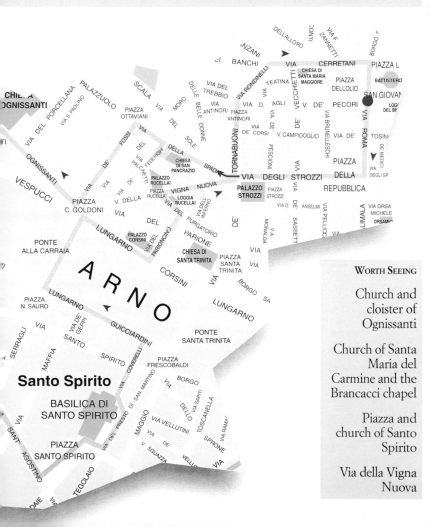

WORTH SEEING

Church and cloister of Ognissanti

Church of Santa Maria del Carmine and the Brancacci chapel

Piazza and church of Santo Spirito

Via della Vigna Nuova

View of Via Strozzi with its famous shops.

Antique shop in Via de' Fossi.

The city could quite simply have been oriented north-south, east-west as was typical in Roman urban planning. For practical reasons, however, the division of land outside the city had to follow the actual geographical lie of the land. Thus Via Strozzi, which follows the urban axis, lies east-west, while Via della Spada, which follows the direction of the plain of Florence, runs north-west, south-east.

The little piazza of San Pancrazio, where the church of the same name now houses a museum (☞ below), is to the left of Via della Spada. Just before the piazza is the entrance to the Cappella Rucellai, which was once part of the church.

The entrance to the Marino Marini Museum in the deconsecrated church of San Pancrazio.

Centre, Venus.

RUCELLAI CHAPEL

The chapel is evidence of the importance that the Rucellai family, whose palace is nearby, had in this area of the city (☞ pp.209-210).

The vast rectangular interior houses the marble *Sanctuary of the Holy Sepulchre,* by Leon Battista Alberti. This unusual monument, completed by the architect in 1474, reproduces the exact proportions of the Holy Sepulchre in Jerusalem.

THE CHURCH OF SAN PANCRAZIO

Documented as early as the 9th century, the church of San Pancrazio was completely rebuilt by the Vallombrosan monks between 1370 and 1454. The present façade is the result of alterations carried out in the mid-18th century and the replacement of elements from Alberti's structure made for the Rucellai chapel. Deconsecrated in 1808, the church was restored in 1988, becoming the Museo Marino Marini. **Marino Marini Museum.** The museum is dedicated to the contemporary artist from Pistoia, Marino Marini (1901-1980) and houses his paintings, sculptures and drawings from the 1920's to the early 1960's. Important works displayed include: a painted plaster cast of a *Man on horseback*

Marino Marini,
Horseman.

(1937) on the ground floor, and, against the large glass panel in the place of the apse, a large bronze *Equestrian Group* (1957-1958); on the mezzanine floor is the *Swimmer* (1932), a young male nude sculpted in wood; on the floor above is the statue *Dancers in a circle,* the work which best represents the artist's later style.

Leaving the museum, we continue to the end of Via della Spada. On the corner of Piazza Ottaviani, to the right is the 16th-century Palazzo Niccolini.

We now turn to the left along Via de' Fossi. The name of the street (meaning ditch) derives from the fact that the course of the Mugnone river, which previously flowed nearer to Via Tornabuoni, was deviated along here when the first city walls were built (1173-1175). The street is renowned for its elegant art and antique shops.

At the end of Via de' Fossi is Piazza Goldoni. Borgo Ognissanti begins immediately on the right.

PIAZZA GOLDONI AND BORGO OGNISSANTI

Piazza Goldoni assumed its present appearance in the mid-19th century, when the Lungarno Nuovo (now Lungarno Vespucci) was made, narrowing the river bed. On the left,

on the corner of Lungarno Corsini, facing into the square, is *Palazzo Ricasoli* (1480-1500), designed by Michelozzo though built after his death. The statue in front of the Carraia Bridge (☛ p. 208) is of Venetian playwright *Carlo Goldoni* (1873), by Ulisse Cambi.

Borgo Ognissanti is on the right, leading out of Piazza Goldoni. This elegant street with its attractive shops and galleries, also has two unusual Liberty-style buildings. The *Casa alla Rovescia* (Upside-Down House), at no. 12, is named after the brackets supporting the terrace and the balustrades, both of which are upside-down; the *Casa galleria* at no. 26 was built in 1911 by Giovanni Michelazzi.

Also on the right side of the street, at no. 20, is the *Spedale di San Giovanni di Dio,* one of the oldest Florentine hospitals, still operative until just a few years ago.

Founded by the Vespucci family in 1380, it was enlarged in the early 18th century, incorporating the house where Amerigo Vespucci was born.

Above, Palazzo Ricasoli, designed by Michelozzi and built after his death (1480-1500). In 1580, when a passageway was built under the road, the palace was linked to an extensive park and a loggia on the river.

Centre page, statue of Carlo Goldoni, *1873 by Ulisse Cambi.*

Right, the 15th-century Palazzo Lenzi has frequently been altered; the projection onto Borgo Ognissanti is an addition. The side facing the piazza was decorated with graffito work by Andrea Feltrini in the 19th century.

The gallery-house, a rare example of art-nouveau by Giovanni Michelazzi (1911).

Below, the church of Ognissanti.

About one hundred yards further ahead is Piazza Ognissanti which, like Piazza Goldoni, is the result of mid-19th-century reconstruction.

On the far side of the piazza, at no. 2, is Palazzo Lenzi. *Built in the 14th century, it was altered several times until the end of the last century, and now houses the French Consulate, as well as the French Institute run by the University of Grenoble. In the middle of the piazza is* Hercules fighting the lion, *a bronze group by Romano Romanelli, placed here in 1937.*

On the right are the church and monastery of Ognissanti, founded in the mid-13th century by the Friars of the monastic order known as the Umiliati, experts in the production of wool. The spacious square in front of the church formed a large terrace over the river, where the Friars had drying and stretching yards, while their mills and machinery lined the banks of the river.

ples of baroque architecture. **Interior.** The building has a transept and single nave.

In the second altar on the right side are three detached frescoes by Domenico Ghirlandaio (1449-1494), portraying the *Pietà,* the *Deposition* and *Our Lady of Mercy.* On the third altar is a painting of the *Virgin with Saints* (1565), by Santi di Tito. Next, frescoed on the wall, is an intense image of *St Augustine* (1480), by Sandro Botticelli. The marble pulpit is decorated with bas-relief *Stories from the Life of St Francis,* by Benedetto da Rovezzano (1474-c.1552).

The *main altar* (1593-1595) with semi-precious stone mosaic, is by Jacopo Ligozzi. The *frescoes* in the dome are by Giovanni da San Giovanni (1592-1636).

In the chapel in the left transept next to the sacristy is the *monk's habit,* reputedly worn by St Francis when he received the stigmata.

CHURCH OF OGNISSANTI

Construction was initiated in 1254. The bell tower dates from the 13th-14th centuries, though the church was completely renovated in the 17th century. The façade (1637) by Matteo Nigetti is one of the earliest exam-

Domenico Ghirlandaio, The Last Supper.

Below and bottom right, details of the Life of Saint Francis, *fresco cycle begun by Jacopo Ligozzi and finished by various artists.*

In the sacristy are fragments of 14th-century *frescoes* by Taddeo Gaddi; above the entrance to the convent is a large *painted cross* by a follower of Giotto.

On the left side, in the fifth altar, is a 14th-century painted wooden *Crucifix*. Between the fourth and the third altars is a fresco of *St Jerome in his study*, by Domenico Ghirlandaio.

Cloister and refectory. The arcaded cloister at no. 42 (on the right leaving the church) is frescoed with *Stories from the Life of St Francis*, begun by Jacopo Ligozzi in 1599 and completed by Giovanni da San Giovanni between 1616 and 1619.

From the right corner of the cloister, opposite the entrance, we reach the old refectory of the monastery; on the far wall is a splendid fresco of the *Last Supper*, (1480) by Domenico Ghirlandaio.

Leaving Piazza Ognissanti, we continue along the Lungarno and cross the river at the Amerigo Vespucci Bridge, built in 1957 to replace a Bailey bridge which had been

there since the end of World War II. *The bridge is situated near the Santa Rosa weir, now the only remaining sign of the structures which produced and used hydraulic energy here as early as the Middle Ages.*

On the other side of the bridge we turn left along Lun-

garno Soderini towards Piazza di Cestello (Cestello *probably being a corrupted form of the Latin* cistercenses *or Cistercians: in fact, it seems that this monastic order once had a settlement here). Continuing straight ahead for a short distance, we come to Piazza del Tiratoio, and turning right into Via Bartolini, we reach the* Antico setificio fiorentino (silk factory) *where silks and*

The cloister of Ognissanti.

The Florentine silk factory.

Previous page, below left, Saint Jerome in his Study *by Domenico Ghrlandaio. Right,* Saint Jerome in his Study *by Sandro Botticelli.*

Above, detail of a 16th-century door with a wide medieval stone vault in a house in Via delle Caldaie. Above, the church of San Frediano in Cestello *and Lungarno Soderini from Ponte alla Carraia, by Emilio Burci, Uffizi, Department of Prints and Drawings.*

The church of San Frediano in Cestello.

Right, the dome of the church of San Frediano in Cestello frescoed by Domenico Gabbiani.

brocades are still produced on 17th-century looms.

On the right (west) side of Piazza di Cestello is the huge Granary of Cosimo III, *or of* Abundance *(1695), built by Giovan Battista Foggini. 'Strategic' reserves of grain, which served to regulate prices and were used to feed the poor in times of famine, were kept here.*

On the other side of the square is the church of San Frediano in Cestello. The entrance is located on the right side of the church, on Via di Cestello.

CHURCH OF SAN FREDIANO IN CESTELLO

Built between 1680 and 1689 by the architect Cerutti, known as Colonello, and crowned with a dome (1698) by Antonio Ferri, the church of San Frediano in Cestello is an attractive example of bright, refined Florentine baroque.

Like many other Florentine churches, the façade is unadorned. The design of the interior is based on a Latin cross, with a single nave and charming stucco decorations. Most of the works of art are 17th- and 18th-century. The dome is frescoed with *Mary Magdalen in Glory* (1702-1718), considered to be Domenico Gabbiani's mas-

terpiece. The massive *main altar*, decorated in marble and semi-precious stone inlay, is 18th-century.

In the left transept, there is a painting of the *Crucifixion with Saints* (1442-1443), by Jacopo del Sellaio. The third chapel on the left side is decorated with *frescoes* (1689) by Pietro Dandini, and contains a 14th-century statue in painted wood, known as the *Smiling Madonna.*

At the end of Via di Cestello is Borgo San Frediano, one of the most picturesque streets of the Oltrarno. On the right, at the far end of the street is the large arch of the San Frediano Gate, *part of the last ring of city walls. Built between 1332 and 1334 as the garrison at the entrance from Via Pisana, it is attributed to Andrea Pisano.*

Continuing in the opposite direction along Borgo San Frediano, we come to the vast Piazza del Carmine. On the far side is the imposing structure of the church of Santa Maria del Carmine.

Local crafts

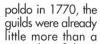
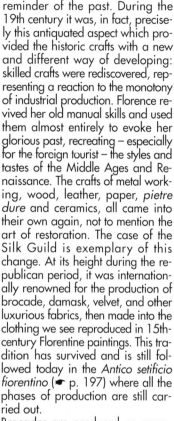

"All Florentines are craftsmen, working and making things with their own hands". Thus the Venetian Marco Foscari reported in 1527, continuing, "and even the heads who govern the state go to their workshops [...] and openly work where everyone can see them". This comment was meant to be a criticism, but in fact it highlighted an aspect of which most Florentines were proud. The citizens of the republican commune had defeated feudal power precisely because their many craftsmen had created such a thriving economy. Florence was a city of workshops and studios: they were to be found everywhere, opening up indiscriminately beside imposing palaces or churches, often with a single craft grouped in one area. This clustering is still reflected in various street names, such as that of the *Archibusieri* (gun-makers), *Ariento* (silversmiths), *Calzaioli* (shoemakers), *Cartolai* (stationers), *Cimatori* (washers of wool cloth), *Conciatori* (leatherworkers), *Fibbiai* (bucklers), *Gomitolo dell'Oro* (gold beaters), *Saponai* (soap makers), *Tessitori* (weavers), *Tintori* (dyers), *Vagellai* (vats of the dyers). There were twenty-one guilds, seven major and fourteen minor ones, and in 1293 the *Ordinances of Justice* established that only those who belonged to a guild could take public office. When the Medici assumed absolute power in the city, the guilds lost much of their political impetus. Ferdinando I created workshops and studios in the Uffizi, housing jewellers, engravers, map makers, goldsmiths, turners, confectioners, clockmakers, distillers and china and porcelain workers. When they were repressed as an institution by Pietro Leopoldo in 1770, the guilds were already little more than a reminder of the past. During the 19th century it was, in fact, precisely this antiquated aspect which provided the historic crafts with a new and different way of developing: skilled crafts were rediscovered, representing a reaction to the monotony of industrial production. Florence revived her old manual skills and used them almost entirely to evoke her glorious past, recreating – especially for the foreign tourist – the styles and tastes of the Middle Ages and Renaissance. The crafts of metal working, wood, leather, paper, *pietre dure* and ceramics, all came into their own again, not to mention the art of restoration. The case of the Silk Guild is exemplary of this change. At its height during the republican period, it was internationally renowned for the production of brocade, damask, velvet, and other luxurious fabrics, then made into the clothing we see reproduced in 15th-century Florentine paintings. This tradition has survived and is still followed today in the *Antico setificio fiorentino* (☞ p. 197) where all the phases of production are still carried out.

Brocades are produced on reproductions of 15th-century handlooms, the width of a Florentine *braccio* (or arm's length, equivalent to 24 inches), as the movement of the shuttle from one side to the other is determined by the length of a person's forearm. A double width can be made on the 17th-century looms to which a Jacquard (1801) or Vincenzi machine (1950's) has been added. Still in perfect working order, and indeed unique for making delicately shaded braiding, is a 15th-century warping machine, the design of which is traditionally attributed to Leonardo da Vinci.

Right, Jacopo da Sellaio, Crucifixion with Saints, *church of San Frediano in Cestello.*

Below, the city gate of San Frediano and a detail of the old gate closely studded with heavy nails.

CHURCH OF SANTA MARIA DEL CARMINE

Founded by the Carmelite monks in the mid-13th century, the church was completed in 1476. It was frequently altered in the 16th and 17th centuries, and in 1771 was partially destroyed by a fire. Giuseppe Ruggieri was responsible for its rebuilding in 1775, and it has remained largely unchanged. Apart from the doorway, the façade has never been decorated.

Interior. Consisting of a single nave with a large transept, the building is 270 ft long and 49 ft wide. In the third chapel on the right is a *Crucifixion* (1560), by Giorgio Vasari; and in the fourth chapel, a *Visitation*, a late work by mannerist painter Aurelio Lomi (1556-1622).

On the far right of the transept is the Brancacci

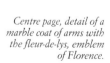

Centre page, detail of a marble coat of arms with the fleur-de-lys, emblem of Florence.

Chapel. There is a separate entrance from the square, to the right of the church.

Behind the altar, in the main chapel of the transept, is the *tomb of Pier Soderini*, by Benedetto da Rovezzano. Soderini, who died in 1522, was elected *gonfaloniere*, or magistrate, of the Florentine Republic after Savonarola had been condemned to death. Although counted among Soderini's friends, Machiavelli was frustrated by his excessively meek and irresolute character, to the point that he composed this pitiful epigram: "The night Pier Soderini died / His soul went to the mouth of Hell, / But Pluto shouted at him: 'Silly soul, / Go up to Limbo where the other babies are!"

At the far left side of the transept is the grand Corsini chapel (1675-1683), which was unscathed by the fire of 1771. Pier Francesco Silvani was commissioned to build it by Bartolomeo and Neri Corsini, in memory of Andrea Corsini — Carmelite bishop of Fiesole during the 14th century and canonized by Pope Urban VIII in 1629.

The chapel contains numerous works by Giovan Bat-

The church of Santa Maria del Carmine (left) and the interior (below).

tista Foggini including, on the right, the *funerary monument to Cardinal Corsini* and above, *St Andrea Corsini leading the Florentines at the Battle of Anghiari* (1685-1687), considered to be the artist's masterpiece. In 1682, Luca Giordano frescoed the dome of the chapel with the *Apotheosis of St Andrea Corsini.*

To the right of the church is the entrance to a large cloister, built at the end of the 16th and beginning of the 17th century. From a vestibule on the far side we enter the sacristy and the Brancacci Chapel.

Built in Gothic style in the late 14th-century, the sacristy is decorated with 15th-century frescoes and mainly 17th-century works of art. The beautiful polyptych representing the Madonna and Child with Saints *is attributed to Andrea di Buonaiuto (14th-century), who also painted the frescoes in the Spanish Chapel at Santa Maria Novella.*

BRANCACCI CHAPEL

The chapel had been under the patronage of the Brancacci family since the 14th century and around 1423, Felice Brancacci commissioned Masolino and Masaccio to decorate it. The two artists worked on it together from 1423-1424, and again from 1427-1428 (when Masaccio left for Rome where he died just a few months later at the age of twenty-seven). Work was still not finished in 1436, when Felice Brancacci –

an enemy of the Medici – fell into disgrace and was exiled. The chapel was then dedicated to the Madonna of the Faithful and the 13th-century *Madonna* on the altar, attributed to Coppo di Marcovaldo, was brought here.

Left unfinished by both Masolino and Masaccio, the frescoes were completed in 1480 by Filippino Lippi. They were damaged by the fire in 1771, but recently underwent complete restoration (1983-1990). The following is a brief description and summary of the cycle.

1. On the left, above, is Masaccio's masterpiece, *The Expulsion of Adam and Eve from Terrestrial Paradise.* With their touching human nudity, the figures of Adam and Eve

View of the frescoes on the left wall of the Brancacci chapel.

*View of the frescoes
on the right wall of
the Brancacci chapel.*

Masaccio, The Expulsion
from Paradise.

Masolino, Saint Peter
preaching.

represent the birth of Renaissance art.

2. Beside, to the right, is the *Payment of the Tribute Money*, the most famous of Masaccio's frescoes and one of the greatest masterpieces ever painted. This large painting illustrates the tale in three parts: in response to the tax collector's request for the tribute money, Jesus (in the centre) shows St Peter a lake where he will find a fish with coins in its mouth; on the left we see the apostle crouching to remove the coins, and on the right, the money is paid to the tax collector.

3. Beside the altar is *St Peter preaching*, by Masolino.

4. On the other side of the altar is the *Baptism of the Neophytes* by Masaccio, with two nude figures: the first is being baptized while the other is standing by, shivering with cold.

5. On the right wall is *St Peter healing the lame man* and *Resurrection of the dead Tabitha*, by Masolino. Noting the vivid portrayal of the houses and streets of 15th-century Florence in the background, art historian Roberto Longhi identified Masaccio's hand in the piece.

6. Next is the *Temptation of Adam and Eve*, by Masolino.

7. On the left, beneath the *Expulsion from Terrestrial Paradise*, is the *Visit of St Paul to St Peter in prison*, by Filippino Lippi.

8. Next is the *Resurrection of Teofilo's son* and *St Peter Enthroned*. The last scene to be painted by Masaccio, it was left unfinished and completed by Filippino Lippi.

9. Next, on the left, is *St Peter, followed by St John, healing the sick with his shadow*, by Masaccio.

10. On the other side of the altar is *St Peter distributing alms* and the *Death of Anania*, by Masaccio. The subject, taken from the *Acts of the Apostles,* reminds Christians that it

Masaccio, Saint Peter, followed by Saint John, healing the sick with his shadow.

Masolino, Saint Peter brings Tabitha to life and heals a lame man.

is their duty to make their possessions available to help the entire community.

11. *The Disputation of Simon the Mystic* and the *Crucifixion of St Peter,* by Filippino Lippi.

12. *The Angel frees St Peter from prison,* by Filippino Lippi.

Leaving Piazza del Carmine, we take the street to the right,

Via Santa Monica, which brings us to the junction with Via dei Serragli and then continues as Via Sant'Agostino. On the left, on the façade of Palazzo Mazzei *(built in the late 15th-early 16th centuries) is a lovely tabernacle depicting* Madonna and Child with Sts Paul and Jerome, *by Bicci di Lorenzo (1373-1452).*

Opening off Via Sant'Agostino on the left, is Piazza Santo Spirito.

PIAZZA SANTO SPIRITO

Dominated by the evocative 18th-century façade of the church, the piazza is presently arranged as garden, with a fountain in the centre.

On the side opposite to the church is a statue of the agronomist *Cosimo Ridolfi*, by Raffaello Romanelli (1856-1928).

The north-western side of the piazza is delimited by the church and monastery of Santo Spirito; the latter is now partially occupied by the offices of the Florentine military authorities.

The eastern side of the square begins with the 16th-

Filippino Lippi, The angel releases Saint Peter from prison *(above);* Saint Peter in prison, visited by Saint Paul.

Detail of 18th-century stone door and window frame decorated with plaster work, on the corner of Via delle Caldaie and Via del Campuccio.

The Origins of the Renaissance -2-

Masaccio (1401-1428)

"To the early development of the gentle style of Lorenzo Monaco and the glowing style of Gentile da Fabriano, enhanced with little naturalistic details, the young Masaccio suddenly introduced a new way of painting, rigorously hostile to the pleasantries of Gothic art". (A. Chastel).

A disciple of Masolino da Panicale – with whom he went to Rome in 1428 – but profoundly influenced by Brunelleschi and Donatello, Masaccio managed, in just ten years, to revolutionize the history of painting as only Giotto before him had done. A close friend of Brunelleschi, he applied the principles of mathematical perspective to painting, creating the illusion of naturalistic space. Argan states that Masaccio's figures "are space made solid and given human form": rejecting the gracious, flowing forms of international Gothic in favour at the time, they seem massive and heavy, realistic and moving in their dramatic and eloquent poses.

The Holy Trinity with the Virgin, St John the Evangelist and Donors (c. 1425). "We can imagine how amazed the Florentines must have been when this wall-painting was unveiled and seemed to have made a hole in the wall through which they could look into a new burial chapel in Brunelleschi's modern style. But perhaps they were even more amazed at the simplicity and grandeur of the figures which were framed by this new architecture". (E.H. Gombrich)

dome which fits into the figure of St Ann in exactly the same way as Brunelleschi's dome fits into the dimensional structure of the 14th-century naves". (G.C. Argan)

The Tribute Money (c. 1424-1427). The most famous of the frescoes in the Brancacci chapel, this is the first great outstanding scene in Renaissance painting. The three stages of the event are shown in a single scene: Jesus is stopped at the entrance to the city by a tax collector who demands the tribute money. In the centre is Jesus, representing the importance of man, surrounded by apostles, set around him in a circle like the columns of Brunelleschi's architecture. The scene shows Peter on the left, on the banks of a lake, removing a silver coin from the mouth of a fish. On the right, the apostle, in obedience to earthly laws, gives the money to the tax collector.

The Virgin and Child with St Ann (c. 1424). "Not since Giotto's time had a figure as majestic and statuesque as St Ann been seen in Florentine painting. Moreover, into the enlarged, dimensional structure of this figure, Masaccio has set a Madonna with the form and even the oval profile of Brunelleschi's

century *Palazzo Guadagni.* The design of the building, crowned with a large, airy loggia, is attributed to Simone del Pollaiolo (known as Cronaca). The façade was beautifully decorated with graffito until the early 20th century.

CHURCH OF SANTO SPIRITO

The plain, unadorned façade of the church of Santo Spirito veils one of the greatest works ever produced by Filippo Brunelleschi, and one of the most sublime pieces of Florentine Renaissance architecture.

Brunelleschi started designing the church in 1428, but only in 1444 was he able to proceed with construction, on the site of an Augustinian church founded in the mid-13th century. After his death in 1446,

the project was taken over first by Antonio Manetti and then by Giovanni da Gaiole and Salvi d'Andrea, completing the Brunelleschian dome between 1479 and 1481. Consecrated in 1481, the church was completed in 1487.

During the last decade of the 15th century, Giuliano da Sangallo designed the sacristy, while Cronaca made the vestibule.

In the early 16th century, Baccio d'Agnolo began the bell tower which was completed in 1541.

The monastery complex was completed around the end of the 16th, beginning of the 17th century by Bartolomeo Ammannati and Alfonso Parigi, responsible for the two cloisters.

Interior. The internal design is in the form of

Interior of the church of
Santo Spirito

Above, the damaged
Crucifixion by
Andrea Orcagna and
Nardo di Cione (late
14th century). Top,
the refectory of Santo
Spirito, once a
printer's workshop.

The baroque high
altar.

a Latin cross, with three
naves divided by thirty-five
monolithic columns with
Corinthian capitals. As in San
Lorenzo, the roof above the
central nave is flat, while the
two side aisles have domed
vaults. A *pietra forte* entablature runs above the arches
which divide the naves.

The structure is very similar
to that of San Lorenzo, but
here the architect introduces
two important variations: the
large dome in the centre of
the transept, and the continuation of the side aisles into the
two wings of the transept.

Around the two side aisles
are forty small, semi-circular
apses, each housing a private
chapel. In the 15th century,
each of these chapels had an
altar panel and a painted
wooden frontal. Over the
centuries, many of these
works have been lost or replaced. However, in the area
of the apse and the left
transept, many of the altars
still have their original 15th-
century appearance.

We begin in the nave on
the right, hosting works dating from the 16th and 17th
centuries. In Chapel II is a
Pietà (1545) by Nanni di
Baccio Bigio, a copy of the
marble group by Michelan-
gelo in St Peter's. In Chapel
IV, *Christ drives the merchants from the Temple*
(1572), by Giovanni
Stradano. The *main altar*
(1599-1607) is an impressive
piece of baroque architecture
in semi-precious stone inlay,
by Giovanni Caccini, assisted
by Gherardo Silvani and
Agostino Ubaldini.

In Chapel VIII, in the right
wing of the transept, is a *Crucifixion with the Virgin and St
John* (17th-century), attributed to Piero Dandini, and a
late 15th-century wooden altar-frontal with *St Francis.*

In Chapel X is a painting of
Our Lady of Charity (late
15th-century), attributed to
the Maestro della Natività
Johnson.

In Chapel XI is a small 14th-
century wooden *Crucifix*; in
XII, a *Virgin and Child with St
John, St Martin and St Catherine Martyr* (1494), a splendid
panel by Filippino Lippi. The
city gate of San Frediano can
be seen in the background.

In Chapel XIV, a railing en-
closes the marble *sarcophagus*
(1458) *of Neri di Gino Capponi* (Florentine politician,
1388-1457), attributed to
Bernardo Rossellino.

In the second chapel in
the apse (XVII) is a *Virgin and
Child with Four Saints* (mid-
14th century), a polyptych
by Maso di Banco. In
Chapel XIX is a painting by
Alessandro Allori (1535-
1607) of the *Martyr Saints.*

Filippino Lippi, Madonna and Child with Saint John, Saint Martin and Saint Catherine.

In Chapel XX is the *Adultress* (1577), also by Allori.

In the left wing of the transept, in Chapel XXIV, is a *Madonna and Child with Two Angels and Sts Bartholomew and John the Evangelist* (late 15th century).

In Chapel XXV is *St Monica founding the Augustinian Order* (second half of the 15th century), attributed to Francesco Botticini.

In Chapel XXVI is the *Virgin and Child Enthroned with Sts Thomas and Peter* (1482), by Cosimo Rosselli.

Chapel XXVII is the Corbinelli Chapel (1492), designed by Andrea Sansovino. Portrayed on the altar-frontal is a *Pietà with the Virgin and St John.*

In Chapel XXX is a *Virgin and Child Enthroned with Saints* (early 16th-century), by Raffaellino del Garbo.

In the left aisle are works by artists dating from the 16th to the 18th centuries. In Chapel XXXIV is a *Virgin with St Ann and other Saints,* by Michele and Ridolfo del Ghirlandaio (first half of the 16th century).

In Chapel XXXV is *St Thomas of Villanova distributing alms* (1625), by Rutilio Manetti, and in Chapel XXXVI-II is a *Resurrection* (1537), by Pier Francesco Foschi.

Vestibule and sacristy. We enter the vestibule from a door beneath the organ. The attractive barrel-vaulted ceiling is caissoned and supported by twelve Corinthian columns. It was made by Cronaca between 1492 and 1494 to a design by Giuliano da Sangallo.

The vestibule leads into the sacristy, also designed by Giuliano da Sangallo (1489-1492). This is one of the major 15th-century, Florentine architectural works, strongly influenced by Brunelleschi. On the altar opposite the entrance is a painting of *St Fiacre healing the sick* (1596), by Alessandro Allori.

Refectory. To the left of the church, at no. 29, is the entrance to the 14th-century refectory of the old monastery. The ceiling has truss beams and the windows have Gothic mullions. On the wall is a *fresco* dating from the second half of the 14th century, attributed to Orcagna. Above is an impressive *Crucifixion with Mary and the pious women*, unfortunately much damaged.

Housed in this large room is a collection of *sculptures, architectural stonework and engraved stone,* dating from the pre-Romanesque period to the late 15th century. They were donated to the city council in 1946 by the antiquarian Salvatore Romano. *Leaving Piazza Santo Spirito,*

The sacristy, built in 1489-92 to a design by Giuliano da Sangallo.

The bell tower of Santo Spirito built by Baccio d'Agnolo in 1503.

View of the Carraia bridge from Lungarno Acciaiuoli.

we take the street to the right of the façade of the church (Via del Presto di San Martino) and, following Via de' Coverelli, we go around the apse of the church. From here we reach the Lungarno Guicciardini and turn left in the direction of Ponte alla Carraia.

From the Lungarno we enjoy an excellent view of the buildings along the river. At no. 7 is Palazzo Guicciardini, rebuilt in the 17th century and then again in the 19th century by Giuseppe Poggi. At no. 9, the 16th-century Palazzo Lanfredini has a façade decorated with graffito by Andrea Feltrini (1477-1548).

PONTE ALLA CARRAIA

Linking Piazza Nazario Sauro and Piazza Goldoni, the Carraia Bridge was first built in 1218, the second bridge over the river after Ponte Vecchio. In 1304, it collapsed under the weight of a crowd that

was watching a performance from it: in fact, from the 13th century on, the section of river between the Santa Trìnita and Carraia bridges was often the scene of water festivals and entertainments. On other occasions the bridge was swept away by the river in flood (1274, 1333 and 1557). After this last disaster, it was rebuilt by Bartolomeo Ammannati (beginning in 1559), who made the structure so solid that it resisted the flood waters for 385 years. In 1944, it was blown up by the retreating Germans, as were all the bridges with the exception of Ponte Vecchio.

It was rebuilt in 1948 to a design by architect Ettore Fagiuoli.

On the other side of the bridge, we turn to the right along Lungarno Corsini. At no. 10 is the grand architectural structure of Palazzo Corsini.

PALAZZO CORSINI

Building was begun under the direction of Pier Francesco Silvani in 1648, then completed after his death by Alfonso Parigi, Pietro Tacca and Anton Maria Ferri.

The design is in three parts, the central section consisting of a two-storey loggia, set back in relation to the rest of the structure. The roof of the building is enhanced by a

The Carraia bridge from Lungarno Soderini.

Thomas Patch, View of the Arno and the Bridge of Santa Trìnita, *Museum of 'Firenze com'era'.*

large balcony, decorated with numerous statues.

The palazzo houses the Corsini Gallery — one of the most important private art collections in Florence. It may only be visited on request.

Corsini Gallery. Started in 1765 by Lorenzo Corsini, the collection contains 14th- and 15th-century master-pieces by Antonello da Messina, Filippino Lippi and the workshop of Luca Signorelli, as well as numer-ous paintings by Italian and foreign artists of the 17th and 18th centuries.

The gallery also houses a valuable collection of 17th-century *furniture* and *deco-rations.*

Just past Palazzo Corsini, the narrow vicolo del Parioncino takes us through to Via del Parione. Crossing this we reach Via del Purgatorio and turning to the left we enter the little triangular Piazzetta de' Rucellai.

Designed by Leon Battista Alberti, the piazza is a gem of Renaissance architecture — the practical application of the theories expounded by this famous humanist in his Latin treatise, De re Ædificatoria *("Architec-ture"). Facing the piazza are the Palazzo Rucellai (oppo-site, on Via della Vigna), and the Rucellai Loggia to the right.*

PALAZZO AND LOGGIA RUCELLAI

Constructed in various phases (from 1455 to the end of the 15th century) and incorporat-ing several pre-existing build-ings, the palazzo is a perfect

John Thomas Serres, View from the Carraia bridge, *Horne Museum.*

The gallery of the antique dealer, Bellini, built by Alfredo Coppedè at the beginning of the 20th century.

Work on Palazzo Corsini was begun in 1648 by Pier Francesco Silvani and was completed by Alfonso Parigi, Pietro Tacca and Anton Maria Ferri.

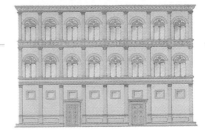

Top, the façade of Palazzo Ruccellai in a reconstruction. Above, a detail of the façade built by Bernardo Rossellino to a design of Leon Battista Alberti. The frieze is decorated with the emblems of Giovanni Rucellai, billowing sails, and of the Medici family, rings with diamonds and feathers.

example of the new role the residences of nobility represented in the city. The defensive element is no longer necessary and the structure now has a purely civil function, blending harmoniously into its urban surroundings. It is not just the power of the family that these palaces now communicate, but also their dignity and decorum. Hence the extraordinary elegance of the façade – with its three horizontal entablatures and three orders with pilasters – built between 1455 and 1458 by Alberti's pupil, Bernardo Rossellino.

The palazzo now houses the archive of the long-standing Florentine photographic business, Alinari. On the ground floor is the *Museum of the History of Photography*, which displays both a permanent collection of

photographic equipment as well as temporary exhibitions.

Designed by Alberti and completed by Rossellino, the graceful loggia (1463-1466) served a social function, the setting for important family events, banquets and festivities.

Continuing along Via della Vigna Nuova to the right we reach the junction with Via della Spada and Via Tornabuoni. From here we return to Piazza del Duomo along Via Strozzi, crossing Piazza della Repubblica and turning left into Via Roma, or by turning left towards Via Rondinelli and then turning right into Via Cerretani.

Carlo Lorenzini, better known by his pen-name Collodi, author of the immortal Pinocchio, lived in the palazzo at no. 7 Via Rondinelli.

Centre page, the palazzo on the corner of Via della Vigna Nuova and Via del Parione.

Right, the Rucellai loggia; the three arches were walled up in 1677 and were re-opened and fitted with glass in 1963.

The River Arno

flows onto the ground, in his left. On several occasions however, the Arno has been overly generous with its supply of water, causing disastrous floods.

The most recent was November 4, 1966 when the river burst its banks, submerging the city under a torrent of water which at some points reached a height of 15 feet above street level. Whirling currents swept cars and tree trunks around the cathedral, and once the water had receded, streets and squares remained covered with mud for more than a month. Some 12,000 families were hit by the flood and 5,000 found themselves homeless.

Dreadful damage had been done to churches, houses, libraries and

The Arno might flow beneath Ponte Vecchio in Florence, but it can also be found in Abruzzo, Lombardy and Trentino. Indeed, there is more than one river with this name in Italy, for the ancient, original meaning of the word, found throughout the Mediterranean area, was *àlveus*, meaning 'the bed of a stream'.

The most famous is, of course, the Florentine Arno, which not only gave birth to the city itself, but also favoured its development. In 1893, when the portico of Piazza della Repubblica was being built, a small marble shrine dating from the 2nd century AD was found, representing the Arno as a god in the form of a sturdy old man, bare-chested and holding a reed in his right hand and a vase from which water

palazzi, as could be seen from the dramatic pictures which the entire world watched in horror, stimulating a spon-

together, usually occurring in the autumn months and in particular, November. During an exceptionally wet August in 1547, however, the Arno deposited an olive tree and a fig tree on Ponte Vecchio, and a huge walnut tree in Piazza San Firenze.

The floods should be considered as unfortunate exceptions to an otherwise tranquil coexistence. Indeed for centuries the Arno has provided Florence with a useful source of energy for grain and fulling

taneous and humanitarian response from people everywhere.

mills. It also gave the city a vital trade route and a useful deposit of sand.

This was not the first time the Arno had chosen November 4th to flood Florence. Already on the same date in 1333, as the medieval historian, Giovanni Villani wrote, the river had "left the city and all the streets and houses and shops on the ground floor, of which there were many in Florence, full of water and stinking mud which it took more than six months to get rid of". Since 1177 about sixty floods, some more serious than others, have been recorded al-

the days when the river water was still unpolluted, rare and tasty kinds of fish could be caught and eaten, such as the delicious lamprey which Boccaccio mentions in the *Decameron*. Not so long ago Florentines held picnics on the riverbanks with boat excursions and swimming parties.

In 1915, there were some ten bathing establishments along the river and even in the early 1960's members of a local swimming club (the *Rari Nantes* – 'occasional swimmers' – a name taken from a verse in Virgil's *Aeneid*) could still train in a fenced-off section of the river itself. Later though, as the Arno fell victim to pollution, it was abandoned by the city's inhabitants and ignored by the tourists, even though some vestige of its former role still exists in the Florentine rowing club, situated immediately beneath the gallery of the Uffizi. Hopes and plans for the river's recuperation are not lacking however: the purity of the water might be improved and along the banks a park could be made where one could sunbathe, walk, run or row but, most especially, enjoy Florence from an unusual and intriguing viewpoint awaiting rediscovery.

8. **Diverse Wanderings**

For the rather disdainful Florentines of the 13th century, the area covered by this itinerary was merely a *"Civitas nova"* — a new town, although it was almost entirely enclosed within the city walls built between 1172-1175 (along the line of Via de' Pucci, Via Bufalini, Via Sant'Egidio) and later again by the 14th-century walls which extended as far as the present inner ring road. This was the area – and also the epoch – most marked by economic growth in Florence, which Dante found so vulgar with its "new people and quick gain," which "pride and intemperance have created" in those "citizens who are polluted now / by Campi, and Certaldo and Fegghine [Figline Valdarno]" (*Inf.*, XVI, 73-74; *Pd.*, XVI, 50-51). Some of these 'villains' remained, becoming an integral part of the social and urban structure, firmly entrenched with their own businesses and palazzi still evident in the densely populated areas around Borgo Pinti and Borgo Àlbizzi.

Less aristocratic are the origins of the area around the church of Sant'Ambrogio, even today a lively, working class quarter. Victim of a 'slum clearance' programmed just before World War II, the neighbourhood is still ani-

Glazed and coloured tondo on the Loggia del Pesce (old fish market). Below, one of the herms of famous literary figures which decorate the façade of Palazzo Valori.

Opposite page, right, fragment of a fresco by Pietro Gerini, The Risen Christ.

mated by Piazza dei Ciompi's Flea Market, as well as Piazza Ghiberti's food market — a smaller version of the one in San Lorenzo.

Decidedly aristocratic, on the other hand, is the adjacent neighbourhood of Piazza d'Azeglio, emerging in the late 19th century in an area that had remained undeveloped for 500 years, as the expansion foreseen by the ambitious extension of the city walls in the 14th century failed to take place. Its position was, in fact, somewhat unusual: lying between the walls and the town center it was, at one and the same time, protected yet on the outskirts, as can still be seen from the presence of the various monasteries and convents. In the area where today one can never find parking space, "horses were taken to be broken and ropemakers made ropes," or one would find "fields of cabbage, lettuce and celery, spread out like carpets". Instead of petrol and diesel fumes, pollution was created around Borgo Pinti by the stench from tallow candle factories which "boiled animal fat in cauldrons and then poured it into tin moulds". Borgo La Croce, instead, "was the place where paintmakers and carpenters went to make their varnishes and polishes, because it was prohibited in the city".

216

The large coat of arms of Leo X by Baccio d'Agnolo, which decorates Palazzo Pucci on the corner of Via de' Servi.

Palazzo Pucci (above) was made by uniting three buildings of different periods; the work was coordinated by Paolo Falconieri during the second half of the 17th century. The central section dates from the century before and was probably designed by Ammannati.

From the north side of the cathedral, almost immediately opposite the 'Porta della Mandorla' (☛ p. 24), we take Via Ricasoli. Near the beginning of the street, on the left, is the neo-classical façade of the Niccolini Theatre. Further ahead, on the corner of Via de' Biffi, is the huge Palazzo Ricasoli, also home to Baron Bettino, prime minister of the Kingdom of Italy when Florence was capital.

The section of the street between Via de' Biffi and Via de' Pucci is marked by the Tabernacle of the Five Lamps, with a fresco by the workshop of Cosimo Rosselli (1439-1507).

We now turn right into Via de' Pucci: here, on the left hand side, over a hundred windows along the entire section between Via Ricasoli and Via de' Servi cover the façade of the group of buildings still owned and occupied by the Pucci family. Three sections

are evident, each representing a different period in the history of the family. In the second half of the 17th century, the various structures were unified and coordinated by Paolo Falconieri; the most important, however, is the 16th-century central palazzo with its impressive vertical sequence of doorway, serliana and balcony, attributed to Ammannati.

Sculpted by Baccio d'Agnolo, the massive coat of arms of Pope Leo X adorns the

The tabernacle of the five lamps is in Via Ricasoli close to the corner of Via de' Pucci. It is decorated with a Virgin and Child, two angels and saints. The arrangement and painting are by the workshop of Cosimo Rosselli (15th century). Above, plaque commemorating Lorenzo Ghiberti whose workshop was in Via Bufalini.

corner of *Via dei Servi.*

We now continue along *Via Bufalini. On the left is a series of important and attractive palazzi, excellently restored by the Cassa di Risparmio di Firenze, a bank which also has its offices there. A plaque at no. 1, on the right, records that "Lorenzo Ghiberti had his workshop*

The hospital of Santa Maria Nuova, left wing. Right, fragment of a fresco by Pietro Gerini, The Risen Christ.

here" at the time when he modelled the Baptistery doors.

Via Bufalini opens onto Piazza Santa Maria Nuova where, on the left, we see the portico of the hospital of the same name.

HOSPITAL OF SANTA MARIA NUOVA

According to Boccaccio, Folco Portinari – the father of Dante's Beatrice – was "one of the most distinguished citizens, and

8. Diverse wanderings

WORTH SEEING

The Museum of 'Firenze Com'era'

Church of Santa Maria dei Pazzi

Synagogue

Flea Market

Casa Buonarroti

A model of Florence at the time of Imperial Rome, made for an exhibition held in the museum of 'Firenze Com'era' (1996-1997). Below, ceramic vase from the late Neolithic necropolis of Ponte San Pietro near Viterbo, and a detail of a Neolithic wall painting from the Grotto di Badisco in Otranto.

Many items in the Museum of 'Firenze Com'era' are not of great economic value, but provide excellent documentation of the development of the city of Florence and surrounding area. Opposite page, above, Giovanni Signorini (first half of the 19th century) View of Florence. Below right, lunette with a view of the Medici villa, La Peggio. The painter, of Flemish origin, was commissioned by the Medici to paint the exterior view of all their grand ducal residences.

blessed with many possessions". In 1288, he had a small hospital built on some land that he owned, just outside the city walls. Gradually it grew in size and prestige, ultimately becoming the most important in the city. Facing onto the piazza is the characteristic late 16th-century loggia, designed by Buontalenti and built by Giulio Parigi. The wing on the left, however, was not added until 1960 by Nello Bemporad.

Inside, the functional modernity of a working hospital coexists with the remaining elements of the original structure: the early 15th-century cloisters and the church of Sant'Egidio. The latter contains 17th-century *paintings,* and a marble *tabernacle* (1450), by Bernardo Rossellino, with a door by Lorenzo Ghiberti.

The building on the other side of the piazza was originally the monastery of the Oblate. Founded in the late 14th century on the ruins of an old brick-yard, it was linked to the hospital of Santa Maria Nuova by an underground passage in 1625 (the ventilation grates

can be seen in the paving of the square). In 1780, the monastery was used as a home for convalescent women. Today, it serves a cultural function, housing the city's historical library and archive, the Museum of Prehistory, and the Historical Topographical Museum "Firenze Com'Era".

The entrance to the Museum of Prehistory is from Via Sant'Egidio, the continuation of Via Bufalini.

MUSEUM OF PREHISTORY

The Museo di Preistoria promises a journey through both time and space, from the early Stone Age up through later periods of prehistory, from Tuscany to North America. The collection includes tools made from stone and bone, ceramics, and copper and bronze weapons.

Carefully preserved and displayed as they were in the 19th-century, the collections could be described as providing a 'history of prehistory'. Items represent some of the earliest paleo-ethnological discoveries and come from sites – such as Le Moustier and La Madeleine in Southern France – which have given their name to fundamental typologies and classifications.

Leaving the museum, we return along Via Sant'Egidio and turn left into Via Folco Portinari, which leads us into Via dell'Oriuolo. At no. 24 is the entrance to the Topographical Museum 'Firenze Com'era'.

Topographical Museum 'Firenze Com'era'

With its vast collection of maps, prints, drawings and paintings, the topographical museum reconstructs the development and urban transformation of Florence from the time of the Renaissance to the end of the 19th century.

Important items include: the famous *Chain Map* with a panorama of the city around 1470; the beautiful *lunettes* by Giusto Utens (1599) cataloguing the Medici villas and gardens; the 18th-century *views of the city*, by Zocchi; Telemaco Signorini's *watercolours*; evocative images of the ghetto, destroyed during the 'slum clearance' of 1885.

From the museum we continue left along Via dell'Oriuolo to the junction with Borgo Pinti on the left. When still a "strada nuova," Borgo Pinti led away from the network of streets at San Pier Maggiore into the countryside, and it maintained its winding rural course even when palazzi and churches were built along both sides.

At no. 13 is the 17th-century Palazzo Roffia; decorating the façade is Florence's first-ever wrought iron balcony. The most impressive sculptures to be cast in Florence – from the equestrian statue of Cosimo I in Piazza Signoria, to the statue of Ferdinando I now in Madrid – passed through the vast doorway of no. 24. Behind this door was, in fact, the

foundry where Giambologna (who also lived nearby in Palazzo Quaratesi*), Pietro Tacca and later Lorenzo Lippi, Matteo Rosselli and Giovan Battista Foggini all worked.*

Palazzo Caccini, *at no. 33, still has the remains of a garden where botanist Matteo Caccini experimented with the cultivation of exotic flowers. At no. 56, past the side of the* church of Santa Maria a Candeli *(façade on Via dei Pilastri), is the* neo-classical Liceo Imperiale, *with two columns and large semi-circular windows, commissioned by Napoleon.*

Just before the junction with Via della Colonna, the church of Santa Maria Maddalena de' Pazzi is on the right.

Santa Maria Maddalena de' Pazzi

"Since there is already a building and house built there for the women who call themselves Repentant or Converted."... So reads the document, dated November 10, 1257, which mentions the convent for the first time. Over 200 years later, in

Thomas Patch, View of the Arno and Ponte Santa Trinita. *Museum of 'Firenze Com'era'.*

Borgo Pinti: the doorway of Palazzo Roffia (17th century), with the first wrought iron balcony to be made in Florence.

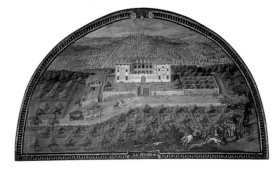

The cloister of Santa Maria Maddalena de' Pazzi (above) in front of the church. Designed by Giuliano da Sangallo, the structure, built on the site of a 13th-century convent, was the first important work of this renowned Renaissance artist (1479). Right, the interior of the church, redecorated during the second half of the 17th century, maintaining the original design. Above right, the Crucifixion (1493-1496), a luminescent fresco by Pietro Perugino who decorated the capitulary room of the convent. Below, Piazza D'Azeglio is a typical example of 19th-century urban planning which lead to the demolition of the city walls and the development of middle-class residential areas around the new suburban avenues.

1479, Giuliano da Sangallo was appointed to rebuild the complex.

The architect, who just a few months later was to be commissioned by Lorenzo the Magnificent to design the villa at Poggio a Caiano, devised an original layout for the church which was subsequently much copied. The single nave had a series of side chapels based on the

niches which, in other churches such as San Marco, contained altars.

According to Vasari, the elegant cloister in front of the church with its Ionic arcading, was also a prototype, representing Sangallo's first complete work. The Renaissance interior was not altered by the sensitive restoration carried out in the second half of the 17th century. Sumptuously decorated in marble, gilded bronze and columns of Sicilian jasper, the main chapel is of particular note: one of the greatest examples of baroque architecture in Florence, it was

made between 1677 and 1685 by Ciro Ferri.

From the sacristy we enter the old chapter house, with a large fresco of the *Crucifixion* (1493-1496), by Perugino. In the background, behind the main figures, is a wonderful open landscape.

Leaving the cloister we continue to the right, following Via della Colonna in the same direction until we reach Piazza d'Azeglio. This part of the street was opened between 1865 and 1869, when the piazza was being built, by cutting through the convent of Santa Maria Maddalena. The long series of open arches now forming one of the walls around the Michelangelo High School indicates the alteration.

Piazza D'Azeglio is a swath of green, created in 1870 by transforming the old 'Mattonaia orchards' into a Romantic park, modelled on the example of English squares. Surrounded by grandly elegant, residences, Palazzo Uzielli *at*

The Cascine Park

"Oh, for a carriage ride through the Cascine in springtime". The very thought of such a pleasure once caused Gian Gastone, the last of the Medici, to feel profoundly homesick while on a protracted visit to Bohemia. An aristocratic prerogative at the time, it was soon to be democratized by the Lorraine dukes. Thus after fulfilling various functions, this pleasant, leafy expanse – two miles long and covering an area of 290 acres – was finally destined to become a public park.

During the Middle Ages it had been a fluvial island – known as the 'Island Estate' – surrounded by the Arno, the Mugnone and the canal which fed the mills at Ognissanti. Purchased by Alessandro de' Medici, the first duke of Florence, the land was used for raising dairy cattle thus giving the area its name (*cascine* means dairy farm). Under Cosimo I, the fields were planted with oaks, ilexes, maples, and elms, becoming a garden where various species of trees and shrubs were cultivated. This aspect continued to be developed as part of the interest in scientific and botanical research which had become an important part of Florentine culture. As new specimens, such as plane trees, limes and chestnuts, became acclimatized there, the Cascine gradually developed from a farm to a park for pleasant walks and drives.

In 1737 it became the property of the Lorraine dinasty, and Pietro Leopoldo subsequently opened it to the public and affirmed its new identity by having suitable buildings made there. In 1787, he commissioned Giuseppe Manetti to build a rural residence for the Grand Duke's court. This grand arcaded building (now housing the Faculties of Agriculture and Forestry) was decorated with medallions of cows' heads as a reminder of the area's original function. Avenues and pathways were laid out and some stylish Neoclassical elements were added: little 'temples' for storing the gardeners' tools, ice-houses in the form of pyramids, fountains with masks including the Narcissus fountain where Percy Bysshe Shelley wrote the *Ode to the West Wind*. During the 19th century, the Cascine became a favorite spot for important celebrations, often with firework displays (a large collection of paintings representing these can be seen in the *Firenze Com'era* Museum: ☞ p. 218). For the Florentine aristocracy, the afternoon carriage ride around the Cascine was absolutely *de rigeur* before a visit to the Caffè Doney on Via Tornabuoni. The original aspect of the area as an island surrounded by river was recalled in 1870 when the city council allowed the Maharajah of Kolhapur, Raiaram Cuttraputti, who had died in Florence while returning to India from England, to be cremated at the junction of the two rivers – the Mugnone and the Arno – as required by Indian ritual. This unusual event is recorded by a pagoda-shaped monument with a bust of the Maharajah (1874) by the English sculptor, Fuller.

The synagogue in Via Farini (1872-1874), in Byzantine-Moorish style. Below left, of Venetian origin (1717) are the Rimonìm, Atarà and Simàn, the items used to cover the Old Testament, kept in the synagogue museum.

no. 3 – with its Liberty reinterpretation of Renaissance principles – was highly controversial when it was built by Paolo Emilio Andrée in 1904.

From the piazza we continue along Via Farini to the Synagogue, *built between 1872 and 1874 in Moorish-Byzantine style, rather originally combined with the typically Florentine feature of 'striped' decorative stonework. Attached to the Synagogue is the* Jewish Museum *of Florence.*

We now turn left into Via dei Pilastri, continuing until we reach the church of Sant'Ambrogio.

CHURCH OF SANT'AMBROGIO

It was 1001 when Vuido di Andrea sold a property to Rainerio di Raimneto, "in a place known as Pietrapiana, near the church of Sant'Ambrogio," which had probably been founded at the time of Lombard rule and belonged to the Bishop of Milan. The church was completely rebuilt in 1266 and from the 15th century on was altered and

Palazzo Uzielli in Piazza D'Azeglio, an unusual architectural mixture combining 16th-century features with features typical of Art-Decò. Below, the façade of the church of Sant'Ambrogio, rebuilt in gothic style at the end of the 19th century. The church has an extremely long history: built in the 7th-8th century, it was rebuilt in the second half of the 13th century and later altered on several occasions. As well as some important paintings, the church has a splendid marble shrine by Mino da Fiesole. Opposite page, above, the market of Sant'Ambrogio, a smaller version of its contemporary, the central market.

renovated several times.

The Gothic façade dates to 1888, but the right side of the church on Via Pietrapiana, with pointed mullioned windows, is original.

The interior has a single nave. The series of 15th-century altars has no connecting element and repeats Michelozzo's design as seen in San Marco and the Rotonda dell'Annunziata. In the 18th century, Giovan Battista Foggini joined the entrance arch of the presbytery to the side chapels in an extremely elegant and discreet manner.

The altars contain paintings dating from the 14th to the 16th centuries: one of the loveliest is the *Saints and Angels,* by Alessio Baldovinetti (1425-1499) in the first chapel on the left. The marble *tabernacle* (1481-1483) in the Chapel of Miracles (to the left of the main chapel) is a masterpiece by Mino da Fiesole. Preserved here is a chalice which reputedly caused a miraculous event, illustrated by Cosimo Rosselli in the *fresco* on the far wall. This painting also shows the façade and surroundings of the church as they were in the late 15th century.

Leaving the church, a short deviation to the left leads to Via de' Macci; from here, the first street to the left (Via del Verrocchio) takes us to Piazza

Ghiberti, with its 19th-century market hall in the center. The market of Sant'Ambrogio *is a smaller version of the city's* Central Market (☞ p.52). Off *the usual tourist track, the market is still organized in traditional fashion, with the fruit and vegetable stalls around the outside (those selling fresh produce directly from the farm are on the right side, looking at the front).*

Retracing our steps, we take Via Pietrapiana (Mino da Fiesole lived and died at Palazzo Francioni-Pampaloni, no. 7), *until we reach Piazza dei Ciompi and the Flea Market (a plaque above the door at no. 11 tells us that "This was the house of Lorenzo Ghiberti, of the [Baptistery] doors").*

FLEA MARKET

Mussolini described the group of medieval houses which filled this square as "picturesquely filthy", only worth handing over to "His Majesty the pickaxe". Thus in 1936 the buildings were demolished as part of the urban renewal which took place in the Santa Croce area, and were replaced in the 1960s by the equally picturesque 'flea market', where old and antique items are sold.

Loggia del Pesce. Designed by Vasari, the Loggia (1567) is decorated with coloured tondi of the Grand

Dukes and marine and fishing subjects. It stood in the Piazza del Mercato Vecchio (today's Piazza della Repubblica) until the 'urban renewal policy' of the 19th century. For several decades it was stored, in pieces, in the monastery of San Marco. In 1955, the Loggia del Pesce was reconstructed where we see it now, on the north side of the Piazza dei Ciompi.

After visiting the market, we continue along Via Buonar-

The Flea Market, (above) and one of the attractive 'stalls' below. On the north side of the market is the Loggia del Pesce. Until the 'clearance' undertaken in the 19th century, the structure was in the Piazza of the Old Market (now Piazza della Repubblica). Left, a glazed tondo on the loggia.

Florentine Cookery -2-

Penne 'strascicate'.

Today it is still possible to enjoy the Florentine cuisine already described (☛ p. 53). Many excellent restaurants and trattorie have skillfully adapted the old, traditional recipes, lightening or embellishing them: respect for tradition does not exclude creative interpretation and is no longer a constraint enforced by poverty. Here are some suggestions for a typical menu.

The appetizers or *antipasti* might include *crostini* with liver spread as well as assorted salamis and sausages: Tuscan salami, ham or *prosciutto* from the Casentino (this has a saltier flavour than other famous Italian hams such as Parma and San Daniele) and delicious *finocchiona* (salami flavoured with fennel seeds), which is known as *sbriciolona* when it has not been left to season. In summertime, instead, *panzanella* is a refreshing starter. This simple, peasant dish is made by soaking dry homemade bread in water, then literally wringing it out and crumbling it until quite fine. It is then mixed with chopped

seasonal vegetables (... ter chicory, fresh ton... toes, cucumber, gre... onions etc.), season... with oil, vinegar, salt a... pepper and garnish... with fresh basil leaves.... November, *fettunta* is mo... with newly-pressed olive oil: sli... of unsalted country bread ... grilled on both sides (if po... ble on an open fire), rubbed with clo... of garlic and topped with generous he... ings of tangy new oil.

One of the most characteristic first cou... es, and a direct result of the tasty inve... tiveness found in tratto... kitchens, is *penne stra...* cate*: the pasta is stirr... over a medium flame v... meat sauce, a drop of n... and fresh Parmes... cheese.

Two of the most clas... soups have a true coun... flavour: *ribollita* (a ve... etable soup with slices... stale, unsalted bre... which soak into it; t... soup gains in flavour c... consistency if it is left... stand and reheated several times) a... *pappa al pomodoro* (tomato bre... soup), made by leaving stale bread... slowly soften, becoming a pulp, in...

Olive oil (centre page... the supreme Tuscan product used in dishe... such as vegetable sou... (left) and the renown... 'ribollita'. Opposite page, below right, a t... stall: customers are never kept waiting...Right, typic... Lenten biscuits.

Ham from the Casentino is enjoyed by those who prefer a more highly flavoured product than the rivals' Parma and San Daniele. Those who enjoy particularly strong tastes should try the boar ham (in the centre of the drawing).

saucepan with ripe tomatoes, water, garlic and pepper. *Pappardelle* served with rich hare or boar sauce are, instead, reminiscent of hunting days.

As far as meat is concerned, steak rules supreme, especially when the beef is derived from the Chianina breed (raised in the Chiana valley, near to Arezzo); roast pork (a loin, left on the bone and cooked in the oven) is also exquisite however. Often quite subtle and surprising are the more ordinary, everyday dishes such as *spezzatino* or stew with potatoes cooked in it, or *lesso rifatto* (beef, boiled then sliced and tossed in a frying pan with oil, tomatoes, garlic and plenty of onions).

Almost impossible to find today as it requires poultry of the highest quality, free-range and home-bred, is the mythical and magnificent *cibrèo* — a kind of stew made with the less-tempting parts of the chicken or fowl (neck, comb, feet, gizzard and liver) cooked slowly together *in bianco* (without tomatoes), then bound with a sauce made of eggs and lemon juice.

Eternal and essential accompaniment to all meals are beans (Florentines prefer the small white *cannellini* beans). These are served simply boiled or *all'uccelletto* — tossed in a saucepan, after being cooked, with garlic cloves fried with sage leaves and a bit of tomato.

In spring, artichokes are at their absolute best. Some Tuscan varieties (such as the famous *morellini*, small and purple) are so tender and tasty that they can be eaten raw, simply dipped in oil, salt and pepper. They are also exquisite when fried.

Among the cakes and sweets associated with specific festivals, one finds the so-called *schiacciata alla Fiorentina* — a deliciously light kind of spongecake flavoured with lemon or orange, made at carnival time. Unusual little chocolate biscuits in the shape of the letters of the alphabet, known as *quaresimali*, are made during Lent.

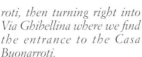

Casa Buonarroti, completed by Michelangelo the younger in 1612, represents the combination of several properties belonging to the family; the master who sculpted the David *lived here for almost ten years. Above, the 'Angel' room and a bust of the great artist attributed to Giambologna. Below, the* Madonna della Scala, *an early work by Michelangelo.*

roti, then turning right into Via Ghibellina where we find the entrance to the Casa Buonarroti.

CASA BUONARROTI

"A dignified house in the city is quite honourable, because we are indeed citizens of most noble descent". In 1546, Michelangelo expressed this wish to his nephew, Leonardo, though the house was not to be entirely finished until 1612, when Michelangelo the Younger made a single house out of several family properties. His famous great-uncle had lived in one of these from 1516 to 1525.

After the death of Cosimo Buonarroti in 1859, the house and collection of art and documents which had been accumulated by the family over the centuries was opened to the public.

In 1965, the Casa Buonarroti was designated as an institute for study and research into the works of Michelangelo, the history of the family and its various collections. The museum also holds temporary exhibitions and has pub-

lished all Michelangelo's papers, as well as the artist's *corpus* of drawings.

In Room 1, on the ground floor, is a *bust of Michelangelo,* probably by Giambologna. The permanent exhibition continues in Rooms 2-5; Room 6 houses various *portraits of Michelangelo*, while the next three rooms contain the artistic and archaeological collections of the family.

On the first floor, some works by Michelangelo are displayed, while other items here commemorate the great artist. The marble *Battle of the Centaurs,* made before 1492, anticipates his *non finito* style, while the *Madonna della Scala* (1492) demonstrates his transition from Donatello's technique and influence to the development of his own individual artistic style.

The *model of the façade of San Lorenzo* is a representation in wood of Michelangelo's design for the decoration, and the *model for a river god* was a figure almost certainly intended for the New Sacristy of San Lorenzo. These plans were never implemented.

Between 1615 and 1637, the most important artists of the day created the *Memorials to Michelangelo* exhibited in the next four rooms. The most interesting is the so-called *gallery*, with a tiled floor in coloured maiolica and beautifully inlaid doors.

Michelangelo the Youn-

ger's study was carved out of the wall separating the two rooms. The library houses some *sketches* by Michelangelo, and is decorated with *frescoes* portraying important Tuscan figures, by Matteo Rosselli, Cecco Bravo and Domenico Pugliani.

Leaving the museum, we turn right along Via Ghibellina where we see various important palazzi: at no. 73, the majestic Palazzo Guicciardini, *restored in 1696; at no. 81 is* Palazzo Sebregondi; *at no. 83, the palazzo where Emilio De Fabris – the architect who designed the façade of the cathedral – died; at no. 87 is* Palazzo Jacometti-Ciofi, *built in the early 18th century.*

Crossing Via Verdi, we continue along Via Ghibellina and turn right into Via Matteo Palmieri (the corner with the imposing 14th-century Palazzo Quaratesi), *which takes us into* Piazza San Pier Maggiore. *Bor-*

go degli Àlbizzi runs along the north (far side) of the square.

PIAZZA SAN PIER MAGGIORE

The bishops of Florence, after being nominated but before taking up residence in Piazza San Giovanni, traditionally entered the city by the San Piero gate, and stayed for one night in the monastery attached to the church which was here. Demolished in 1784 on the orders of Grand Duke Pietro Leopoldo, all that remains is part of the façade commissioned in 1638 from Matteo Nigetti by Luca Àlbizzi. The two rows of arches at the sides were filled in and now house some shops, while

The west side of Piazza San Pier Maggiore. In the foreground are the corbels of Palazzo Corbizzi, flanked by the 14th-century Donati tower at the beginning of Via Matteo Palmieri. Below, the San Piero arch which leads to the junction of Via dell'Oriuolo, Borgo Pinti and Via San'Egidio. Beneath the arch are shops and a characteristic wine shop. The two lateral arches, now bricked up, of what was once the church of San Pier Maggiore also house shops (below). The church, one of the oldest in Florence, was demolished on the orders of grand duke Pietro Leopoldo in 1784. The new bishops of Florence used to stay in the monastery here on entering the city by the nearby San Piero gate, to prepare themselves for the ceremonial entrance to the bishop's palace in Piazza San Giovanni.

A view of Borgo degli Albizzi and the road leading to the old San Piero gate, an extension of the decumanus which crossed Roman Florence. There are numerous noble residences along this road. Below right, the 16th-century doorway of Palazzo Ramirez de Montalvo, designed by Bartolomeo Ammannati for a Spanish aristocrat in the retinue of Eleonora di Toledo, wife of Cosimo I. Note the attractive graffito work on the façade, recently restored. Below, one of the herms of famous literary figures which decorate the façade of Palazzo Valori. With little respect for the famous personages represented, the townsfolk renamed the building Palazzo dei Visacci (mugs).

The race of the barbary horses took place along Borgo degli Albizzi on the feast day of Saint John the Baptist, the city's patron saint (24th June). Right, the grand duke's stand in a painting by Antonio Cioci (1792).

a street passes through what was once the central nave of one of Florence's oldest churches.

On the opposite side of the square is *Palazzo Corbizzi*, with its attractive corbels; alongside is the impressive *Donati Tower;* to the left of the church is the *Volta di San Piero,* an unusual little passageway housing several shops.

BORGO DEGLI ÀLBIZZI

Every year during the St John Palio, riderless Berber horses (locally known as *bàrberi*) raced along this street. Starting from Porta al Prato, the finishing post

was in Piazza San Pier Maggiore, representing an absolutely straight line through the center of the grid of Roman streets; Borgo degli Àlbizzi was thus the eastern extension of the main east-west axis.

The importance of the street is clear from the quality of the palazzi on both sides, many of which (no. 9, 11, 12 and 14) belonged to the Àlbizzi — a wealthy and important family and long-time rivals of the Medici. At no. 18 is *Palazzo Valori,* also known as *Palazzo dei Visacci* ("palace of the mugs") after the figures of famous writers and philosophers on the façade, such as Dante, Petrarch, Boccaccio, Monsignor Della Casa (who wrote a famous *Galateo*, or book of etiquette), Leon Battista Alberti and Francesco Guicciardini. Also important are the 16th-century *Palazzo Valori* (no. 23), *Palazzo Tenagli* (no. 27) and especially, with its wonderful graffito decoration, *Palazzo Matteucci Ramirez de Montalvo* (no. 26), designed by Bartolomeo Ammannati.

At the end of Borgo degli Àlbizzi we turn right into Via del Proconsolo, and from here we return once more to Piazza del Duomo.

Famous visitors of the past

"Coming over the Trìnita bridge and passing by Palazzo Strozzi, the traveller could well believe the year to be 1500," wrote Stendhal in 1827. Even a century earlier, however, Florence had formed part of the Grand Tour which represents the origins of modern "tourism".

By now, Florentines were more often hosts than visitors. They had travelled the world as merchants, bankers and explorers: the riches they had found and made, both intellectual and financial, had been brought home and invested in those monuments and institutions which have made Florence one of the greatest cultural centers in the world.

Since then, the city has developed and promoted a new resource, no longer based on goods and merchandise, but on memory — a history liberally appropriated and consumed by an endless gallery of illustrious personalities "If only you could see this place! One should live and die here," Mozart wrote to his mother. And according to Anatole France, "The God who made the hills of Florence was an artist. He was a goldsmith, an engraver of medals, a sculptor and a painter. He was a Florentine". Unfavourable reports are few and far between, though John Ruskin, for example, probably expected Florence to be more of an escape and refuge: "Of all the places I have visited, it is the most irritating and annoying for anyone whose spirit is inclined to meditation". For Henry James, on the contrary, in Florence "one can leave the modern world behind [...]. The predominant images we all have of old Florence, are of constant happiness, the feeling of something solid and human which offers us a way of living which is still plausible". Full enjoyment of the Florentine way of life was, however, reserved for the privileged few. Byron travelled with seven servants and five carriages. The Countess of Blessington recommended the use of a large wagon which would carry absolutely everything: a brass bedstead, armchairs and sofas, kitchen utensils "and lastly hatboxes for fragile headwear". In complete contrast, Johann G. Seume arrived in Florence on foot in 1802. However they arrived, the 19th-century travellers could stay in one of the city's few large hotels, or rather in the more tranquil *pensioni* or guesthouses, often run by foreigners: the *Hombert* in Palazzo Spini Feroni, for example, or the *Benois* on the Lungarno Serristori. It was also obligatory to frequent the correct cultural circles, from the reading room established by Giovan Pietro Vieusseux to the Duchess of Albany's 'salon'. In this golden age of tourism, the problem of crowded museums did not exist. Until 1831, one was quite free to bring easel, palette and brushes into the Uffizi to copy the masterpieces and even to remove them from the walls oneself, if necessary. Later on, a permit was required which also advised the artists and copiers to come "always in decent dress" and even prohibited "jackets and any other kind of indoor gown". Of all the various nationalities in the city, the 'English colony' was the most numerous. At the upper end of society, Sir Horace Mann, the English representative at the Tuscan court, complained, "Too many English turn up in this city of Florence! They will be the ruin of me if I have to invite all of them to lunch". At the lower end of the scale, 'English' had become a synonym for 'foreigner,' as revealed by the famous anecdote of the Florentine cab driver who commented, "A bunch of English arrived yesterday, but you couldn't tell if they were Russians or Germans".

9. **The Climb from San Niccolò to San Miniato**

Sculpted shrine in Costa Scarpuccia.

With the Belvedere Fort above and the Arno below, our route, covering a large and sweeping triangle on the edge of the city, begins and ends on one bank of the river but explores primarily the other. Its main characteristics are dictated by the natural lay of the land, formed by a modest but sudden climb upwards to reach what is, today, a vast terrace and delightful viewpoint.

The original function of the area was, however, as a bastion to overlook the city and control the population, evident from the 16th-century walls which enclosed the church of San Miniato and the fort built around the Palazzina di Belvedere. During the second half of the 19th century, the primarily scenic aspect of the area was enhanced and developed by the construction of the panoramic winding avenue of Viale dei Colli.

The viewpoint overlooks an area of the Oltrarno which was developed primarily during the 13th century. According to Stefani, these small hamlets had no need of protective walls, being "quite strong, as the houses

were all enclosed around the outer side by ditches and fences". Intense industrial and commercial activity took place along the bank of the river for many centuries. Just past Ponte alle Grazie was the 'Porticciola' (little harbour), still indicated today by a flight of stone steps. Tree trunks from the Casentino, sent downstream on the current, were collected here and boats loaded with rolls of wool, processed further upstream, were moored here. When these industries had ceased, gardens and embankments were created and the area assumed a primarily panoramic aspect and role as a viewpoint, culminating in the vast piazza above — more of a monument to tourism than to Michelangelo. From here, Romain Rolland, looking over the towers and domes of the city, confessed to feeling "pleasure mingled with regret, in enjoying these things. Why was I not born here? Why are we not Florentine?"

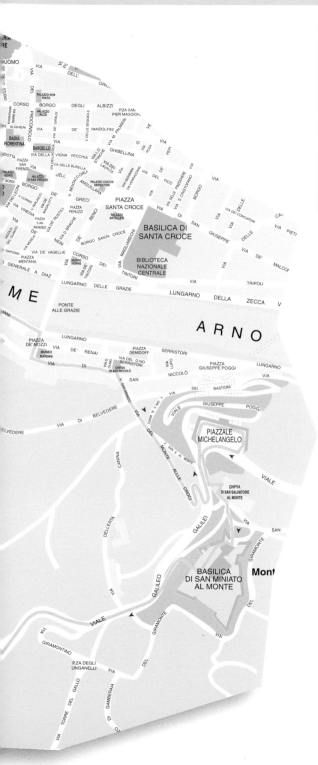

The loggia of the Uffizi Gallery seen from Lungarno Torrigiani. To the left is the portico of the Lungarno degli Archibusieri which houses the Vasari corridor.

Palazzo Torrigiani (below) designed by Baccio d'Agnolo and built by his son Domenico in the late 16th century. The Lutheran church faces onto the little garden which was opened to the public in 1901. Below, Ponte alle Grazie seen from the right bank of the Arno.

From Piazza del Duomo, we reach Ponte Vecchio by following Via Roma - Piazza della Repubblica - Via Calimala - Mercato Nuovo - Via Por Santa Maria (☞ p. 158) On the other side of the bridge, we turn left along the modern section of Via de' Bardi, built over the ruins left by German mines in 1944. We then follow Lungarno Torrigiani, enjoying an excellent view of the opposite side of the river, The Vasari corridor and the Ponte Vecchio.

Just before Ponte alle Grazie is a small public garden with a neo-Gothic Lutheran Church and the back of Palazzo Torrigiani on one side.

PONTE ALLE GRAZIE

During the Middle Ages, this stretch of the left bank was known as the 'San Niccolò sandbank', being subject to seasonal flooding. It was reached by crossing the Rubaconte Bridge (named after the *Podestà* who had it built in 1237). The bridge was later re-baptized as "alle Grazie," as, among the various

14th-century tabernacles built along the bridge, one contained a venerated image of *Madonna delle Grazie*, by the school of Giotto.

Destroyed by German bombs in 1944, it was rebuilt in its present form – with five arches and jutting pavements – in 1957.

Ambassadors, princes and cardinals all crossed the Rubaconte bridge as they travelled through Florence, often staying as guests of the Mozzi, a rich banking family connected to the Vatican court. Turning right into the piazza named after the family, we find Palazzo Mozzi at no. 2, one of the few palazzi in Florence to have maintained its typically 13th/14th-century characteristics, despite various alterations. Other aristocratic residences in this area are: Palazzo Lensi-Nencioni (no. 3); Palazzo Torrigiani-Nasi (no. 4), decorated with graffito; Palazzo Torrigiani (no. 5) (first half of the 16th century), by Domenico di Baccio d'Agnolo; and the Bardini Museum (at no. 1).

BARDINI MUSEUM

The windows of the neo-classical palazzo which houses the Museo Bardini are made from altars taken from a demolished church in Pistoia. The palace was built over the 13th-century church and monastery of San Ghirigoro della Pace, the only reminder of which is the plaque in Gothic script on the left side of the façade.

The building perfectly reflects the character of its creator and owner, Stefano Bardini (1836-1922). A talented and enthusiastic antique dealer at the end of the 19th and beginning of the 20th centuries, Bardini accrued an enormous and heterogeneous private collection which he bequeathed to the city of Florence on his death. **Ground floor.** There are nine rooms on the ground floor (Rooms 3, 4 and 5, housing the Corsi gallery, are presently closed). Displayed here are architectural fragments and exhibits of various kinds and different periods. Rooms 1 and 2 are dedicated to Etruscan and Roman art. Interesting parapets of medieval wells can be found in Room 6. In Room 7 is a figure of *Charity*, by Tino da Camaino; Room 8, columns, capitals and other architectural fragments. In Room 9 are a Roman porphyry basin and medieval stone fireplaces.

Mezzanine. (Room 10) Funerary monuments in stone, headstones, tablets and glazed terracotta by the school of Della Robbia are displayed here.

First floor. Large Indian rugs are hung along the stairs leading to the first floor. The items in the ten rooms here are further evidence of Bardini's eclectic tastes as a collector. Exhibits include: architectural elements such as doors and carved and painted wooden ceilings; furniture (in Room 16, a magnificent sacristy cupboard); thematic collections such as weapons in Room 13; medallions, coins and bronze bas-reliefs in Room 15; and musical instruments in Room 19. Especially important is the collection of mainly sacred works of art, both paintings and sculptures, by artists including Cenni di Francesco, Donatello, Benedetto da Maiano, Matteo Civitali, Giovanni di San Giovanni, Domenico Beccafumi.

Above centre, Donatello, Madonna and Child. *Above, the Neo-classic style building which houses the Bardini Museum in Piazza de' Mozzi. The cornices of the windows on the first floor are altar frontals taken from a church in Pistoia, demolished in the 19th century.*

Interesting sculptures are housed on the ground floor of the Bardini Museum. Above is a 12th-century lion from the base of a pulpit of a romanesque church. Left, Andrea della Robbia, altar frontal portraying the Madonna and Child *with cherubs and worshipping angels.*

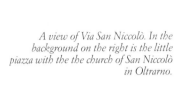

A view of Via San Niccolò. In the background on the right is the little piazza with the the church of San Niccolò in Oltrarno.

The gate of San Niccolò is in an attractive location on the banks of the Arno. Built in 1324, it is the only one to have maintained its original height. The others were partially 'buried' during the 19th century by the stone and material left by demolition of the 14th-century city walls. Below, the façade of San Niccolò Oltrarno seen from Via San Miniato. The San Miniato gate leads up to Via del Monte alle Croci which brings us to Viale dei Colli, just a few metres from Piazzale Michelangelo.

Piazza de' Mozzi leads into Via San Niccolò, which has all the characteristics typical of a medieval 'borgo'. The population growth in this area, particularly during the second half of the 13th century, was a direct result of the wool mills and manufacturing carried on slightly further upstream.

On either side of the street, as far as Via dell'Olmo, is an impressive series of palazzi. At no. 107, for example, is Palazzo Nasi *(with 15th-century graffito on the façade);* Palazzo Stiozzi-Ridolfi *at no. 99 has a 16th-century façade, attributed to Baccio d'Agnolo; at no. 87 is the* Quaratesi Tower-House; *at no. 56 is* Palazzo Demidoff, *altered in the 17th century by Giulio Parigi; at no. 54 is the 16th-century* Palazzo Vitelli. *Shortly after we come to the church of San Niccolò.*

CHURCH OF SAN NICCOLÒ

Mentioned in records as early as the 12th century, the church of San Niccolò was rebuilt in Gothic style during the second half of the 14th century. To the left of the doorway on the simple façade, a small, engraved marble hand on a stone plaque indicates the level the Arno reached here during the flood of 1557.

Interior. The church has a single nave with a truss beamed ceiling. Around the walls and on the inner façade are 16th-century stone altars and *paintings*, by Alessandro Allori, del Poppi, Empoli and Jacopo Coppi. There are remnants of 15th-century *frescoes* in altars I and II on the right. The wooden *Crucifix* in the second altar is attributed to Michelozzo, as is the *tabernacle* in the sacristy. The *fresco* in the lunette is possibly by Piero del Pollaiolo.

Michelangelo hid in a cell beneath the bell tower in 1530 when, after the siege and fall of the Republic, imperial soldiers entered the city.

From here the road continues to the city gate, also called San Niccolò (this is the only gate in the 14th-century walls to have preserved at its original height). The series of houses gradually takes on a more working-class appearance as they become narrower, and the palazzi at no. 23, 34 and 36 are fine 15th-century buildings.

From the church, however, our itinerary continues to the right, passing under the Porta

a San Miniato then up the steep steps of Via del Monte alle Croci. The

The gate of San Miniato looking towards the city. The passageway on top of the wall is supported by suspended arches (below).

road is characterized by the Via Crucis made by the Franciscan monks of the church of San Salvatore (☛ p. 239).

At the end of the Via Crucis, we reach the Viale dei Colli; turning to the left, we come to Piazzale Michelangelo.

PIAZZALE MICHELANGELO

Built in 1875, this renowned balcony over Florence introduced the tourist-oriented concept of a 'scenic viewpoint' to the city for the first time. It was created by Giuseppe Poggi as part of the overall design for Viale dei Colli, representing, however, one of his less successful innovations as it is awkwardly situated within the context of the two Romanesque churches of San Miniato and San Salvatore, just above.

The monument in the middle of the square is an anthology of some of Michelangelo's most famous works, consisting of bronze reproductions of the David and the allegorical figures on the

Medici tombs in San Lorenzo. Poggi had originally intended that the entire piazza would become a museum dedicated to Michelangelo. In fact, the spacious loggia at the back of the square was intended to house plaster casts of the great artist's masterpieces. Instead, as Poggi himself wrote somewhat bitterly, "it was destined to become no more than an ordinary café-restaurant". And such it has remained.

Above, the Via Crucis, leading to the church of San Salvatore al Monte. Above left, the view from Piazzale Michelangelo. Centre, the monument to Michelangelo (1871) consists of bronze copies of David and the funerary statues in the Medici chapel. Left, a painter with his work. Below, loggia designed by Giuseppe Poggi (1873).

Retracing our steps towards the back of the loggia, we climb the stairs (the

"What could barely have been achieved in several decades in other places, has been done here, as if by magic, in just a few years". Thus commented a reporter for the *Kölnische Zeitung* in October, 1876, describing the changes which had taken place in Florence between 1865 and 1871, when the city had been the capital of Italy. The changes might have been impressive, but they had certainly been neither painless nor without controversy. In just a few months, Florence had had to house approximately 30,000 government officials and other new residents, increasing the population from 114,568 in 1861 to 146,441 inhabitants at the end of 1865, and 194,001 in 1870. With buildings both new and variously modified, a total of 51,380 new houses had been created. Room was made available to house the institutions of state and government by expropriating several church properties and buildings: thus the Minstery of Education was located in the monastery of San Firenze, the Treasury in the Badìa, the Naval Command in the monastery of the Missionary Fathers near the Arno. The walls were demolished as part of Giuseppe Poggi's vast and comprehensive urban plan, sponsored not only by Italian banks, but also from foreign interests. Insurance companies such as the Gresham Life Assurance Society and industrial interests such as the Moncenis Railway Company set up agencies in the city. Local newspapers with such playful names as *Lo Zenzero*, *La Chiacchiera*, *Il Lampione* (Ginger, Chatterbox and the Lamp Post) were soon joined by the *Gazzetta d'Italia* and *Il Corriere Italiano*. Foreign representatives and diplomats arrived from Turin: the doyen of the diplomatic corps, the American George Perkins Marh, took up residence in a villa near San Gervasio, while Rustem Bey, the representative of the *Sublime Porta* – the Ottoman Empire – ventured forth from his home on Via de' Serragli sporting a red fez.

All this took place in an urban context which had changed little since the 1500's. Adapted to a pre-industrial situation, the structures were quite inadequate for the pressing needs of modernity which demanded new services and functions, parks, drainage and sanitary systems, roads and streets to cope efficiently with the new situation. In 1861, there were only three factories employing more than 100 workers. Local production methods remained rooted in the old craft workshops with no more than ten labourers. It is therefore not surprising that so much sudden innovation produced a profound imbalance and widespread discontent in which, as Giuseppe Guerzoni describes: "Everything is changed, overturned, upset. Florence has become a city for all except for the Florentines: foreigners from all over the place, traders of all kinds, have installed themselves in our homes, have taken our best places and thrown us out and now they are sucking out the very marrow and throwing us the bones".

Subjective reactions aside, it is true that with the transfer of the capital to Rome in 1871, it was at last possible to bring the urge for 'improvement' under control. Within a year, the population was reduced to 167,999 and the devastating economic consequences, which were felt for many years, began to become evident. In March 1878, faced with a debt – enormous for the times – of 23,635,390 lire, the council was forced to declare bankruptcy. A few days later, a measure was approved obliging the Florentines to pay a total of almost 2,000,000 lire a year for the next 55 years.

The south side and (below) the façade of the church of San Salvatore al Monte (1499-1504) by Simone del Pollaiolo, 'Il Cronaca'.

continuation of the Via Crucis leading to the church of San Salvatore al Monte.

CHURCH OF SAN SALVATORE AL MONTE

According to art historian Adolfo Venturi, Michelangelo is said to have called this church "my pretty country maid", referring to the "sparkling and almost gaudy note of color" introduced into the vigorous structure by the "deep cornices of *pietra serena* on the pure white walls". Today the effect of this contrast, also found in the interior, has been almost entirely lost due to heavy-handed restoration which replaced the bright white with a less suitable ochre color.

The church was built by Cronaca between 1499 and 1504, replacing an earlier building which had gradually collapsed due to geological instability.

The façade is of a gracious simplicity, based on the design of the tympanum which is repeated over the doorway and the three windows. The interior has a large single nave with side chapels; in the left transept, over a doorway, is a glazed terracotta *Deposition*, by Giovanni della Robbia (1469-1529).

Leaving the church, we continue up to the left, soon arriving at the church of San Miniato al Monte.

CHURCH OF SAN MINIATO AL MONTE

Together with the Baptistery of San Giovanni, San Miniato al Monte represents the finest Romanesque architecture in Florence, located on the *'mons florentinus'* where the first Christian communities dug their catacombs.

It was built between 1018 and 1027 as a church for the Cluniac Benedictine monks, replacing a 4th-century chapel (which had existed as early as the Carolingian period) dedicated to Minias, the first Christian martyr. The bell tower collapsed in 1499, and was rebuilt to a design by Baccio d'Agnolo in 1524. Six years later, during the siege of Florence, two small cannons were placed here to fire on the imperial troops. Michelangelo transformed the entire hillside into a fortress, incorporating the monastery and surrounding it with bulwarks which continued down to the church of

The church of San Miniato al Monte (below left, the façade) was built from 1120-1130 over an early Christian church also dedicated to the martyred saint. The decoration, like that of the cathedral and the baptistery, is of white and green marble. Above, a detail of the north side; in the background is the sturdy bell tower designed by Baccio d'Agnolo. During the siege of Florence (1530), Michelangelo turned it into an artillery station and protected it from enemy fire by tying mattresses around the walls.

The mosaic in the vault of the apse, portraying Christ in Glory with Mary and Saint Minias *(mid 13th century).*

The central aisle of the church seen from the apse. In the foreground is the top of the elegant tabernacle built by Michelozzo in 1448; the structure contains several paintings by Agnolo Gaddi (late 14th century). Below, the attractive pulpit with the lectern supported by a caryatid and an eagle, the symbol of Saint John. Right, the wooden truss beam ceiling painted with coloured decorations.

San Salvatore al Monte. In 1868, the steps designed by Giuseppe Poggi to link the church to Via-le dei Colli were built.

Façade. The dominant feature is the geometric pattern created by the contrast of the green and white marbles. The first order has three doorways and five blind arches, rounded at the top, resting on Corinthian half-columns. The second order corresponds only to the central nave and is divided into three sections by grooved pilaster strips; in the central section is a window with a tympanum and a gold-leaf mosaic portraying *Christ Enthroned between the Virgin Mary and St Minias* (13th-century, but much restored). Nine small arches with inlayed symbolic figures decorate the pediment; in the pinnacle is a gilded copper coat of arms of the Calimala Guild (an eagle with a bale of cloth in its talons) who financed the church.

Interior. Inside, the church is on three levels (the crypt, main floor and raised presbytery), and has three naves formed by columns and pairs of clustered pilasters which are joined by an arch across the nave. The exposed beams of the ceiling are polychrome. The nave is paved with beautiful marble inlay, forming designs and pat-terns which are part of a coherent decorative scheme evident throughout the church. As art critic Toesca describes: "The various architectural elements are highlighted by white and green marble and are decorated with marble inlay which does not, however affect the overall sense of space, but is subordinate to the architectural outline. The decoration of San Miniato is based not so much on the contrast of colors and clean outlines, but rather on the harmonious proportions of separate yet ordered spaces, so that it seems to actually be a part of the building and not something imposed on it".

One should not, however, confuse the original decorations (which include the triumphal arch and semi-circu-

Michelozzo's 15th-century tabernacle; the vault is decorated with glazed terracotta caissons by the Della Robbia workshop.

Probably 13th-century, the altar in the crypt contains bones which Bishop Hildebrand identified as those of the martyr Minias. Centre page, Jacopo del Casentino, San Miniato altar panel; the figure of the saint, holding the palm leaf of martyrdom, is surrounded by eight episodes of his life.

lar apse) with the 19th-century ones which cover the walls. The Corinthian and Composite capitals are classical; the terracotta capitals with leaves of aquatic plants, painted white, are Romanesque.

At the end of the central nave is the Chapel of the Crucifix. The caissons in the vault of Michelozzo's *tabernacle* (1448) are decorated with white glazed terracotta on a blue background (Della Rob-bia workshop), and inside are paintings of *Sts John Gualberto and Minias,* the *Annunciation* and the *Passion* (1394-1396).

In the right nave are 13th- and 14th-century *frescoes.*

From the presbytery we enter the sacristy — a large square hall with cross-vaulted ceiling (1387). In the vault and lunettes are noteworthy frescoes representing *Scenes from the Life of St Benedict,* by Spinello Aretino (1350-1410) and assistants.

Returning to the presbytery, on the right is an altar with a pointed panel painting illustrating *Scenes from the Life of St Minias* (1320), Jacopo da Casentino's masterpiece. The presbytery is divided into three naves and has a lovely high marble screen, inlayed and

carved choir stalls and a Romanesque altar with a terracotta *Crucifix,* attributed to Luca della Robbia (c.1400-1482).

In the vault of the apse is a huge 13th-century mosaic, frequently restored, portraying *Christ Blessing between the Virgin Mary and St Minias* and the *Symbols of the Evangelists.*

In the 12th-century crypt, the vaults rest on thirty-six marble columns (taken from Florentine buildings of the Roman period), arran-ged to form seven short naves. In the vaults of the presbytery are gold-leaf *paintings* (1341), by Taddeo Gaddi.

Cardinal of Portugal's Chapel. In the left nave is the Cappella del Cardinale di Portogallo (1473). This structure was added to the church at a later date and is a prime example of the prevailing style in all artistic forms during the second half of the 15th century.

The architectural design, clearly inspired by the Old Sacristy in San Lorenzo, is by Antonio di Manetto, a pupil of Brunelleschi. The vault is decorated with four glazed terracotta *panels,* by Luca della Robbia. The *Cardinal's monument* on the right is a fine piece by Bernardo Rossellino. In a niche in the left arch is a painting of the *Annunciation* (1466-1467), by

Viale dei Colli. There are splendid views across the city on the walk from Piazzale Michelangelo and Via San Leonardo.

Via San Leonardo is one of the most characteristic old streets of the city. Beyond the old walls and the villas on either side are gardens and olive groves. The different alternating greens of the olive and the cypress are one of the most characteristic features of the hills around Florence. Below, a plaque commemorating the Russian musician, Tchaikovsky, who lived in the villa on the corner of Via San Leonardo and Viale dei Colli in 1878. Further ahead, on the other side of the road was the house and studio of Ottone Rosai, a famous Florentine artist of the first half of the 20th century.

Alessio Baldinovetti. On the right of the church is the 14th-century Bishop's Palace, which is not open to the public. To the left is the entrance to the monumental 19th-century cemetery, known as that of the 'Porte Sante' (Holy Gates).

We now return back down the stairs in front of the church to Viale dei Colli, and turn left in the opposite direction to Piazzale Michelangelo. The view is best enjoyed by crossing the road to the opposite, right-hand side.

VIALE DEI COLLI

The gently climbing curves of Viale dei Colli are in sharp contrast to the rugged, rustic appearance of the older roads (Via San Salvatore al Monte, Via di San Miniato, Via del Erta Canina, Costa San Giorgio) previously linking Florence to San Miniato and the neighbouring hillsides.

The creation of Viale dei Colli transformed into a pleasant walk a route once demanding the physical sacrifice of a pilgrimage. In laying out the new avenues, Poggi and his collaborators also made extensive and novel use of features such as benches, balusters, supporting walls, flowerbeds and hedges, attractively and unobtrusively positioned. "Poggi here seems uninhibited by his professional prag-

matism," notes the architectural historian, Franco Borsi, "opening a dialogue between architecture-nature, antique-modern, that cannot help but emerge as his greatest strength".

From San Miniato we descend to the level of the viale, enjoying a wonderful and ever changing panorama. Reaching Via San Leonardo we turn to the right: the little church of the same name lies on the last stretch of the road on the right-hand side.

VIA SAN LEONARDO

Winding and flat, the road runs like a public corridor between the elegant private residences just visible between the olive trees on the other side of low stone walls, often (in keeping with tradition) enhanced with patterned or 'combed' plasterwork. This singularly beautiful and evocative area was frequently commemorated by 20th-century Florentine writers, including Giovanni Papini and Vasco Pratolini. On the corner of the avenue, on the left, is the villa where the Russian composer Tchaikovsky lived and composed in 1878. Further ahead, at no. 49, is the house and studio of the contemporary artist Ottone Rosai.

CHURCH OF SAN LEONARDO

Built in the 11th or 12th century but victim to periodic, clumsy restorations, the little church interrupts the sequence of villas. Inside one finds the splendid *pulpit* from which Dante, Boccaccio and St Anthony spoke when it was still in the church of San Piero Scheraggio (later incorporated into the Uffizi). It was reassembled here in 1782 and was placed in its present location in 1921, on the sixth centenary of Dante's death.

At the end of Via San Leonardo, immediately before the 14th-century Porta a San Giorgio (with a fresco in the inner vault depicting Madonna and Child Enthroned with Sts Leonard and George, *by Bicci di Lorenzo) is the massive bulk of Fort Belvedere (☛ p. 247).*

Leaving the fort, we pass under the arch of the gate and continue along the steep and twisting Costa a San Giorgio. Gradually the villas and gardens give way to narrow,

closely-built medieval structures. At no. 17 is Galileo's house*, decorated with an image of the scientist and the family coat of arms. We now turn right down the equally steep Costa Scarpuccia (to the left is the picturesque little Via*

del Canneto, with numerous terracotta arches across it) until reaching Via de' Bardi.

VIA DE' BARDI

"A flea-ridden hamlet" where "vile, common people lived" was how the 14th-century historian, Giovanni Villani, referred to this area. He described how, in the Oltrarno of the mid-11th century, three hamlets had grown up around the end of the Ponte Vecchio, the other two being Santa Felìcita and San Jacopo (☛ p. 182-183).

From Costa Scarpuccia we turn to the left where we immediately find the *church of Santa Lucia de' Màgnoli,* dating from the 11th century, but periodically rebuilt and restored. The church has a single nave and at the first altar is a panel painting of *St Lucy,* by Pietro Lorenzetti (c.1280-1348).

Just beyond the church, on the other side of the street, a

Pietro Lorenzetti, Santa Lucia *(14th century). Below, façade of the church of Santa Lucia de' Màgnoli, where the work is housed.*

plaque commemorates Cosimo I's edict of 1565, forbidding further building in the area. In fact, the "flea-ridden hamlet" was also morphologically unstable: the combination of pressure from the Magnoli hillside and the frequent flooding of the river Arno had caused disastrous landslides here. In 1284, more than fifty houses collapsed, and on December 12, 1547, another eighteen gave way (including Palazzo Bardi and Palazzo Del Nero). According to an unconfirmed tale, the architect Buontalenti was found

The Stibbert Museum

Frederick, also known as Federico, Stibbert was born in Florence in 1838 and died there in 1906. He was the son of Giulia Cafaggi, a Florentine, and Thomas, a lieutenant-colonel in the British army. He was educated at Harrow and, though he frequented the highest ranks of European aristocracy, he loved his Florentine home and roots most of all. An Englishman of both eclectic and eccentric character. In 1866, attracted by the image of the 'Hero of Two Worlds,' he enrolled in Garibaldi's army and was awarded a silver medal. An art collector, but also an artist, he became a member of the Florentine Academy of Fine Arts in 1868. He succeeded in increasing the wealth he had inherited through successful business dealings, including considerable investments in the shares of Tuscan financial enterprises which had recently been formed. Culture and money, used with intelligence during his long and frequent journeys, enabled him to create his extraordinary collection of over 50,000 items, left on his death to the English government which later granted it to the city of Florence. Above all, the Stibbert Museum is a monument to its founder and to a period style, as too are the Horne Museum (☛ p. 149) and the Bardini Museum (☛ p. 234). Indeed, all three are the houses of 19th-century collectors which, rather than highlighting some innate quality or aspect of the single items, reflect an individual's passion in recreating a historical setting, fascinating in its exactness and detail even when resorting to imitation or copies. The two principal themes of the Stibbert Museum should be seen in this light: weapons and costumes are displayed in over sixty rooms, specifically created to accommodate them by completely transforming a historic villa, once the property of the Davanzati family. The building was both

Sculpted shrine in Costa Scarpuccia. Right,
Palazzo Capponi, built by Lorenzo di Bicci
for Niccolò da Uzzano; the 14th-century
Palazzo Canigiani (below), was built over
the old hospital of Santa Lucia.

here as a baby, miraculously unscathed amidst the ruins of his family home.

Further ahead, the immense façades of *Palazzo Canigiani* (no. 30-32) and *Palazzo Capponi* (no. 36-38) are most imposing. The unusual look of the former was created when, during the 15th century, three pre-existing buildings were incorporated into one: the large fan-shaped arches on the ground floor date back, in fact, to the 14th-century. The latter, which also has a parallel façade on the Lungarno Torrigiani, is still in that restrained late-Gothic style which Michelozzo was later fully to exploit and develop.

Slightly further ahead, from the modern section of Via de' Bardi, we retrace our steps back to Piazza del Duomo.

inadequate and too small to house the enormous collection and was consequently altered between 1880 and 1890 by a group of artists who worked in the most important aristocratic residences in Florence and throughout Italy. The most outstanding example of the 'Stibbert Style' is the rightly famous 'cavalcade'. Dramatically and theatrically arranged in a vast room decorated by Gaetano Bianchi, is a procession of ten horsemen dressed in 16th-century armour, twelve armed soldiers on foot and four Islamic horsemen. There are also dozens of complete suits of armour displayed on mannequins. The European and Islamic items are of particular importance and rarity, while the Far Eastern, and especially the Japanese, are some of the most important examples in the world. The costume collection is also of considerable value and interest, including, in particular, many 18th-century items, as well as the apparel worn by Napoleon in 1805 when he was crowned king of Italy. Stibbert's interest in armoury and costume can also be identified in the numerous, valuable paintings on display. These include works by Sano di Pietro, Neri di Bicci, Benedetto Ghirlandaio, Alessandro Allori, Luca Giordano, Justus Sustermans, as well as an *Annunciation* similar in style to the work of Coppo di Marcovaldo. The furnishings are also noteworthy, especially a circular table in malachite made for Gerolamo Bonaparte; all the furnishings displayed however, represent an eclectic collection of high quality antiques of all kinds, from bronzes to umbrellas, from candlesticks to fans, from combs to clocks, and walking sticks to maps. The villa is surrounded by a romantic park, one of the most unspoiled and original Italianate gardens, with a little lake and many exotic plants.
[Entrance: via Stibbert 26; ☛ T3/F1. Opening times 9-13; closed on Thursdays]

The Medici fortresses

Florence's two fortresses are the result of both political tyranny and new engineering skills. In fact the Medici, having regained control of the city after the siege of 1530, built the San Giovanni and the Belvedere fortresses to protect themselves against internal uprisings rather than from foreign aggression. Moreover, the old medieval design (high defensive walls with sturdy square towers at intervals) was no longer adequate. With the invention of fire-arms which could be used from all angles, low, thick walls protected by ramparts and with a more sophisticated geometrical design were required.

Fortezza da Basso.

The San Giovanni fortress, later known as 'da Basso' (lower), compared to the position of the other fortress, was built by Antonio da Sangallo the Younger for Duke Alessandro to meet the requirements described above. The ramparts of this huge pentagonal structure have remained at their original height of just 39 feet on the side facing the railway station. The moat which surrounded it was filled in to maintain the level of the new boulevards during the second half of the 19th century, using stone and rubble from the demolished 14th-century city walls. During the construction of the fortress itself,

Aerial view of Fortezza da Basso. Both this and the Belvedere fort were built more to contain unrest within the city than for defence against the rather improbable possibility of attack from outside. In fact the walls are stronger and deeper on the south side which faces towards Florence (above, a section of the wall).

the 13th-century Porta a Faenza was incorporated into the keep on Viale Strozzi. The splendid stone walls here, facing towards the city to keep an eye on its restless inhabitants, have ashlars sculpted to a diamond-shaped point, alternating with hemispherical blocks. All that remains of the original buildings inside, in an area covering approximately 10 hectares, is the octago-

nal guard house, with a brick herring-bone patterned roof. The low, modern buildings, partially underground, were recently designed and built by contemporary architect Pierluigi Spadolini. Important exhibitions and conferences are held here as well as an annual Crafts Exhibition.

Forte di Belvedere. This fortress was built later, high above the city. As architectural historian Giorgio Fanelli notes: "It is the completion and conclusion of that creative organization of internal space and panoramic or linear views which developed throughout the 16th century with the Fortezza da Basso, Cosimo's ramparts in the Oltrarno and the fortifications of San Miniato". Indeed, where guns and cannons once scrutinized the centre of Florence from this fortress, visitors and tourists now enjoy the views over the city. This aesthetic aspect of a defensive structure had already been most attractively

put into practice in the 'palazzina' located in the centre of the star-shaped structure. The ground floor of this elegant building is enhanced by the use of a portico with an architrave along the entire façade, identical on both sides, thus providing magnificent and varied views across the city and the surrounding hills. The palazzina (1560-1570) is attributed to Ammannati, probably assisted by Buontalenti who, with Don Giovanni de' Medici, designed the later structure of the fort (1590 onwards) for Ferdinando I. Situated at an altitude of 250 feet above the city, the fort has three walls with ramparts and two 'pincer' walls. Entrance is from a gateway on the east side, from where a ramp leads up to the level of the ramparts. A walk around the walls of the watch provides wonderful, continually changing views. The palazzina and grounds are now frequently used for art exhibitions.

Left, the 'palazzina' of the Belvedere fort: designed by Bartolomeo Ammannati, it was built some twenty years before the fortress (1590). Easily reached from the Boboli Gardens, it provided protection for the Medici in case of rioting. Above, the city walls near to the fortress.

10. **Fiesole, the Lofty Ancestor**

In the beginning was Fiesole, and it is, in fact, from this hilltown that the Florentines descended, "… that ungrateful and malignant race / which descended from the Fiesole of old / and still have rock and mountain in their blood," as Dante described them (*Inferno*, XV, 61-63). The hill has been inhabited ever since the Iron Age, and one of the most important Etruscan cities was situated here. Dante's invective also alludes to one of the most vital aspects of Fiesole: it was the very "rock and mountain" – the *pietra serena* quarried and worked here since time immemorial – to give the town its color. Many are the sculptors who descended from these hills to work in Florence: Giuliano da Maiano, Mino da Fiesole, Desiderio da Settignano… Fiesole developed between the 6th and 5th centuries BC, taking in the area extending from the hill of San Francesco to the hill of San Apollinare, where the central Piazza Mino now stands. The town was surrounded by massive defensive walls a mile and a

Imperial Roman sculpture. Fiesole, Civic Museum.

half long. From the 3rd century BC it was a Roman city and ally, and during the 1st century BC participated with many other cities and Italic peoples in the revolution known as the Social War, during which it was taken and burnt by Lucius Cato in 90 BC. During the civil war, the town was on the side of Marius, and upon his defeat was awarded to a group of veterans from Sulla's army, against whom the citizens revolted in 78 BC. However, Fiesole did gradually become an entirely Roman town, particularly with the rebuilding which took place after its destruction in the 1st century. During the Augustan period, the city extended to the north, with the theatre and the baths. These were rediscovered in the 19th century in a field where, for centuries, ruins and 'underground vaults' had been unearthed. In the Middle Ages, Fiesole was supplanted by Florence, and was finally conquered in 1125. Already in Early Christian times, the higher part of the town, which could be more easily defended, had been gradually abandoned. It has been renowned for its beauty ever since Boccaccio's day, and was immortalized by the writer in both the *Decameron* and the *Ninfale Fiesolano*. The Medici, too, appreciated the tranquil hills of Fiesole, and not only had Michelozzo build them a villa there, but also completely restored the Badìa at San Domenico. From the 18th century on, famous foreigners and Italians built villas and created gardens on this gracious hillside. Today, important cultural institutes are located here, such as the European University Institute, the Primo Conte Foundation, and research centers belonging to Harvard and Stanford universities.

Ancient Etruscan votive statue in bronze. Fiesole, Civic Museum.

Portico of the church of San Domenico, designed by Matteo Nigetti (17th century).

Fra' Angelico, Madonna and Child with angels and Saints Barnabas, Dominic, Thomas Aquinas and Peter (detail).

To reach Fiesole, we take no 7 bus from Piazza San Marco. Before getting off at the end of the line in Piazza Mino, it is worth stopping briefly half-way in the tiny village of· San Domenico where there is a Dominican church and monastery.

CHURCH AND MONASTERY OF SAN DOMENICO

The Dominican church was founded in 1406 by Fra' Giovanni di Domenico Baccini, and was subsequently enlarged and altered until the 17th century.

The church has an elegant 17th-century portico by Matteo Nigetti. The interior has a single nave with three 15th- and 16th-century chapels on each side, and is decorated with many paintings mostly dating from the 17th to 19th centuries.

Fra' Angelico lived in the adjacent monastery, and around 1430 painted a triptych for the church portraying the *Virgin and Child, Praying Angels and Sts Barnabas, Dominic, Thomas d'Aquinas and Peter the Martyr* now at the first altar on the left. It was altered in 1501 by Lorenzo di Credi, who added the landscape and the buildings in the background making it into a rectangular panel.

In the chapter room of the monastery is another work by

10. Fiesole, the Lofty Ancestor

Fra' Angelico, a frescoed *Crucifix*, dated 1430, and a detached fresco of the *Virgin and Child* with its original synopsis, by the workshop of Fra' Angelico.

In the hospice is a painting by Fra' Paolino da Pistoia, a follower of Savonarola, representing *Savonarola and his two companions indicate Florence to Christ and the Virgin* (early 16th-century).

Leaving the monastery, we continue along the narrow road opposite the church and reach the Badìa Fiesolana on the left.

BADÌA FIESOLANA

Without doubt, the Badìa Fiesolana is the most important religious building in the outskirts of Florence. Originally the residence of the Bishops of Fiesole, it was built on the spot where, according to tradition, St Romulus was martyred. Around the year 1000, Bishop Jacopo il Bavaro decided to abandon it, moving to the greater safety afforded by the massive protective walls of the *civitas* of Fiesole. Around 1028, however – during the period of reform and upheaval which affected the churches of Florence and Fiesole – the same bishop decided to turn it into a monastery, handing it over to the monks from Camaldoli. He had two motives for doing so: firstly, to prevent the building from falling into ruin; and secondly, to create a new

spiritual center outside the city walls and therefore free from political control.

For several centuries during the Middle Ages, both the Badia and the town of Fiesole fell into a state of decline. Florence was gradually gaining control of the surrounding countryside and clearly had no interest in encouraging reminders of Fiesole's longstanding autonomy.

It was Cosimo the Elder who restored the church and monastery to their original splendour. Indeed, he was so fond of the Badia that he had an apartment made for himself and spent the last eight years of his life there (1456-1464). He also created an important library which became one of the focal points of Florentine humanism. During this period the Badia became an immense building site and almost seems to have remained such, as the exterior and façade have never been completed, while the interior has been subject to various modifications and restorations.

In 1753, Abbot Montelatici founded the *Accademia dei Georgòfili* here — the oldest Academy of Agricultural Sciences in Europe. Later, Grand Duke Pietro Leopoldo suppressed the monastery and the library was annexed to the Laurentian Library. During the same period further restoration work was carried out. Various alterations took place during the 19th century, and at one point, the building was even subdivid-

Detail of the romanesque façade of the Badìa Fiesolana. The green and white marble repeats the decorative patterns seen on the baptistery of Florence and the façade of San Miniato. The romanesque part is incorporated into the Renaissance façade (below) commissioned by Cosimo the Elder, but left unfinished after his death (1464).

Piazza Mino seen from Palazzo Pretorio. On the right is San Romolo and opposite, the Bishop's Seminary.

The façade of Palazzo Pretorio with its attractive loggia. Below, a detail of the entrance where, over the centuries, successive magistrates of the town placed their coats of arms. Below, the elegant Bishop's Palace (second half of the 17th century).

ed into private apartments. Finally, the Piarist Fathers opened a school there, and consequently some modern buildings were added in 1955.

The Piarist school was closed in 1972 and since 1976 the Badia has been the home of the European University Institute. The splendid Romanesque façade (second half of the 12th century) in white and green marble from Prato framed by the larger 15th-century stone one, reflects the lengthy history of these buildings.

The single nave of the interior is Brunelleschian in style and dates from the restoration carried out under Cosimo the Elder. In the altars are 17th-and 18th-century paintings.

To the right of the church is the entrance to the monastery, now the European University Institute, with a splendid Renaissance cloister. In the old refectory, now a conference room, is a large fresco of *Christ served by angels* (1629), by Giovanni da San Giovanni.

After visiting the Badia we retrace our steps to the main road and take the bus up to Piazza

Mino, where the forum of the old Roman city used to stand.

To the west of the piazza is a large 17th-century Seminary; *to the east, slightly raised, is the* Palazzo Pretorio, *now housing the city council. The façade is decorated with the coats of arms of the* Podestà. *Beside is the small* church of Santa Maria Primerana, *first recorded in 966 and completely renovated in mannerist style at the end of the 16th century. On the north side are the* Bishop's Palace, *founded in the 11th century and rebuilt in 1675, and the vast cathedral dedicated to St Romulus.*

CATHEDRAL OF SAN ROMOLO

Dedicated to the martyred Bishop of Fiesole, Romulus, the cathedral was founded in the 11th century when the bishop's seat was moved here from the Badìa. It was enlarged during the 13th century, restored during the second half of the 14th century and completely renovated between 1878 and 1883 by the architect Michelangelo Maiorfi (responsible for the façade of dressed stone). The tall slender bell tower has 13th-century foundations, and was enhanced in 1738 with the addition of the crenellated gallery.

The interior has three naves with stone columns and contains some important works of art, especially sculpture, clearly reflecting the local tradition of quarrying and working stone.

Above the central door of the church is a polychrome terracotta statue of *St Romulus* (early 16th century), by Giovanni della Robbia.

On the second column to the right is a 15th-century *pulpit*. At the end of the central nave is the green and white altar frontal which was in the Badia Fiesolana, signed by 'Maestro Costantino' and dated 1273. The column supports a 14th-century wooden *Crucifix*.

In the presbytery is the Salutati chapel, with two works by Mino da Fiesole: the *tomb of Bishop Leonardo Salutati* (d. 1466) and the *altar frontal*.

On the main altar is a polyptych of the *Virgin Enthroned with Child and Saints* (mid-15th century), by Bicci di Lorenzo. In the Canons' Chapel is a marble altar frontal (late 15th century) by Andrea Ferrucci, with statues of *St Romulus* and *St Matthew*.

In the 13th-century crypt is a granite *baptismal font* (16th century) by Francesco del Tadda, whose *self-portrait* (1576) can be seen in the left nave.

Immediately behind the apse of the cathedral, at the beginning of Via Giovanni Duprè, is the Bandini Museum — a small treasure trove of medieval painting. A ticket for

Santa Maria Primerana, dating from the 10th century and completely rebuilt in the 16th century. Below, the cathedral of San Romolo.

the Civic Museum also grants entrance to the Bandini, the archaeological site and the Costantini Antiquarium.

BANDINI MUSEUM

Founded in 1913, the Museum contains works collected in the 18th century of the 'primitive' painters — those preceding the Renaissance. These were collected by Angelo Maria Bandini a scholarly church canon, who then left them to the diocese of Fiesole. Consisting mainly of paintings from the Tuscan school of the 13th to the 15th centuries, the collection also contains Byzantine and Gothic ivory bas-reliefs dating from the 11th century and some minor arts and sculptures, including a marble *Virgin and Child* (second half of the

The sombre interior of San Romolo. The three naves are divided by plain columns and the roof is of wooden truss beams.

Below, the Bandini Museum which houses some important paintings dating from the 13th to the 15th centuries.

Above, two rooms in the Primo Conti Foundation. On the right, the entrance to Villa Le Coste where the Foundation is housed.

Above, Taddeo Gaddi (13th century), Annunciation, Bandini Museum. Right, a view of the hill of Fiesole.

14th century) by the school of Nino Pisano.

The most important works are the thirty-four paintings by 14th-century artists such as Taddeo Gaddi and Bernardo Daddi, Nardo and Jacopo di Cione; and the twenty-five paintings dating from the late 14th and 15th centuries, including works by Giovanni del Biondo, Giovanni del Ponte, Lorenzo Monaco and Jacopo del Sellaio.

Leaving the Bandini Museum, we continue downwards along Via Giovanni Duprè – from which we can see a section of Etruscan wall on the

right – to reach the 16th-century Villa Le Coste. *Here one finds the* Primo Conti Foundation, *housing the interesting personal archive of the contemporary artist (1900-1988), proponent of the Futurist movement from a very young age. In the neighboring* Museo delle avanguardie storiche "Primo Conti," *one finds samples of the artist's finest work, as well as excellent documentation of the 20th-century artistic avant-garde movements in Italy.*

Returning to the beginning of Via Duprè, opposite the Bandini Museum is the entrance to the archaeological site. From here one enjoys a wonderful view of the steep valley of the Mugnone and the Mugello mountains. Excavations begun at the end of the 19th century and continued after the World War II *have brought to light many remains of both the Etruscan and the Roman city; exhibited in the museum are items dating from these periods.*

ARCHAEOLOGICAL SITE

At the center of the Area Archeologica, set into the hillside, is the Roman theatre, built during the Augustan period and capable of holding 3,000 people. The theatre is still packed with audiences every year, enjoying the ballet, theatre, films and concerts of the *Estate Fiesolana* (Fiesole Summer Festival).

Along a path to the right of the theatre are the remains of the baths, probably rebuilt in the 2nd-3rd centuries. Here we can also see the Etruscan walls which ran along the northern side of the town: almost seventeen feet high, they are made of enormous blocks of stone. On the other side of the baths are the remains of the Roman temple built in the 1st century AD on the ruins of an earlier Etruscan temple (beginning of the 3rd century BC) which was destroyed by fire. The entrance consists of a flight of seven steps, seventy-five feet wide.

Civic Museum. Founded in 1873, the Museo Civico is located immediately to the right just inside the entrance to the site. The present building, in the shape of a small Tuscan-style temple, dates from 1914. Displayed are artifacts dating from early history up to the Etruscan and Roman periods, as well as from the early Middle Ages (with indications of the Lombard dominion) and late Middle Ages. The collection includes some funerary urns excavated in Chiusi and Volterra, and some archaic and

Above, the entrance to the archaeological site. Top left, the ruins of the stage of the Roman theatre; above left are the ruins of the baths, and on the right, a general view of the theatre. Below, the entrance to the Civic Museum inside the archaeological site. Left, an Etruscan stele (Fiesole, 5th century B.C.). Below, an Etruscan chamber tomb.

256

*Left, funerary urn in terrcotta
(Etruscan-Roman art, 2nd century
B.C.). Fiesole, Civic Museum. Below,
Imperial Roman sculpture. Fiesole,
Civic Museum. Below left, votive
bronze figure representing* Hercules
(Etruscan art, 5th century B.C.).

classical Greek ceramics from
the central and southern Etruscan area.

*Leaving the archaeological site
and continuing along Via Por-
tigiani, at no. 9 is the* Costantini Antiquarium, *also part of
the Civic Museum. The collection consists of approximately
150 ceramic items from
Greece, Etruria and Magna
Grecia, donated to the town
by Alfiero Costantini in 1985.*

*Almost opposite the anti-
quarium is* Palazzina Mangani
*where art exhibitions are fre-
quently held.*

*Returning along Via Porti-
giani and continuing along
Via Sermei, we come to Via
del Bargellino: after a few
yards, to the left, is a little
road leading to two* Etruscan
tombs, *the only remains of
what was once a large necrop-*

olis dating from the Hellenic
era (4th century BC).

We now return to Piazza
Mino; from here we follow
the narrow street of San
Francesco between the Bishop's Palace and the Seminary;
this leads up to the old acropolis of Fiesole.

HILL OF SAN FRANCESCO

Boasting a magnificent view
of Florence and the valley below, the hill of San Francesco
also hosts the basilica of San-
t'Alessandro and the basilica
and monastery of San
Francesco.
Church of Sant'Alessandro.
According to tradition, the
basilica was built in the 6th
century, on the site of a pagan
temple. Rebuilt after 1000 AD,
it was altered several times in
the 16th, 17th and early 19th
centuries. An extensive
restoration was completed in
1978. The interior has three
naves, supported by sixteen
authentic Roman columns. In
the oratory beside are a *panel
painting,* by Gerino da Pistoia, and 16th-century detached frescoes with *Scenes
from the Life of Mary.*

Above the basilica we
reach the top of the hill where
the Etruscan and Roman
acropolis was and, during the
Middle Ages, the fortress defending the town. In the small
square are the church and
monastery of San Francesco.

Left and right, two views of the steep Via di San Francesco which ascends the hill of the same name.

Church and Monastery of San Francesco.

Built in the 14th century, the Franciscan monks altered and extended the structure when they moved here in 1399. In 1907, the church was renovated by architect Giuseppe Castellucci.

The works of art inside include an *Annunciation*, by Raffaellino del Garbo (1466-1524/25) at the second altar on the left, and 16th-century inlaid stalls in the presbytery. In the Sant'Antonio chapel, entered from the sacristy, is a terracotta crib by the school of Della Robbia; above the entrance is a 17th-century fresco from the Tuscan school, portraying the *Meeting of St Francis and St Dominic.*

The 15th-century cloister is also entered from the sacristy. From here we descend into the small but noteworthy *Ethnographical Franciscan Missionary Museum* where antique Chinese items are displayed (bronzes, textiles, ivory, ceramics), as well as an Egyptian mummy. The remains of the massive Etruscan defensive walls can be seen from the museum.

Rather than taking the bus back to Florence directly from Piazza Mino, we can walk back down to San Domenico following an interesting and picturesque route along part of the old road to Fiesole, the Via Vecchia Fiesolana. This begins just below the south side of the seminary. There are numerous attractive villas along this steep little country road: to the right, just before the end of the road, is the lovely medieval 'Riposo dei vescovi'. According to tradition, this beautiful building – altered during the Renaissance and restored at the end of the 19th century – was a resting place for prelates on their way to take over the bishopric of Fiesole.

Above, a view of the pretty Via Vecchia Fiesolana. In the two photos below: on the left, the hill of San Francesco with the churches of Sant'Alessandro and Santa Cecilia; on the right, the cloister of the monastery of San Francesco, which houses a small but interesting Ethnographic Museum.

The Medici villas

Careggi. This 14th-century mansion was bought by Giovanni di Bicci, founder of the Medici dynasty, in 1417. Cosimo the Elder, who died here in 1464, commissioned Michelozzo to redesign the building. The architect succeeded in transforming an old, fortified farmhouse into a villa, while preserving elements of the original style, such as the crenellated gallery that crowns the central part of the building. Lorenzo the Magnificent was particularly fond of the villa and its garden, and it was here that philosopher Marsilio Ficino founded the famous Platonic Academy. Sacked in 1529, after the Medici had been ousted from Florence, the villa was renovated in 1532 by Duke Alessandro. Work was completed under Cosimo I, who had Pontormo and Bronzino decorate some of the rooms with frescoes, now sadly lost.
[Entrance: Viale Pieraccini 17. Opening times 9-13/ 15-18; closed on Saturdays and Sundays. To book 4277981].

La Petraia. Dating from the 14th-century, the mansion was purchased by the Medici in 1530. It was completely rebuilt between 1576 and 1589 by Ferdinando I to a design by Buontalenti, who planned a rectangular building with an inner courtyard, preserving the sturdy tower in the center of the medieval structure. Volterrano decorated the inner courtyard with a fresco cycle (1636-1648) illustrating the history of the Medici family. The garden maintains its charm notwithstanding the considerable alterations made to it when Vittorio Emanuele II lived here, during the period when Florence was capital of Italy. The garden is laid out on three levels, ascending towards the adjacent hillside. The middle level is occupied by an immense fishpond. The upper level hosts the *fountain of Venus-Fiorenza*, made by Tribolo in the mid-16th century and originally located at the Villa of Castello.
[Entrance: Via della Pietraia 40. Opening times 9-17,30; closed 1st May].

Castello. While the Villa of Careggi dates back to the period of Medici control of the Florentine Republic, the Villa of Castello was contemporary to the establishment of the Grand Ducal dynasty. It was bought and rebuilt in 1477 by Lorenzo the Magnificent's second cousins, Lorenzo and Giovanni. The villa was sacked when the Medici were exiled from Florence in 1527, but when Cosimo I took control of the city in 1537, he had it rebuilt according to a design by Vasari. Michel de Montaigne believed the garden, with its graceful fountain and sculpture of *Hercules and Antaeus* in the center, to be one of the most beautiful in Europe. The garden was designed by Tribolo, who directed the project from 1538 until his death. Subsequently, both Buontalenti and Ammannati worked on the garden. According to the original design, never actually completed, the garden would constitute an immense allegory of the prince's triumph, reproducing various features of the Tuscan countryside, including rivers and mountains.
Since 1974, the villa has been the seat of the Accademia della Crusca, founded in 1583 to compile the first dictionary of the Italian language.
[Entrance: Via di Castello. Garden only open to the public 9-17.30; closed 1st May].

The Certosa at Galluzzo

The monastery lies outside Porta Romana, on Via Senese, just beyond the suburb of Galluzzo. Towering and majestic, it looks almost like a fortress built high on the hill dominating the valley of the Ema. When it was suppressed by the French in 1810, who then occupied the Tuscan Grand Duchy, the inventory listed no less than five hundred works of art, many of which have never since been traced. The Certosa was founded in 1342 by Niccolò Acciaioli, a Florentine noble and High

Steward of Roberto, King of Naples. Despite the fact that the rules of the Carthusian order, as established by the founder, St Bruno, dictated poverty and separation from worldly possessions, Acciaioli ordered a large palace to be built beside the monastery. On his death in 1365, the ground and first floors of the building, designed by two friars, Jacopo Passavanti and Jacopo Talenti, had been built. It was completed around the mid-16th century. Since 1960, the first floor has housed a picture gallery. Amongst the many important works of art exhibited are five detached lunettes frescoed by Jacopo Pontormo, who came to live in the monastery from 1523 to 1525 in order to escape the plague. The paintings depict the *Sermon in the Garden, Christ before Pontius Pilate*, the *Resurrection*, the *Road to Calvary* and the *Deposition*.

The extensive monastic complex covers the entire summit of the hill, and is composed of various buildings which, viewed from outside, give the impression of a compact, single entity. The impression is entirely different from inside, where the sensation is that of an expansive terrace overlooking the splendid hills around Florence. From a large square the entrance leads up to the church of San Lorenzo, founded in the 14th century and modified in the 16th century. The façade is decorated with *bas-reliefs* and *statues* by Giovanni Fancelli; inside are works by 16th- and 17th-century Florentine and Tuscan painters, including Rutilio Manetti and Bartolomeo Atticciati.

In the monastery church are works by Bernardino Poccetti and, on three of the walls, late 16th-century stalls in carved and inlaid walnut. Beside the church is the Monk's cloister, altered in the mid-16th century; this leads into the Great Cloister, built several decades earlier. Around three sides are the monks cells, opening onto an extremely fine loggia. In the spandrels of the arches are sixty-six coloured terracotta tondi by the workshop of Giovanni della Robbia with *Old Testament Prophets, Saints, Apostles* and *Evangelists*.

[Entrance: Buca di Certosa 2. Opening times 9-12/ 16-19; closed on Mondays].

USEFUL INFORMATION

Bakeries. Florentine bakers make various kinds of bread ranging from the traditional Tuscan (unsalted) kind to the ubiquitous pizza. Well worth trying are the local *schiacciata* (flat bread, drizzled with oil) and *pandiramerino* (flavoured with rosemary). Traditional specialities also appear according to the season: in Autumn there is *schiacciata all'uva* (filled with a grape jam) and *castagnaccio* (made with sweet chestnut flour); at Christmas time there are *cavallucci* and *ricciarelli* (made with dried fruits) - really of Sienese origin, but popular in Florence; at carneval time there are *schiacciata all fiorentina* (lemon sponge cake) and *cenci* (fritters); for Saint Joseph's day (19th March), *fritelle* (small fried rice cakes), and during the Easter period *quaresimali* (lenten cakes). *Il Forno*, Via San Gallo 147r; *Pane e focacce*, Via de' Macci 65r; *Panetteria*, Via de' Neri 5r; *Panificio*, Via della Spada 39r; *Panificio Chiappi*, Borgo la Croce 43-45r; *Sartoni*, Via de' Cerchi 34r; *Quattrocchi*, Via Santa Monica 3r; *Il Fornaio di Galli*, Via Matteo Palmieri 24r and Via Faenza 39r.

Banks. The following opening hours apply: Monday-Friday 9.00-13.15; 14.30 (or 14.45)-15.30 (or 15.45). Many currency exchanges can be found in the centre. Be sure to ask what commission is applied before changing cheques or cash. Many shops and restaurants accept credit cards.

Boat rental on the river Arno. *Lidò*, Lungarno Pecori Giraldi 1; *Società Canottieri Firenze*, Lungarno F. Ferrucci 2.

Cafés and cake shops. ☛ box on p. 264.

Car rental. The main car rental companies have several branches in the city. Thus here we list only the address and telephone number of the main office. They are also to be found at the 'Amerigo Vespucci' airport, Florence. *Avis,* Borgo Ognissanti128r, tel. 239.882.6; *Eurodollar,* Via il Prato 80r, tel. 238.248.0/1; *Hertz,* Via Palazzuolo 94, tel. 282.260; *Maggiore,* Via Maso Finiguerra 31r, tel. 294.578.

Chemists (24-hour). *Comunale 13,* inside Santa Maria Novella Station; *Molteni,* Via Calzaiuoli 7r (on the corner with Via Porta Rossa); *All'Insegna del Moro,* Piazza San Giovanni 20r.

Children. Parents with young children should call in at the Ludoteca centrale, Piazza Santissima Annunziata 13, tel. 247.838.6, for toys and games. Open every morning (except Wednesday) from 9.00 until 13.00; open in the afternoon from 15.00 to 19.00 (Tuesday and Friday for children over six years old, Monday and Thursday for younger children). Several parks also provide a play area where families can relax: Piazza d'Azeglio, Borgo Allegri, the horticultural garden in Via Vittorio Emanuele II 4, the Cascine park, the garden at the Fortezza da Basso (the park is located beside the Fortezza between Viale Strozzi and Viale

Spartaco Lavagnini).

Consulates. Austria Via de' Servi 9, tel. 238.200.8
Belgium Via dei Servi 28, tel. 282.094
Chile Via Alamanni 25, tel. 214.131
China Via Fontana 34, tel. 351.680
Costa Rica Via Giambologna 10, tel. 573.603
Denmark Via dei Servi 13, tel. 211.007
Dominican Republic Via Milano 23 (Prato) tel. (0574)607.518
Finland Via Strozzi 6, tel. 293.228
France Piazza Ognissanti 2, tel. 230.255.6
Germany Lungarno A. Vespucci 30, tel. 294.722
Great Britain Lungarno Corsini 2, tel. 284.133-289.556
Haiti Via Cerretani 2, tel. 282.683
Honduras Via de' Bardi 30, tel. 234.251.9
Hungary Via Belgio 2, tel. 653.181.7
Ivory Coast Via Santo Spirito 9r, tel. 294.837
Luxembourg Via Bartolomei 4, tel. 473.219
Malta Via dell'Oriuolo 45, tel. 217.875; Via dei Servi 13, tel. 230.293.7
Mexico Via dell'Arte della Lana 4, tel. 217.831
Monaco (Principality of) Via Cherubini 18, tel. 587.897
The Netherlands Via Cavour 81, tel. 475.249
Norway Via G.Capponi 26, tel. 247.932.1
Panama Via Respighi 8, tel. 351.493; Via Mayer 19, tel. 473.904
Paraguay Via dell'Erta Canina 66, tel. 234.502.0
Peru Via della Mattonaia 17, tel. 234.334.5
Romania Borgo Pinti 20, tel. 240.601
San Marino Via Roma 3, tel. 210.864
South Africa Piazza dei Saltarelli 1, tel. 281.863
Spain Via G. la Pira 21, tel. 217.110
Sweden Via della Scala 4, tel. 239.686.5
Turkey Via Nazionale 7, tel. 294.893
United States of America *switchboard* tel. 239.827.6-217.605-280.261; *information service and cultural affairs* Lungarno A.Vespucci 46, tel. 294.921-283.780-284.088; *cultural exchanges* tel. 216.531; *commercial affairs* Lungarno A. Vespucci 38, tel. 211.676.
Venezuela Via Giambologna 10, tel. 588.082
Department stores. *Coin,* Via dei Calzaiuoli 56r; *Coop,* Via Nazionale 32r; *La Rinascente,* Piazza della Repubblica 1; *Oviesse,* Via Gioberti 158r and Via Nazionale 29; *Upim,* Via Gioberti 70 and Via dello Statuto 19r.
Discotheques and Night Clubs. *Meccanò,* Viale degli Olmi 1, Cascine park; *Tenax,* Via Pratese 47; *Villa Kasar,* Lungarno Colombo 23r; *Full Up,* Via della Vigna Vecchia 21r (music for all tastes); *Dolce Zucchero,* Via Pandolfini 36-38r (piano bar open until late at night with two rooms and small discotheque); *Caffedecò,* Piazza della Libertà 45-46r (open from morning until late at night); *Jackie O',* Via dell'Erta Canina 24a (a classic night club); *Lido,* Lungarno Pecori Giraldi 1 (one of the

most popular nightclubs, pedal boats can also be hired from here); *Cassiopea*, Via Aretina 7r (large enough for live groups to hold concerts); *Teatro sull'Acqua*, Lungarno Pecori Giraldi 3 (only open in the summertime).

Guided tours. ☞ entry 'Tourist Guides'.

Health Services. Switchboard for ambulance calls 212.222; *emergency service,* tel. 118; *Santa Maria Nuova Hospital*, Piazza Santa Maria Nuova 1, tel. 275.81; *Meyer Pediatric Hospital*, Via Luca Giordano 13, tel. 566.21.

Hotels (☞ p. 268). If you are planning to visit Florence you really need to book in advance. If you did not so beforehand, or simply were not able to, here are a few helpful suggestions. Firstly the *APT* (Azienda di promozione turistica di Firenze) (☞ Tourist Information) distributes free of charge its annual publication, *Firenze, Guida all'ospitalità* (Florence Hotel Information) containing a complete list of all the hotels, *pensioni*, camping sites and youth hostels in the city and surrounding area, including a full description of their services and facilities, with current prices.

Information is also available from the *ITA*, Tourist Hotel Information, which has three offices: one inside the station of Santa Maria Novella, tel. 282.893; another on the A11 motorway, Firenze-Mare at the Agip service station at Peretola, tel. 421.1800; a third is located on the A1 motorway, at the Chianti Est service station, tel. 621.349.

Those who would like to rent a room in a private house (with the possibility of having meals with the guest family) can contact *AGAP* in Via de' Neri 9, tel. and fax 284.100.

Ice cream shops. One of the most popular genuine Italian specialities. There are plenty of good ice cream shops in Florence; here are just some of them: *Aquilone*, Via don Puliti 21; *Badiani*, Viale dei Mille 20r; *Baroncini*, Via Celso 3r; *Carabè*, Via Ricasoli 60r; *Cavini*, Piazza delle Cure 19-23r; *Ciolli*, Via Ramazzini 35-37r; *Frilli*, Via San Miniato 5r; *Orso Bianco*, Via di Caciolle 6; *Perché no?*, Via dei Tavolini 19r; *Pinguino*, Via Q. Sella 6d; *Villani*, Via San Domenico 8; *Vivoli*, Via Isola delle Stinche 7r.

Local cheeses ☞ box on p. 270.

Markets. Food markets: stalls inside the *San Lorenzo central market*, Via dell'Ariento (every morning from 7.00 to 14.00 except for Sunday and public holidays); *Sant'Ambrogio*, Piazza Ghiberti (same hours as the central market for the stalls both inside and outside the building); *Santo Spirito market*, Piazza Santo Spirito (every morning except Sundays and public holidays; all day on the second Sunday of every month); *Le Cure*, Piazza delle Cure (every morning except Sunday and public holidays). Clothing, leather and straw goods: *Straw Market*, Piazza del Mercato Nuovo (every day from 9.00 to 18.30 pm. except Sunday and public holidays). Second-hand furniture, household articles and books: *Flea market*, Piazza dei Ciompi (every day from 9.00 to 19.30 pm. On the last Sunday of every month the stalls extend into the sur-

rounding streets). Clothing, shoes and leather: *San Lorenzo market*, Via del canto de' Nelli, Via dell'Ariento e Via Sant'Antonino (every day from 9.00 to 19.30). Clothing, shoes and household goods: the *Cascine market*, Viale degli Olmi (every Tuesday morning). Plants and flowers: *Flower market*, under the portico in Piazza della Repubblica (every Thursday morning).

Opening times of main churches. ☞ box p. 272.

Opening times of main museums. ☞ box p. 272.

Pizza. ☞ box p. 267.

Police and Fire Brigade. Italy has two separate police forces, the Polizia di Stato (a non-military force) and the Carabinieri (fulfilling a double role as both military and judicial police). Either force may be called on when necessary, such as in the case of theft (☞ entry) or other emergencies and problems.

Questura (headquarters of the State Police), Via Zara, 2, tel. 497.71.

Commissariato di Polizia di Stato, Piazza Duomo 5, tel 497.71

Carabinieri, emergency number, tel. 112.

Centralized emergency number, tel. 113.

The *Polizia Stradale* (tel. 577.777) is responsible for all matters concerning road traffic and circulation. Road accidents should be reported to them (or to the *Polizia Municipale,* * below) for assistance and for the necessary report.

In addition to these state forces, the Municipal Police (*Polizia Municipale,* also known as the *Vigili Urbani*) tel. 328.31, are not only responsible for traffic in the city, but also fulfil several other roles. One may refer to them for matters concerning prices and services.

Vigili del Fuoco (Fire Brigade) tel. 115.

Post Offices. All post offices are open from Monday to Saturday from 8.15 to 13.30; some, including the main Post Office (Via Pelliceria, 3) and the Post Office in Via Pietrapiana, 53, are open all day from 8.15 to 18.00.

Stamps can be bought in Post Offices and to-bacconists' shops.

For information on the postal services, ring 160.

Restaurants and Trattorie. ☞ box on p. 265.

Self-service petrol stations. *AGIP*, Via Antonio del Pollaiolo; *Tamoil*, Via Senese; *ESSO*, Viale Europa; *IP*, Via Baccio da Montelupo; *Mobiloil*, Via Pratese.

Shopping. ☞ box on p. 271.

SOS for Tourists. The APT tourist information office (Via Cavour1r) provides assistance and advice for all problems (open 10.00 - 13.00 & 15.00 - 18.00; tel. 276.038.2). At present the service is only operative from April to October, but it is hoped that it willl soon be active all year round.

Street numbering. According to a rule which applies in almost all of Europe, street numbers usually start from the principle geographical feature of the city, in this case, the river. If the street or square is parallel to the river Arno, the numbering of the buildings starts towards the source and increases in the direction of the outlet; if perpendicular, numbering starts from the river bank and increases away from it. Even numbers are on the right side and uneven on the left.

In Florence a double sequence of street numbering exists. Shops and businesses are identified by the letter 'r' after the number. This signifies 'red'. Private residences are numbered in black. Thus a street may have two number 18's, at times at considerable distance one from the other; 18r (as in the addresses given here) is a shop or business, while 18 is a private house.

Supermarkets. There are few food supermarkets in the city centre; these are mainly located in the immediate suburbs. *Coop,* Via Cimabue 49, Via Gian Paolo Orsini, 41r, Via Salvi Cristiani 16, Via Gramsci 18, Fiesole; *Conad,* Via dei Servi 56r and Via Scipione Ammirato 94/b; *Esselunga*, Via Massaccio 274-276, Via Canova 164, Viale de Amicis 89/b.

Taxis. All taxis are white and are identified by a sign on the roof and a name and identification number on the front doors. When free, they will stop if hailed. Radio taxis can be called by phone using one of the following number: 439.0; 424.2; 479.8. The main taxi ranks are in Piazza Duomo (at the back of the cathedral), in Piazza della Repubblica and in Piazza Stazione. If you are near any of the secondary taxi ranks it is worth calling the number directly. They can be found at: Piazza Alberti, tel. 679.872; Piazza Beccaria, tel. 234.361.4; Piazza delle Cure, tel. 579.035; Piazza F. Ferrucci, tel. 681.164.4; Piazza Giorgini, tel. 471.530; Piazza Mino (Fiesole), tel. 592.04; Piazza Puccini, tel. 361.100; Piazza San Marco, tel. 284.124; Piazzale di Porta Romana, tel. 220.528; Via Bronzino (on corner of Via A. del Pollaiolo), tel. 705.100; Via di Novoli, tel. 537.999.3; Viale Calatafimi, tel. 605.794; Viale Mazzini, tel. 242.601; Viale Morgagni, tel. 416.800.

Tea, Coffee and Confectionery. *Lanzo Caffè,* Via de' Neri 69r. Regional Italian produce and a wide variety of coffees. *Traversi «La Sorgente delle delizie»,* Via Cavour 30a. Well stocked with chocolate and sweets. *Caffè e Delizie di Lisa,* Viale don Minzoni 52r. Exquisite chocolate truffles.

Telephones. Public telephones are located all over the city, however, poor maintenance is a problem and frequently many are out of service. Avoid machines which only take coins (both the least practical and least reliable) and use telephone cards instead. Cards, available at various prices, are sold in tobacconist shops. Otherwise there is a public telephone office in Via Cavour. The user is assigned a cabin and pays the cost of the call at the end. To make an operator call, dial 10 for national connections and 170 for international.

Temperatures. Don't give too much credence to the myth of blue skies and an eternal balmy spring - you will only risk arriving in Florence with too light a wardrobe and probably without a raincoat and umbrella too! If so, you will be poorly equipped, because the city, lying at the foot of the Apennine chain is barely affected by the mild influence of the sea, although it is not far away (less than 100 kilometres). The climate is continental with extremes of temperature in summer and winter and heavy rainfall in spring and autumn. In summer the temperature during the day, aggravated by the lumidity which is felt even at night, can easily reach 36-37° C with occasional, but not exceptional peaks of 40°C and above, while in January and February it can often drop below 0°C.

Theatres. Florence's theatres provide a wide range of entertainment from prose to opera, symphonic and chamber music, ballet and jazz. Information on the programmes offered is published every day in the local entertainment pages of the *Repubblica, Nazione* and *Unità* newspapers, and is also available from *Box Office*, Via Faenza, 139r, tel. 210.804, where bookings can be made and tickets bought.

Theft. Like any other large tourist centre, Florence has a high rate of petty crime. There are three common types of theft: pickpockets on the bus, especially at rush hour; bag-snatching, where the thief, on a scooter, grabs the victim's hand or shoulder bag violently as he passes; thefts in the historic centre especially while waiting in a queue to enter a museum or church. Here is some advice to minimize the possibility: be particularly cautious while travelling by bus; do not keep large sums of money, traveller's cheques, credit cards or personal documents in your bag; if you find you have to wait for any length of time in one place, keep your camera in your hand and be very wary of anyone who approaches you without clear reason.

Obviously it is preferable to change small amounts of money at a time and to use a bank to do so.

Tourist guides. *Agt Firenze,* Via Roma 4, tel. 230.288.3, fax 238.279.0; *Centro Guide Turismo,* Via Ghibellina 110, tel. 288.448, fax 288.476; *Guide Turistiche Fiorentine*, Via Ugo Corsi 25, tel. and fax 422.090.1.

Tourist information. *APT* (Azienda Provinciale per il Turismo). The central office (Via A. Manzoni 16) only provides information by correspondance (fax 055/234.6286). On the spot information is available at: *APT,* Via Cavour 1r, tel. 290.832/3; *APT,* arrivals area in the 'Amerigo Vespucci' airport, tel. 315.874. *City of Florence Tourist Office*: Chiasso de' Baroncelli 17-19r, tel. 230.212.4 and Piazza Stazione (beneath the metal canopy outside on the arrivals side) tel. 212.245.

Traffic and Car Parks. Given the size of the city, walking or using the bus are the best ways of getting around. In any case, trying to drive in the centre is a veritable challenge. A ZTL (traffic free zone) exists from 8.30 in the morning to 18.30 (except Sunday and public holidays). Parking is prohibited in this area between those hours and you may find that your car has been fined or, worse, towed away. There are, however, many periferal car parks: those at the Parterre (on the far side of Piazza Libertà), Via del Gelsomino 11 and Piazza Stazione are covered pay-parks. Many others, also pay-parks but uncovered, are located all over the city: Viale Mazzini, Piazza Donatello, Piazza Savonarola, Piazza della Libertà, Lungarno Torrigiani, Lungarno della Zecca Vecchia, Piazza Poggi. Others, such as Via Massaccio, and Via Ferdinando Paolieri, have parking meters. Take care also not to park overnight in an area where rectangular No Parking (Divieto di Sosta) signs indicate a weekday between 0-6am., when street cleaning takes place. This too can lead to a fine and removal of the vehicle.

Transport. A list follows of the various means of transport availale for urban, provincial and intercity transport, both long distance and local.

- *Urban transport.* The Florentine bus service is run by the ATAF company, Viale dei Mille 115, tel. 565.01. The buses are a bright orange colour. Maps of all the routes are available from the ATAF information office, Piazza Stazione (located below the metal canopy on the arrivals side). Bus tickets must be bought before boarding and stamped on the bus using the machine by the door. Tickets can be bought from tobacconists, many bars and newstands and are available as follows:
- valid for 60 minutes;
- valid for 120 minutes;
- multiple (*multiplo*) for four journeys, each valid 60 minutes;
- 24-hour tourist ticket.

If staying in the city for a month or more, it is a good idea to take out a monthly subscription. Simply take a passport photograph to the 'Ufficio Abbonamenti' ATAF, Piazza Stazione (at the far end of the canopy on the arrivals side).

The number 62 bus links Santa Maria Novella station to the Amerigo Vespucci airport at Peretola. This service functions from 6am. to 10pm. and leaves at frequencies between 10 minutes at rush hour and 30 minutes at slack times. The number 7 bus links Santa Maria station to Fiesole.

- *Coaches* (provincial and regional buses). Several bus companies provide an extensive network linking towns and cities throughout the province of Florence and the entire Tuscan region. The main bus companies are: *CAP* and *COPIT*, Largo Fratelli Alinari 9, tel. 214.637; *Lazzi*, Piazza Stazione 4 (on the corner of Piazza Adua), tel. 215.154; *SITA*, Via Santa Caterina da Siena 15, tel. 214.721.

- *Trains.* Most regrettably it has to be said that although the FS (ferrovie dello Stato) were made into a limited company some time ago, they still unfortunately preserve much of the bureaucracy and inefficiency of many Italian state bodies. Luckily, to compensate for these defects is the courtesy of the staff, who manage always to be patient and helpful in dealing with passengers.

Tickets can be bought not only in the station, but also in some travel agencies (☞ entry) with no extra, or only a minimal, charge. To ensure a seat on long distance trains, (*espressi, interregionali* and *Eurostar*) it is necessary to make and pay for a reservation. Moreover, for the *Eurostar* trains, whose rapidity is often more a fantasy than a fact, a supplement applies. This can be issued separately or added on to the price of the basic ticket. Those without a supplement will be fined. Another fine can be imposed on those who forget to stamp their ticket at the yellow machines at the head of the platforms. And don't forget that if you have a return ticket, it must be stamped a second time on the return trip. Almost all trains leave from *Santa Maria Novella*, (tel. 245.1). Local trains and some high speed trains may stop at *Rifredi*, (tel. 411.138); mainly local and interregional trains stop at *Campo di Marte* (tel. 234.434).

- *Airlines.* Although small, the Amerigo Vespucci airport at Peretola (information office tel. 373.498) has good connections. For information on flights, contact the offices of the various airlines: *Aerolinas Argentinas*, Via dei Neri 19, tel. 289.166; *Air France,* Borgo Santi Apostoli 9, tel. 284.304; *Alia*, Borgo San Jacopo 2, tel. 283.219; *Alitalia* Lungarno Vespucci 10-12r, tel. 278.81; *Cimair (Sabena, Garuda, Icelandair, Cyprus Airways, Korean Airlines),* Via Tornabuoni 1, tel. 282.282 and 293.031; *Kuwait Airways*, Via Calimaruzza 3, tel. 294.854; *Meridiana*, Lungarno Soderini 1, tel. 230.233.4; *Olympic Airways,* Via Por Santa Maria 4, tel. 292.733; *SAS*, Lungarno Acciaioli 8, tel. 238.270.1; *Thai*, Via de' Vecchietti 4, tel. 294.372; *TWA*, Via de' Vecchietti 4, tel. 239.685.6.

Travel Agencies. *CIT*, Via Cavour 56r; *CIT*, Piazza della Stazione 51r; *Lazzi Express*, Piazza Adua 4r; *Amico Travel Box*, Via dell'Oriuolo 52-54; *Salviati e Santori*, Via Lambertesca 21 r; *TST* Viaggi 2000, Borgo de' Greci 5.

Tripe. A Florentine speciality not favoured by all. These are the locations of the various stalls throughout the city: Piazza de' Cimatori (on the corner with Via Dante Alighieri); Piazza del Mercato Nuovo (opposite no. 4); the square at Porta Romana (between Viale Machiavelli and Via Romana); Piazza delle Cure; Piazza Tanucci; Via Gioberti (between Via Cimabue and Piazza Beccaria); Viale Giannotti (on the corner with Via G. Caponsacchi).

Wine. ☞ box on p. 267.

CAFÉS & CAKE SHOPS

Caffelatte,
Via degli Alfani 39r.
This bar, with a magnificent marble counter, has been selling milk and coffee since 1921. Have a seat and sip a delicious milky coffee with a piece of home-made cake.

Calamai,
Via dell'Agnolo 113r.
Attractive, high-class bar.

Caponeri,
Via F. Valori 4r.
Excellent profiteroles and pastries. No coffee bar.

Castaldini,
Viale dei Mille 47r.
The millefeuilles are delicious, but try the other sweet treats too.

Cosi,
Borgo degli Àlbizzi 11r.
The cream cakes are a real treat at teatime.

Crociani,
Piazza Dalmazia 37r.
Lots of delicious little cakes and lovely Sicilian cannoli.

Dolci & Dolcezze,
Piazza Beccaria 9r and Via del Corso 41r.
This patisserie has introduced imaginative new ideas to Florentine cake lovers.

Donnini,
Piazza della Repubblica 15r.
Wonderful patisserie.

Gaetano,
Via Torre degli Agli 2.
Always crowded but worth the effort!

Giacosa,
Via Tornabuoni 83 r.
They make one of the best coffees in town.

Giorgio,
Via Duccio da Boninsegna 36.
Elegant bar, excellent cakes.

Gualtieri,
Via Senese 18r. *Charmingly old-fashioned. Good traditional specialities.*

Italiano,
Via Condotta 56r.
Pause for a tea, coffee or drink, or have a bite to eat upstairs at lunchtime.

Minni,
Via A. Giacomini 16.
Their speciality is little doughnuts (called bomboloni in Florence) served hot at five in the afternoon. A good selection of sweets and savouries is available all day.

Piansa,
Borgo Pinti 18r and Viale Europa 128.
These two comfortable bars were opened by a coffee specialist and importer - so great coffee as well as snacks.

Rivoire,
Piazza della Signoria 5r.
Try their steaming cups of hot chocolate.

Robiglio,
Via dei Servi 112r, Via Tosinghi 11r and Viale S. Lavagnini 18r.
Delicious sweets and savouries. Try the savoury pastries filled with ham.

Scudieri,
Piazza San Giovanni 19r.
The best savoury croissants.

Stefania,
Via Marconi 26r.
Excellent patisserie.

Alcedo,
Via A. Gramsci 26. Fiesole.
Good service, good quality.

Restaurants And Trattorie

Italians generally do not start the day with a big breakfast, on the whole a cappuccino and a brioche are sufficient. While lunch used to be quite a substantial meal, most people now only have time for a light snack and few can still enjoy the luxury of actually going home for their midday meal. Many bars in the centre now prepare pasta dishes and light second courses, but also have a large choice of substantial sandwiches. More traditionally, some prefer to eat a boiled egg or a crostino, perhaps in a 'mescita' (☛ p. 267), with a glass of wine, or simply standing at one of the characteristic stalls selling the classic tripe sandwich. Purists, however, have not yet given up the habit of a pause - even if not too lengthy - in a trattoria. The trattoria is generally less expensive than a restaurant; moreover, you do not have to pay a service charge and rarely the 'coperto' - a sort of modest tax on the table setting, and a rather dubious Italian practice which happily seems to be dying out.
To enjoy fully the pleasures of the table, it is best to save your main meal until the evening. Don't forget that the more modest trattorie do not accept bookings, so it is best to get there early (about 7.30-8pm).

🍴 under 30,000 lire
🍴 🍴 30,000-60,000 lire
🍴 🍴 🍴 60,000-100,000 lire
🍴 🍴 🍴 🍴 over 100,000 lire

🍴 Da Gastone «alle mossacce»
Via del Proconsolo 55r
Tel. 294.361
closed Saturday and Sunday
☛ T. 4/F5
In the Florentine dialect mossacce means a gruff, uncouth gesture, probably accompanied by language which one would not use in good company. That is the treatment customers who think they will linger over their meal can expect from the owner here, for the place is small and very popular. Needless to say you cannot reserve a table and you will be squeezed in where there is room. Apart from such minor drawbacks, the typically Florentine dishes are very tasty.

🍴 Carlino «diladdarno»
Via de' Serragli 108r
Tel. 225.001
closed Monday and Tuesday
☛ T. 2/D6
'Diladdarno' is vernacular for 'the other side of the Arno'. Typically Tuscan home cooking. Worth trying the desserts too.

🍴 Mario
Via Rosina 2r
Tel. 218.550
closed in the evenings and on Sunday
☛ T. 3/F4
No table reservations here either - the trattoria is small and you just have to queue, but it is worth the effort. Typically Tuscan food and wine. On Fridays fish, bought fresh in the nearby San Lorenzo market, is served.

🍴 Da Benvenuto
Via Mosca 16r (On the corner of Via de' Neri)
Tel. 214.833
closed Sunday and Wednesday
☛ T. 4/F6
A good old family-style trattoria, with attractive decor. Loriano Pallini is the proud owner of a vegetable garden and he makes good use of its seasonal produce. Here too the menu is mainly traditional (excellent bollito misto - mixed boiled meats - and baccalà - stockfish - on Fridays) with some house specialities too, however, such as the cappellacci al tartufo (pasta with truffle sauce). The cooking is tasty, but light, avoiding some of the bad habits one occasionally comes across in Florence, such as the use of fried oil in some dishes. A good choice of wines, including some non-Tuscan, and some of top quality.

🍴 Acquacotta
Via dei Pilastri 51r
Tel. 242.907
closed Tuesday evening and Wednesday
☛ T. 4/G5
This trattoria is named after a typical Tuscan dish from the area of the Maremma which consists of a vegetable soup served with an egg poached in it and garnished with toasted bread.

🍴 Pentola dell'Oro
Via di Mezzo 24-26r
Tel. 241.821
closed Sunday and public holidays
☛ T. 4/G5
The manager of this club for gourmets, Alessi, is renowned for his creative style of cooking which reinterprets traditional Tuscan dishes. Open for lunch and in the evening, to enter you will have to become a member of Endas, a national recreational association. A membership card costs a moderate L.10,000 and Alessi's prices are most reasonable too. Once you have enjoyed your meal the Endas card entitles you to discounts at theatres, cinemas and exhibitions.

🍴 Il Guscio
Via dell'Orto 49
Tel. 224.421
open only in the evenings; closed Sunday

T. 2/D5

Home cooking from various regions of Italy, enhanced by some clever and interesting innovations. Over fifty different types of wine to choose from, including some good French ones.

Sergio Gozzi

Piazza San Lorenzo 8r
Tel. 281.941
closed Sunday and in the evenings.
T. 3/F4

Sergio is the talented chef in this family-run trattoria. There is always something new to try on the menu, from best quality fish to zuppa di farro (wheat and bean soup).

Sabatino

Borgo San Frediano 39r
Tel. 284.625
closed Saturday and Sunday
T. 2/D5

This lively family-run trattoria opened in 1950 and its style and charm remain unchanged. Simple home cooking - excellent chick peas and beans with oil. Best to book in the evening.

Buca dell'Orafo

Volta de' Girolami 28r
Tel. 213.619
closed Sunday and Monday
T. 4/F6

In Florence the cellar of an aristocratic palace which has a door on to the street, is known as a buca (a hole or pit). Open since 1945 this is a favourite of Florentines and tourists alike for both its excellent cooking (fried brains, beef stew, tripe and fresh pasta) and the family atmosphere. Piero, one of the owners, can immediately recognize the best steaks for producing a delicious bistecca alla fiorentina and is quite capable of sending it straight back to the butcher if it is not up to standard.

Angiolino

Via Santo Spirito 36r
Tel. 239.8976
closed Monday and Sunday evening
T. 4/E6

A lovely antique cast iron stove adds to the pleasant atmosphere in this typically Florentine trattoria, with its vaulted ceilings, old tables and characteristic bar at the entrance. You will find a balanced menu and good cooking with an excellent choice of wines.

Palle d'Oro

Via Sant'Antonino 73r
Tel. 288.383
closed Sunday
T. 3/F4

At lunchtime you can choose between a meal served at table or a quick snack at the bar for a fixed price. In the evening there is waiter service only and the menu changes too. A more international selection takes the place of mainly southern Italian dishes. On Friday, fish specialities are available.

Sostanza detto «il troia»

Via del Porcellana 25r
Tel. 212.691
closed Saturday and Sunday
T. 4/E5

This trattoria opened in 1869 and has maintained an old-fashioned look and atmosphere: the marble counter and the chairs are beautiful. It owes its name troia (slut) to the first owner who apparently had the rather unpleasant habit of touching the guests with his hands still greasy from the kitchen. The menu is typically Florentine: delicious bistecca alla fiorentina; a spectacular artichoke pie; wonderful baccalà (stockfish) on Friday. Don't forget to book.

Alfredo

viale don Minzoni 3r
Tel. 578.291
closed Monday
T. 3/G2

It is advisable to book as the restaurant is small. The atmosphere is warm and welcoming, the menu traditional with occasional exotic experiments.

Pane e Vino

Via San Niccolò 70a/r
Tel. 247.695.6
closed Sunday
T. 4/G6

Pane e Vino came into existence twenty years ago as a wine bar with cold buffet in a suburb of the city. Chef Barbara Zattoni is inventive without extremes and the menu is one of the best examples of new Florentine cookery. As well as the classics, the wine list offers some interesting choices at good prices. The style is informal and Gilberto Pierazzuoli, the manager-cum-sommelier, with the help of his brother, Ubaldo, is always willing to help and advise.

Taverna del Bronzino

Via delle Ruote 27r
Tel. 495.220
closed Sunday
T. 3/F3

Both the menu and wine list offer a wide choice. Dishes from various regions of Italy, as well as the classics, and many interesting variations are available. Though the setting is elegant, the atmosphere is informal.

Enoteca Pinchiorri

Via Ghibellina 87
Tel. 242.777
closed Wednesday lunchtime, Sunday and Monday
T. 4/G5

Filled with bottles of rare wines, this is one of the best stocked cellars in Europe. There is a rather French flavour to all the cooking, even the local and regional dishes, and probably the continuing official recognition the Enoteca from beyond the Alps is due to this. The setting is elegant and the atmosphere formal. One can dine in the garden in summertime. The sample menu costs L. 150,000, excluding wine.

PIZZERIE

The pizza - a Neapolitan invention now popular throughout all Italy, thanks to its lightness and convenience. A good pizza - and Florence boasts quite a few experts in the skill - can take the place of an evening meal or, even better, lunch when a long pause in a restaurant or trattoria would be too time consuming.

¶ Pizzaiuolo
Via dei Macci 113r
Tel. 241.171
closed Sunday
☛ T. 4/G5
First-class pizzas. The owner is a genuine Neapolitan. You will need to book, as their pizza is so good they are always full up.

¶ Santa Lucia
Via del Ponte alle Mosse 102r
Tel. 353.255
closed Wednesday
☛ T. 1/C3
Good pizza served until late at night.

¶ Spera
Via della Cernaia 9r
Tel. 495.286
closed Monday; open only in the evening on Saturday and Sunday
☛ T. 3/F2
Signor Spera was a first rate amateur boxer in the past, even reaching the world finals in the ban-

tamweight category. When he decided to hang up the gloves, he started to prepare knock-out pizzas instead. There is a fixed price menu available at lunchtime too and it is well worth trying the seafood and vegetarian antipasti. They don't accept bookings so you should get there early, especially in the evenings.

¶ Firenze Nova
Via Benedetto Dei 122
Tel. 411.937
closed Monday
☛ T. 1/C1 beyond Via ponte di Mezzo
As well as pizza you shouldn't miss the house speciality - delicious fish.

¶ La Greppia
Lungarno F. Ferrucci 4-8
Tel. 681.234.1
closed Monday
☛ T. 5/I6
Open until two in the morning. You can eat your food while enjoying the wonderful view over the Arno.

WINE BARS & WINE SELLERS

¶ Cantinetta dei Verrazzano
Via de' Tavolini 20r
Tel. 268.590
closed Sunday and public holidays
☛ T. 4/F5
The oil, wines and spirits all come from the estate and castle of Verrazzano near Greve in Chianti. As well as savouring the wines and grappa and enjoying an excellent coffee, you can also have a bite to eat. The warm schiacciata sandwiches and the unusual little snacks are all most tempting.

¶ Antica Mescita
Via San Niccolò 60r
Tel. 234.283.6
closed Sunday
☛ T. 4/G6
Typical Florentine food served in a warm and friendly setting. Booking is necessary in the evenings. After supper it stays open as a bar.

¶ ¶ Enoteca bar Fuori Porta
Via del Monte alle Croci 10r
Tel. 234.248.3
closed Saturday and Sunday
☛ T. 4/G7
An excellent and wide range of Italian and foreign wines and spirits. At lunchtime you can enjoy good home cooking served at table for as little as L. 20,000. In the evening only snacks are available -

tasty cold meats, hams, salame and pickles. Next door, the well stocked shop sells wines and liqueurs.

Zanobini
Via Sant'Antonino 47r
Tel. 239.685.0
closed Sunday and Wednesday
☛ T. 3/F4
The street this mescita is in used to be called Cella di Ciardo after the vast cellar (in Latin cella) which Ciardo the wine dealer used to have here. The original porticoed shop has now disappeared. The present proprietors have been selling wine and oil from their farm 'Le Lame' here since 1944. The traditions of good wine and good crack, even if a bit ribald or even coarse at times, though always good humoured, create the thoroughly Florentine atmosphere.

¶ Fiaschetteria Vecchio Casentino
Via de' Neri 17r
Tel. 217.411
closed Monday
☛ T. 4/F6
Strictly Tuscan food: ribollita (bread soup), salsiccia and beans, excellent cold sliced meats. You can have a quick snack or enjoy a glass of wine and appetizer at the bar.

¶ Casa del Vino
Via dell'Ariento 16r

closed Sunday
☛ T. 3/F4
This bar opened in the 19th century and still has the original wood furnishings. The good atmosphere is due to the interesting mix of locals and habitués who, however, all have the same interest in wine and good chat. A wide range of wines, spirits, oil, snacks and sandwiches.

⅋ Vini del Chianti «I fratellini»
Via de' Cimatori 38r
closed Sunday
☛ T. 4/F5
The bar opened in 1875 and has always been run by two brothers: the name means 'younger brothers'. There is no room to sit as the little bar has actually been set up in the doorway to the cellar. Only Tuscan wines are served accompanied, if you wish, by crostini, slices of ham, salami and local specialities.

⅋ Antico Noè
Volta di San Piero 6r
sometimes closed on Sunday

☛ T. 4/G5
Wash a tasty antipasto down with a good glass of red Tuscan wine at the bar. They make wonderful sandwiches too, filled with typical Tuscan meats and ingredients such as cold meats and sausage (like the delicious briciolona), tripe, crostini with Tuscan paté, roast pork or veal, vegetables preserved in oil or vinegar.

Bonatti
Via Gioberti 66r
Tel. 660.050
☛ T. 5/I5
One of the best stocked wine shops in the city where the frieindly owners are always at hand with good advice.

Internazionale De Rham
Via Campofiore 110
Tel. 661.665
☛ T. 6/I6
Slightly off the beaten track but worth a visit anyway. Specialists in wine exportation.

HOTELS & PENSIONS

Prices given are for double rooms with bathroom.
Asterisks indicate the maximum price in Lire as follows:
* = 100,000; ** = 150,000; *** = 200,000; **** = 250,000; ***** = 300,000; ****** = 400,000;
******* = 600,000.
AC Credit cards accepted.
☛ Breakfast included.

Villa il Castagno *
Via Andrea del Castagno 31
Tel. 571.701
☛ T.5/H3
A very simple but charming hotel. Eighteen rooms all with private bathroom.

Teti & Prestige *
Via Porta Rossa 5
Tel. 239.843.5 Fax 239.824.8
☛ T.4/E5
Small, family-run hotel in the heart of Florence.

Firenze * ☛
Piazza dei Donati 4
Tel. 214.203 fax 212.370
☛ T.4/F5
Charming hotel in a wonderful position.

Il Granduca * ☛
Via Pier Capponi 13
Tel 572.803 fax 579.252
☛ T.5/H3
Twenty-room hotel, just outside the historic centre, but in a good strategic position.

Ferrucci *
Via di Ricorboli 2
Tel. 658.098.2 fax 689.664
☛ T.6/I7

With only a very few rooms it is almost like living in a family.

Residenza Johanna ** ☛
Via B. Lupi 14
Tel. 481.896 fax 482.721
☛ T.3/F3
Eleven rooms almost all with private facilities. Extremely well kept and surrounded by gardens.

Pensione Bencistà ** ☛
Via Benedetto da Maiano 4, Fiesole
Tel. & fax 591.63
Situated on a hill above Florence, this is the ideal place for those who have children. Not all the 44 rooms have private baths. Prices are for each individual and include full board.

Ariston** ☛ AC
Via Fiesolana 40
Tel. 247.669.3 fax 247.698.0
☛ T.4/G5
Small hotel with 29 rooms, all with private bathroom.

Rita Major**
Via della Mattonaia 43
Tel. 247.7990 fax 247.835.8
☛ T.5/H4
Hotel with a private garden and a reading room.

Bodoni ** ☛
Via Martiri del Popolo 27
Tel. 240.741 fax 244.432
☛ T.4/G5
Some of the rooms look out over the Loggia del Pesce in Piazza dei Ciompi.

Chiazza ** ☛
Borgo Pinti 5
Tel. 248.036.3 fax 234.688.8
☛ T.3/G4
Small hotel in one of the most characteristic areas of the city.

Classic *** ☛ AC
☛ T.2/D8
Hotel in a 19-th century villa surrounded by trees and gardens. Most attractive and welcoming.

Silla *** ☛ AC
Via de' Renai 5
Tel. 234.288.8 fax 234.143.7
☛ T.4/G6
Of architectural interest, the building dates from the 16th century; attractive views, quiet and relaxing.

Porta Rossa *** ☛
Via Porta Rossa 19
Tel. 287.551 fax 282.179
☛ T.4/E5
There has been a hotel here since 1389. Each of the 85 rooms is decorated differently. The entrance has a beautiful vaulted ceiling.

David **** ☛ AC
Viale Michelangelo 1
Tel. 681.169.5 fax 680.602
☛ T.6/H7
A peaceful spot to stay, not far from the centre. All of the 26 rooms have a view over the garden.

Palazzo Benci **** ☛ AC
Via Faenza 6 r
Tel 217.049/238.282.1/213.848 fax 288.308
☛ T.3/E4
Thirty-five rooms all with private bathroom, television and frigo bar. Some of the rooms have a good view of the Medici chapels.

Villa Liberty **** ☛ AC
Viale Michelangelo 40
Tel. 681.058.1/683.819 fax 681.259.5
☛ T.6/H7
Fifteen rooms and two suites in Liberty style with art-nouveau furnishings. Rooms on the first floor have frescoed ceilings and those on the second, exposed beams. The Hotel City in Via Sant'Antonino 18 has the same management and the same rates.

Tel. 211.543 fax 295.451.
☛ T.3/E4

Loggiato dei Serviti ***** ☛ AC
Piazza Santissima Annunziata 3
Tel. 289.592/3/4 fax 289.595
☛ T.3/G4
Twenty-nine rooms , including four suites, in a delightful 16th-century building. No two rooms are the same and the furnishings and decoration are all in excellent taste.

Villa Aurora ***** ☛ AC
Piazza Mino 39, Fiesole
Tel. 591.00/592.92 fax 595.87
☛ Fiesole
Built in the 1860's as a theatre and opera house and transformed at the end of the 19th century into a hotel. All 28 rooms have full services and some on the first floor have a splendid view of Florence.

J and J ****** ☛ AC
Via di Mezzo 20
Tel. 234.500.5 fax 240.282
☛ T.4/G5
Once a monastery, this hotel still preserves the original plasterwork, frescoes and lovely cloister with a well. The nineteen rooms, including two suites, are exquisitely furnished down to the last detail. The view from some of the rooms is quite magnificent. The beautifully presented buffet-style breakfast will satisfy all tastes, whether you prefer a classic start to the day or decide to try out some traditional Tuscan foods.

Regency & Relais Le Jardin ******* ☛ AC
Piazza M. d'Azeglio 3
Tel. 245.247 fax 234.293.8
☛ T.5/H4
This late 19th-century villa has 34 rooms and 5 suites all beautifully and tastefully decorated, and with every possible facility. The atmosphere is refined and welcoming: in the summer clients can breakfast in the garden. The restaurant is open at lunchtime and in the evening to non-residents as well. Closed on Sunday, the menu is mainly Tuscan and Italian, though the style is that of nouvelle cuisine.

Villa Cora ******* ☛ AC
Viale Machiavelli 18
Tel. 229.845.1 fax 229.086
☛ T.4/E8
This elegant villa, located on a wooded hillside and boasting an attractive swimming pool, has 48 rooms, 16 of which are suites. A stylish and welcoming hotel. The restaurant, the 'Taverna Machiavelli', has a mainly Tuscan menu with some delicious international dishes too.

HOSTELS, CAMPSITES AND COUNTRY FARMS

There is an alternative to staying in a hotel; some Florentine convents accomodate visitors and pilgrims.

Suore Oblate dello Spirito Santo *
Via Nazionale 8
Tel. 239.820.2 - ☛ T.3/F3

Suore del Sacro Cuore *
Via della Piazzola 4
Tel. 574.466.2 - ☛ T.5/I2
Prices are for full board, though half board is also available, and are per person.

Villa Maria Santissima Assunta *
Via delle Forbici 38
Tel. 577.690 - ☛ T.5/I2
Prices are per person and are available for full or half board.

Several hostels and campsites also exist, all in convenient and often scenic positions.

Campeggio Comunale
Viale Michelangelo 80
Tel. 681.197.7 / 689.348 - ☛ T.6/H7

Campeggio panoramico Fiesole
Via Permonda 1
Tel. 599.069 fax 591.86

Camping internazionale Firenze
Via San Crsitofano 2. Località Bottai
Tel. 202.277.0 / 237.341.2

Camping Ostello villa Camerata
Viale A. Righi 2-4
Tel. 601.451 fax 610.300 - ☛ T.5/M2

Ostello Santa Monica
Via Santa Monica 6
Tel. 268.338 / 239.670.4 fax 280.185
☛ T.2/D6

Ostello archi rossi
Via Faenza 94r
Tel. 290.804 - ☛ T.3/E4

'Agriturismo' is another accommodation possibility. These are generally simply furnished rooms or small flats outside the city in the sur-rounding countryside. The lodgings are usually in farms and converted farm buildings. Specific guides are available from bookshops.

Le Macine
Viuzzo del Pozzetto 1
Tel. 653.108.9 - ☛ T.6/M8 from Viale Europa
Three independent single-room flats inside the farmhouse. All comforts, including a swimming pool.

La Fattoressa
Via Volterrana 58
Tel. 204.841.8
Small farmstead producing fruit and vegetables, near to the Certosa del Galluzzo.

Il Termine
Località Ferrone, Impruneta
Tel. 207.037
Delightful farm surrounded by peaceful countryside.

Fattoria Il Milione
Via di Giogoli 12/14
Via della Greve 7/9
Tel. 204.871.3
A group of old farmhouses, carefully renovated and equipped with swimming pool and play area for children.

Fattoria Poggiopiano
Via dei Bassi 13 Girone. Fiesole.
Tel. 659.302.0
Seven kilometres from the centre of Florence, this splendid old farmhouse is the ideal place for total relaxation.

Fattoria di Maiano
Località Maiano di Fiesole
Tel. 599.600
Once a monastery, located on the hills above Florence, the building has now been converted into a series of flats.

La Massa e i Sodi
Via della Torricella 4. Località Valle. Fiesole
Tel. 659.901.0
A farm situated deep in the countryside and equipped with a swimming pool.

GROCERS' SHOPS AND DELICATESSENS

I formaggi di Giulia
Via V. Emanuele II 2r (on the corner of Via XX Settembre).
Giorgio Bartolozzi won't mind at all if we call him old-fashioned: his honesty, helpfulness and dedication to his trade all seem to belong to another era. Every summer he gives up part of his much-deserved holiday to tour Italy in search of rare and special cheeses. Whether Tuscan pecorino or Pasubio, Caporetto or burrata, Bra or gorgonzola imperiale they are all quite superb. The cold meats and salumi are equally good.

Procacci
Via Tornabuoni 64r.
Luxury delicatessen. Lots of tasty delicacies, including delicious sandwiches to eat at the bar with a flute of white wine.

Pegna
Via dello Studio 26r.
Supermarket style, but with an old-fashioned and genteel atmosphere. They stock absolutely everything.

Orizi
Via del Parione 19r
A grocer's shop which produces delicious hot meals at lunch time.

Tassini
Borgo Santissimi Apostoli 24r
Fabulous delicatessen and specialities with a quite unique choice of salami and cheeses.

Friggitoria Luisa
Via Sant'Antonino 50r
One of the few surviving 'deep fry' shops with a wide choice of tasty nibbles.

Caseficio Salicella
Via Madonna della Querce 23b
Bufala mozzarella (the very best) and a wide range of cheeses and top quality produce from Lucca and Campania.

Ciatti
Via Panicale 19r.
There are wonderful marble basins for the stockfish to soak in, while the dried fillets hang from the ceiling. Anchovies, herring, rice and beans are all available here. The shop opened in the early years of this century and offers an amazing variety of goods.

Giuliano
Via dei Neri 5r.
The counter is filled with tempting delicacies.

SHOPPING

Antiques. Magnificent examples of antique furniture, carpets, paintings and decorative items are to be found in the major antique shops in Via Maggio, Via dei Fossi and Borgo Ognissanti.

Bookshops. *Centro Di*, Via de' Renai 20r; *Salimbeni*, Via M. Palmieri 14-16r; *Seeber*, Via Tornabuoni 70r; *Lef*, Via Ricasoli 105-107r; *Marzocco*, Via Martelli 22r; *Del Porcellino*, Piazza del Mercato Nuovo 6; *Cima*, Borgo Albizzi 37r; *Viaggio*, Borgo Albizzi 41r; *Feltrinelli*, Via Cerretani 30r; *After Dark*, Via de' Ginori 47r; *Falciani*, Via Tosinghi 44r; *Condotta 29*, Via Condotta 29; *Edison*, Piazza della Repubblica 13r; *Paperback Exchange*, Via Fiesolana, 31r; *Art & Libri*, Via de' Fossi 32r.. Antique books and prints: *Ippogrifo*, Via della Vigna Nuova 5r. Children's books: *Cooperativa dei ragazzi*, Via San Gallo 27r; *Il Marzocchino*, Via Martelli 14r; *l'Albero Mago*, Viale Petrarca 84r.

Clothes. The most stylish shops are in Via Tornabuoni, Via della Vigna Nuova, Via Tosinghi, Via Calzaiuoli e Via Roma.

Embroidery. *TAF*, Via Por Santa Maria 22r; *Cirri*, Via Por Santa Maria 40r; *Città di San Gallo*, Via Por Santa Maria 60r; *Loretta Caponi*, Piazza Antinori 22r; *Baroni*, Via Tornabuoni 29r.

Hand made items. Local Florentine goods and products: *Solo a Firenze*, Borgo Santissimi Apostoli 37r; terracotta and ceramics: *Sbigoli*, Via Sant'Egidio 4r, *Silvano Andreini*, Borgo Albizi 63r; paper goods: *Giannini*, Piazza Pitti 37r; exclusive hand-woven furnishing fabrics: *Lisio*, Via de' Fossi 45 r, *Antico setificio fiorentino*, Via Bartolini 4; artistic mosaic work: *Ugolini*, Lungarno Acciaiuoli 66r, *Pitti mosaici*, Piazza Pitti 17r; violin makers: *Carlo Vettori*, Via Guelfa 3, *Lazzara Jamie*, Via dei Leoni 4r; smokers accessories: *Corselli*, Via Ghibellina 132r; artistic glass work: *Locchi*, Via Burchiello 10. The little streets in the three areas of San Niccolò, Santa Croce and San Frediano are full of leather workers, framers, carpenters and restorers.

Hats. *Borsalino*, Via Porta Rossa 40r and Via Calzaiuoli 22r; *Tina*, Via de' Pucci 23r; *Pananti*, Borgo la Croce 3c.

Herbalists and Chemists. *Bottega di Lungavita*, Via Ghibellina 126r; *De Herbore*, Via del Proconsolo 6 a/b; *Officina Profumo-Farmaceutica di Santa Maria Novella*, Via della Scala 16 (historical institution: ☞ p. 55); *Farmacia Santissima Annunziata*, Via de' Servi 80r (fine cosmetics made in their laboratory with natural ingredients) .

Jewellery. *Torrini*, Piazza Duomo 10r; *Favilli*, Piazza Duomo 16r; *Bottega Orafa Artigiana*, Via F. Zannetti 14-16r; *Buccellati*, Via Tornabuoni 71r; *Gherardi*, Ponte Vecchio 8r; *Befani e Tai*, Via Vacchereccia 13r; *Morelli*, Borgo la Croce 77r; *Meli*, Costa San Giorgio 11r.

Leather goods. *Il Bisonte*, Via del Parione 11.

Silverware. *Brandimarte*, Via Bartolini 18 r; *Il Leone*, Via San Giovanni 13-15 r; *Ottanelli*, Viale dei Mille 90; *Roselli*, Via U. Rattazzi 2r; *Zaccaro*, Sdrucciolo de' Pitti 12-14 r.

Other items. Wine growing and production: *Bizzarri*, Via Condotta 32r; household goods: *Bartolini*, Via de' Servi 30r. Old-fashioned emporium, originally established to import English foodstuffs: *Old England Stores*, Via de' Vecchietti 28r. Porcelain: *Richard Ginori*, Via Rondinelli 17r.

OPENING TIMES OF MAIN MUSEUMS

Accademia (Galleria dell'Accademia) 8.30-18.50 / Sunday 8.30-13.50 (closed Monday)

Archaeology Museum 9.00-14.00 / Sunday 9.00-13.00 (closed first, third and fifth Sundays of month and second and fourth Mondays)

Argenti Museum (Palazzo Pitti) 9.00-14.00 (closed Monday)

Bardini Museum 9.00-14.00 / Sunday 8.00-13.00 (closed Wednesday)

Bargello Museum 8.30-13.50 including Sunday (closed first, third and fifth Sundays of month and second and fourth Mondays of month)

Benozzo Gozzoli chapel (palazzo Medici Riccardi) 9.00-13.00 and 15.00-18.00 / Sunday 9.00-13.00 (closed Wednesday)

Bòboli Gardens From 9.00 until one hour before sunset / from June to September 9.00-19.00 (closed first and fourth Mondays of month)

Brancacci chapel 10.00-17.00 / Sunday 13.00-17.00 (closed Tuesday)

Casa Buonarroti 9.30-13.30 / Sunday 9.30-13.30 (closed Tuesday)

Cathedral Dome 9.30-18.20 (closed Sunday and public holidays)

Cathedral Museum (Museo dell'Opera del Duomo) 9.00-18.00

Corsini Gallery only open on application

Costume Gallery (Palazzo Pitti) 9.00-14.00 including Sunday (closed Monday)

Etnographic Museum (Palazzo Non Finito) Thursday-Saturday 9.00-13.00 / open third Sunday of month

«Firenze com'era» Museum 9.00-14.00 / Sunday 8.00-13.00 (closed Thursday)

Gallery of Modern Art (Palazzo Pitti) 9.00-14.00 including Sunday (closed first, third and fifth Mondays of month)

Giotto's Belltower (Campanile) summer 9.00-18.50 / winter 9.00-16.20 including Sunday.

Horne Museum 9.00-13.00 (closed Sunday and public holidays)

La Specola Museum 9.00-12.00 / Sunday 9.00-13.00 (closed Wednesday)

Laurentian Library 9.00-13.00 (closed Sunday and public holidays)

Marino Marini Museum 10.00-17.00 / Sunday 10.00-13.00 (closed Tuesday and Sunday in summer)

Medici chapels 8.30-13.50 including Sunday (closed first, third and fifth Mondays of month)

Natural History Museum 9.00-12.00 Monday, Wednesday, Friday and Saturday

Opificio delle Pietre Dure 9.00-17.30 (closed Sunday and public holidays)

Palatine Gallery 8.30-18.50 / Sunday 8.30-13.50 (closed Monday)

Palazzo Davanzati closed for restoration

Palazzo Vecchio 9.00-19.00 / Sunday 8.00-13.00 (closed Thursday)

Pazzi chapel 10.00-12.30 and 14.30-18.30

San Marco Museum 8.30-13.50 including Sunday (closed first, third and fifth Sundays of month and second and fourth Mondays of month)

Santa Croce Museum summer 10.00-12.30 and 14.30-18.30 including Sunday / winter 10.00-12.30 and 15.00-17.00 including Sunday (closed Wednesday)

Santa Maria Novella Museum 9.00-14.00 / Sunday 8.00-13.00 (closed Friday)

Uffizi Gallery Tuesday-Saturday 8.30-18.50 / Sunday 8.30-13.50 (closed Monday)

OPENING TIMES OF MAIN CHURCHES

Badìa Fiesolana only open Sunday morning

Badìa Fiorentina Tuesday - Thursday 17.00-19.00

Baptistery summer 13.30-18.30 (Sunday 8.30-13.30); winter 13.30-17.30

Carmine Saturday 8.00-17.30; Sunday 8.00-12.00 and 17.30-18.00

Cathedral see: Santa Maria del Fiore

Ognissanti 8.00-12.00 and 16.00-18.30

Orsanmichele 9.00-12.00 and 16.00-18.00

San Felice in Piazza Sunday 8.00-11.30; weekdays 8.00-19.00

San Firenze Saturday 8.00-19.00; Sunday 8.00-12.00 and 15.30-19.00

San Frediano in Cestello 9.00-12.00 and 16.30-17.30; Sunday 16.30-19.30

San Lorenzo 7.00-12.00 and 15.30-18.30

San Marco 7.00-12.30 and 16.00-20.00

San Miniato al Monte summer 8.00-12.00 and 14.00-19.00 / winter 8.00-12.00 and 14.30-18.00

San Niccolò Sunday only 9.30-11.30

San Salvatore al Monte Saturday 17.30-18; Sunday 8.30-17.30

Sant'Ambrogio Sunday only 8.00-11.30

Santa Croce summer 8.00-18.30; winter 8.00-12.30 and 15.00-18.30 (Sunday 15.00-18.00)

Santa Felicita 8.00-12.00 and 15.30-18.30

Santa Maria del Fiore 10.00-17.00; first Saturday of month 10.00-15.30; Sunday 13.00-17.00

Santa Maria Maddalena de' Pazzi 9.00-12.00 and 17.00-19.00

Santa Maria Maggiore; Saturday 8.00-19.00; Sunday 7.30-12.30; 19-21

Santa Maria Novella 7.00-11.30 and 15.30-18.00

Santa Trìnita 7.30-12.00 and 16.00-19.00

Santissima Annunziata 7.30-12.30 and 16.00-18.30

Santo Spirito 8.30-12.00 and 16.00-17.30

GLOSSARY OF ART TERMS

Acanthus. The acanthus leaf was used as a decorative motif on the Corinthian capital and later on the Composite capital. The form is a stylized version of the plant's long, slender leaves and pointed flowers.

Aedicule. Small structure intended to house a sacred image or statue. It may also be a niche set into the external wall of a building.

Altar frontal. Decoration of the front of an altar table, often either a relief sculpture or inlay. Usually made of marble but precious materials such as ivory or silver may also be used. Sometimes called antependium.

Altar panel. Large painting of a religious subject, situated above an altar in a church.

Alto-rilievo (High relief). Technique of sculpting in which the figures are considerably raised or detached from the background. In a bas-relief the figures are only slightly raised from the surface.

Amber. Derived from Arabic, amber is a fossilized resin, reddish-yellow in colour and more or less transparent. It has been used from ancient times to make trinkets and jewellery.

Antependium. ☞ Altar frontal.

Apse. A semi-circular or polygonal projection of a building, with a half dome or conch (bowl-shaped vault). In churches it is at the end of the central nave (sometimes also at the end of the side naves or transept) and houses the main altar and the choir. Two identical, facing apses are known as a double apse and where, as in some Romanesque churches, there are three, a triple apse.

Apsidiole. A small projecting apse forming part of the main apse. A typical element of Gothic and Cluniac architecture.

Arch. An architectural structure supported by columns or pilasters. The classical elements of an arch are: 1) intrados - the underside or soffit of an arch; 2) keystone - a central wedge-shaped block in the upper curved section; 3) extrados - the outer curve of the arch; 4) the impost - the blocks or bands on either side, from which the arch springs; 5) the span - the distance between the two sides. Various types of arches exist, according to the form of the curve: round arch - semicircular with the centre on the springing line; segmental arch - where the span is less than the diameter and the curve is semi-circular; drop arch - where the span is greater than the radii; pointed arch - having two arcs drawn from centres on the springing line; horseshoe - where the blocks at the springing line turn inwards; trefoil arch - rising from the apexes of two half arches; flying buttress - the two sides rest on staggered imposts.

Architrave. The lowest of the three main elements of an entablature. Also a moulded frame around a door or window.

Art Nouveau. Highly decorative artistic style, popular at the end of the 19th and beginning of the 20th century. Heavy use is made of ornamentally curving lines and shapes derived from flower and plant motifs.

Ashlar. Large square block of stone usually used as quoins on the outer corners of buildings decorated with rustication.

Atlas. Male version of a *caryatide,* a sculpted figure used instead of a column to support an entablature. Also called telamon.

Attic. Decorative architectural element situated above the cornice of a building and concealing the roof from view.

Baptismal font. Usually made of stone or marble and of various shapes, containing the holy water used during the ritual of baptism (☞ baptistery).

Baptistery. Religious building of circular design where the baptismal font is housed. Usually built beside or in front of a church or cathedral.

Baroque. Style of art popular in Italy and throughout Europe in the 17th century. It consisted of rich and elaborate detail and complex design. The term possibly derived from the Spanish *barrueca* (a rare type of pearl with an uneven shape) which later assumed the French form, *baroque.*

Base or basement. Lowest part of a building on which the entire structure rests. Also the lowest element of an order supporting the shaft of a column.

Basilica. In ancient Rome the basilica was a public building which served several purposes of an institutional nature, both civil and religious. The building was generally rectangular and was divided by colonnades. The wall at one end formed a semicircular or rectangular apse. The term later came to mean a Christian church which adopted the same design as the Roman basilica.

Bas-relief. ☞ Alto rilievo.

Baths. Roman baths consisted of a complex of buildings which were used as public baths and meeting place. They usually consisted of a series of rooms containing basins, baths and pools with warm, tepid and cold water (known as the calidarium, the tepidarium and the frigidarium); there was also a laconicum (a steam bath) and a apodyterium (changing room).

Battlements. A form of indented parapet around the top of castles and towers which may either be defensive or decorative. A Guelf battlement was rectangular while the solid upright blocks (merlons) of a Ghibelline battlement were further indented with a 'V' shape.

Bay. Space limited by two adjacent weight-bearing structures (columns, pilasters etc.). In churches the bay is also an area of the nave defined by four adjacent columns or pilasters in facing pairs. Here, the bay generally has a cross vault (☞ vault).

Bell tower (Campanile). Structure in the shape of a tower, often incorporated into the outer wall of a church, though it may also be free-standing. The church bells are housed in the upper section.

Bottega (it.). Derived from the Latin apothèca, in turn derived from the Greek term apothèke. Room or rooms inside a building, opening onto the street and used for either a commercial activity or as an artist's or craftsman's workshop.

Bracket. ☞ Corbel.

Bronze. Metal resulting from the fusion of copper and tin, occasionally with the addition of other metals. Used for figurines and statues.

Byzantine art. Figurative art which came into being around the 4th century A.D. in the eastern Roman empire. The name derives from Byzantium, another name for Constantinople, the eastern capital. The style continued for over one thousand years, surviving until the fall of Constantinople to the Turks in 1453. The earliest works of art date from the 6th century when Byzantine art developed its own particular style (I Golden Age). Following a lengthy period of decline caused by the spread of iconoclasm which forbade the representation of religious subjects, it flourished once more during the reign of the Macedonian dynasty (867-1057, II Golden Age) and under the dynasty of the Palaeologus Emperors (1261-1453 Byzantine Renaissance). Byzantine art produced architectural works of art (Hagia Sophia in Constantinople, 7th-century, the Basilica of S. Apollinare Nuovo and S. Apollinare in Classe in Ravenna, 8th-9th century), magnificent mosaics (Ravenna, the cathedral of Monreale in Palermo), as well as icons and illuminated manuscripts.

Campanile. ☞ Bell tower.

Cantoria. Choir gallery, usually raised, for the choir of singers in a church.

Cardo. Latin term for the main road running in a north-south direction through a town or city and crossing the *decumanus* which ran from west to east.

Carroccio (it.). In the 'free comunes' during the Middle Ages, the carroccio was a large wagon with four wheels drawn by oxen and symbolized the independence of the city. During periods of war, it was brought to the battlefield decorated with all the emblems and insignia of the city, the war bell and an altar.

Cartoon. A charcoal drawing made on card used in the making of large works of art, especially frescoes. The outline is then nicked out with a small knife or pricked out with an awl and placed on the surface to be painted. The form is then dusted with coal powder which leaves the outline of the picture to be painted on the surface.

Cathedral. The main church of a bishopric. The bishop officiates at the religious ceremonies and practices his spiritual teachings here.

Càvea. Semicircular area of a Roman theatre or amphitheatre occupied by rows of seats for the public.

Cenacolo (it.). Derived from the Latin *coenaculum* - a room where one ate. Subsequently the term used for the room where Christ and his disciples ate the Last Supper and consequently paintings representing this scene.

Chapel. The name derives from the oratory in Charlemagne's palace at Aquisgrana in Germany, where the cape of Saint Martin of Tours was housed. In the nave of a church it represents a niche containing an altar dedicated to a saint.

Chapter house. Large room in a cathedral or monastery where the chapter (governing body) met to discuss and decide on matters concerning the religious community.

Chasuble. Outer vestment worn by officiating priest at mass.

Chisel (Cesello). The cesello is a small chisel with a rounded tip used for engraving images or decorations on metal and stone.

Choir. Section of a church situated behind the main altar, furnished with stalls and intended for members of the choir.

Choir stalls. Canopied and carved seats for the choir and officiating clergy in a church.

Cloister. Internal courtyard of a monastery or convent with a portico of slender columns supporting a roof and resting on a low wall.

Coffered (Caissoned) ceiling. Square or polygonal panels set into a ceiling and often decorated with ornamental motifs.

Commesso. Decorative pattern on a large, flat surface - usually a floor - consisting of the inlay of small unevenly shaped and variously coloured stones.

Composite order. An order of Roman architecture characterized by a capital - much used in triumphal arches - consisting of acanthus leaves and large volutes. It is a combination of elements of both the Ionic and the Corinthian orders.

Corbel. Architectural element which projects from a wall and supports beams and cornices.

Corinthian order. Architectural order which originated in Corinth around the 5th century B.C. The Corinthian capital is decorated with acanthus leaves from which small volutes emerge.

Cornice. Horizontal decorative element found where the wall meets the ceiling. Also the uppermost main division of an entablature (☞).

Cornucopia. Vase in the shape of a horn, filled with fruit and decorated with flowers. A classic symbol of abundance.

Crosier. Staff, resembling a shepherd's crook, carried by bishops and abbots as a symbol of office.

Cross vault. ☛ Vault.

Cross window. Divided into four sections by a mullion and a transom.

Crypt. Underground chamber or vault, usually beneath the presbytery of a church and used for burial or sometimes as an oratory.

Cupola ☛ Dome.

Decumanus. ☛ Cardo.

Dentils. A series of small rectangular blocks, similar to a row of teeth, decorating Corinthian, Ionic and Composite cornices.

Dome (Cupola). Curved or spherical vault (may also be semi-circular with an oval section) mainly found in religious buildings. The cupola rests on a 'drum' with a polygonal or cylindrical external structure and is crowned by a lantern (☛) through which light is admitted to the interior.

Dressing. Stone surface of a building, worked to a finish, whether smooth or moulded. Also the decorative stonework around any of the openings.

Drop arch. ☛ Arch.

Drum. ☛ Dome.

Enamel. A siliceous substance made from a mixture of feldspar, quartz, carbonate and sodium chloride. Used to decorate ceramics and metals. Metals may be decorated using the *cloisonné* technique whereby the paste is set into small mountings created by metal thread, or using the *champlevé* technique, where the paste is set into dents made by a punch on the surface of the metal.

Entablature. Arrangement of three horizontal members - architrave (☛), frieze (☛) and cornice (☛) - supported by columns or pilasters.

Extrados. Outer curve of an arch with a structural or purely decorative function (☛ arch).

Ex-voto. Object, often a small painting, offered to a saint to express gratitude.

Flamboyant Gothic. Style of Gothic architecture which came into being at the end of the 14th and beginning of the 15th centuries. It developed in similar fashion in many European countries and was characterized, especially in painting and the applied arts, by an extremely linear decorative style and a purity of colour. Flamboyant Gothic may have derived from the influence of Simone Martini's later work on French artists during his period in Avignon.

Fòndaco (it.) Store/Warehouse. In the early Middle Ages the term signified a building used not only as a hotel but also as a trading centre for merchants during their period of residence in foreign countries.

Fresco. A technique of painting which consists of applying diluted paint to fresh, damp lime plaster. This method creates a chemical reaction which, in drying, transforms the lime of the plaster into calcium carbonate. The result is a smooth and resistant surface which incorporates the pigment with the material of the wall.

Frieze. The middle of the three main elements of an entablature (☛). A horizontal band with cornice (☛) above and architrave (☛) below. In the Doric order it consists of metope - a square panel sculpted with figures - and triglyph - panels with three vertical grooves. In the other orders the band of the frieze is usually continuous and is entirely decorated with sculpted figures.

Gallery. A long room or corridor, usually on the upper floor and extending the full length of a building. In church architecture, an open upper storey over an aisle (☛).

Gipsoteca (it.) A collection of plaster moulds used to produce series of statues, bas-reliefs, medallions etc.

Gothic. Style which influenced first architecture and later painting, sculpture and the minor arts. It developed in France during the mid-12th century and spread throughout Europe and Italy from the 13th to the 15th centuries. Gothic sculpture is characterized by a pure, verical line and delicate interpretation; in architecture the pointed arch, ribbed vault and flying buttresses are typical features.

Graffiti. A decorative design made by scratching the plaster of a wall, or the surface of a stone, metal, ceramics or layer of painting, to reveal the contrasting colour of the background. Alternatively the outline made may be filled with a material of a different colour.

Grezzo (it.). The base, raw material to be used in producing an item; also painting, sculpture etc. in unfinished, 'roughed out' stage.

Grotesque. Derived from the term *grotto* which was used in the 16th century to describe the ruins of the *Domus Aurea* (Nero's palace in Rome). It describes painted or stucco decoration in a style frequent in ancient Rome which represented imaginary and fantastic motifs (plants interwoven with mythical or semi-human and animal figures).

Herm. A tapering pilaster which, in ancient Greece, was sculpted with the head of a god (usually Hermes). More generally, it now indicates any sculpture representing a human bust.

High-relief. ☛ Alto rilievo.

Horseshoe arch. ☛ Arch.

Icon. Religious image painted on a panel, typical of Byzantine religious and artistic culture (☛ Byzantine). The Russian church later adopted these as items of worship and devotion.

Impost. Block or slab from which an arch springs.

Inlaid work. Technique of inlaying pieces of stone or wood (marquetry) of different colours to create a design or picture.

Intrados. The inner curve or underside of an arch. Also known as a soffit.

'Kneeling' windows. Typical feature of Renaissance buildings, the window is framed by columns, entablature and tympanum, all resting on two corbels or brackets.

Lantern. Crowning element of a dome (☞), usually circular or polygonal, admitting light to the interior of the building.

Lesene. ☞ Pilaster-strip.

Lintel. Outer edge of an arch which may be purely decorative or structural in function.

Loggia. Part of a building, or sometimes an entire structure, open on one or more sides, with a roof supported by pilasters or columns. Often used as a meeting place or market.

Lunette. Semi-circular space decorated with frescoes or mosaics usually situated above doors or windows where the vault (☞) joins the walls. Also used to describe a semicircular section above a painting or bas-relief.

Macchiaioli. Group of Italian impressionist painters who used a technique of 'spots' (macchie) of colour. The school came into being in Florence between 1857 and 1867; some of its most important exponents were Giovanni Fattori, Telemaco Signorini and Silvestro Lega.

Mannerism. A highly formalized and elegant form of art which came into being in 16th-century Italy. With Mannerism, methodical use of the principles of variety and complexity developed into an extrovert display of artistic virtuosity.

Marquetry. Technique consisting of the inlay of ornamental woods, metals, ivory and other decorative materials, arranged to form designs and patterns.

Matronèo (it.). Internal loggia or gallery, usually above the side naves of early Christian or Romanesque churches, reserved for women.

Medallion. Small bas-relief, often made of metal.

Monochrome. Used to describe a figurative image executed in a single colour, or shades of a single colour.

Monolithic column. A column made from a single block of stone, rather than in several sections.

Mosaic. Decorative design covering a large, flat surface - often a floor - made of inlay arranged in a regular pattern according to the form and colour of various stones used.

Moulding. Decorative feature added to an architectural element which may be simple or enriched in design.

Mullion. Window divided into two vertical

parts by a small column or pilaster. Frequently found in Romanesque, Gothic and Renaissance buildings.

Nave. The main body or central aisle of a church which may be enclosed by walls (church with a single nave), by columns or by pilasters (church with three or five naves where the central one is usually higher and wider).

Niche. ☞ Aedicule.

Oculus. Oval or circular opening or window in a wall or dome.

Opus tassellatum. Type of floor made entirely from small square-shaped pieces of marble and stone, usually of different colours.

Oratory. Chapel or other building belonging to a church or monastery, used either for private worship or associations of brethren.

Order. Architectural style defined by the type of column and entablature (☞). The column is divided into three main elements: the base, shaft and capital. The entablature consists of architrave, frieze and cornice. Three classical Greek orders developed (Doric, Ionic and Corinthian) and two Roman orders (Tuscan and Composite).

Ovulo. A convex moulding in the shape of a quarter circle which forms a horizontal band: usually a decorative member in a Corinthian or Doric cornice.

Panel. Decorative element of various shapes and material (marble, stone, bronze, wood) which has been sculpted, carved or painted with figures or scenes and used on doors, walls or cornices.

Perspective. Technique of representing three-dimensional space on a flat or relief surface giving a sense of depth. Linear perspective foreshortens objects as they recede into the distance with lines converging to a vanishing point. Aerial perspective is based on contrasts of colour and shade, which are stronger in the foreground and fainter in the distance.

Pilaster-strip. Flat column, slightly projecting from a wall. Has a purely decorative function.

Pillar. Vertical structural member which bears a load - arches (☞), architraves (☞) or vaults (☞). It may be square, oblong or polygonal in shape. Romanesque pillars are usually cruciform with a column on each of the four sides; Gothic pillars generally consist of a 'cluster' of columns.

Pinnacle. Element which crowns a façade, dome etc. Often used in Gothic architecture sometimes as a purely decorative feature on doorways.

Plan. Horizontal layout of a building. Churches often have the form of a cross with two sections at right angles to each other. If the sections are of the same length and cross at the centre, they form a Greek cross; if one section is shorter than the other, intersecting it at about a third of its length, they form a Latin cross. If the shorter arm crosses the end of the longer section, the form is known as a Tau or Saint Anthony's cross.

Pointed arch. ☞ Arch.

Polychrome. Item made with, or decorated in several colours.

Polyptych. Painting or panel in more than three sections which are hinged together. Three paintings or panels are known as a tryptych. These paintings often formed altar panels (☞).

Presbytery. Area of a church around the main altar. Reserved for the clergy, it is separated from the central nave by a balustrade.

Projection. Architectural element projecting from the wall of a building (frieze, balcony, bracket, butress etc.).

Pulpit. Elevated platform or reading desk in a church (occasionally also located externally) from which a sermon is preached.

Reliquary. Urn or container for the relics of a saint or martyr.

Ribbed vault. A form of cross vaulting in which the weight of the segments is evenly distributed over raised stone ribs.

Rock crystal. A kind of quartz of transparant and neutral appearance, used before glass was developed to make household articles and ornaments.

Romanesque. A style of the figurative arts - especially sculpture - and of architecture which flourished throughout western Europe from the end of the 10th century until the middle of the 12th century (in Italy until the early decades of the 13th century). Typical features of the Romanesque style are: simple pillars often alternating with composite pillars; cross or barrel vault ceilings; external pilaster strips and buttresses; bays separated by transverse arches supported by clustered columns.

Rosette. A circular design or ornament which resembles a formalized rose; may be painted, sculpted or moulded.

Rotunda. A round building often covered with a dome. A large round room or hall, generally in the centre of a building.

Round arch. ☞ Arch.

Rustication. A method of treating masonry. Large, rectangular blocks of stone project from the wall with deeply emphasized joints. Lightly hewn blocks are known as 'boasted' or 'droved' ashlars.

Sacristy. Room attached to a church for the storage of sacred vessels and vestments. Usually also a robing room for the clergy.

Sarcophagus. Coffin in stone, marble or other material. Roman sarcophagi were decorated with bas-relief sculptures on the sides, while Etruscan sarcophagi generally had a statue of the deceased, in a reclining position as though at a banquet, on top.

Segmental arch. ☞ Arch.

Seraph. Angel belonging to the highest order in the celestial heirarchy, the seraphim. Often depicted surrounding the figure of God in adoration.

Serliana. A triple opening. The central part is arched, while the two lateral sections have a straight upper frame. The term is derived from the name of an architect from Bologna, Sebastiano Serlio (1475-1555), who proposed the design in his manual of architecture, but it was already known in Roman times.

Spandrel. Triangular surface between the vault of a dome and the supporting elements. Also the triangular surface, with curved sides, between two adjacent arches and the horizontal moulding above.

Stained glass. Coloured or stained glass used especially in church windows to form figures or decorations. The colour is derived from metalllic oxide added during manufacture. Small pieces of the coloured glass are set into a framework to compose the design or image.

Street bench. Stone seat built into the base of the external wall of some palaces and residences.

Tabernacle. Niche (☞) or aedicule (☞) in the shape of a small temple containing a sacred image. Also used for the ciborium, receptacle in the centre of the altar for the Sacrament.

Tapestry. Large tapestries usually portraying historical events, legends and figures. They were edged with decorative borders woven in wool, silk, gold and silver thread. The Italian word *arazzo* is derived from the name of the French city, Arras, once one of the most important centres for cloth production.

Telamon. ☞ Atlas.

Terracotta, glazed. Pottery or china decorated with a vitreous finish obtained by combining silica (found in clay) and lead oxide. The pottery thus becomes impermeable and lustrous.

Tower-house. A tall, fortified house which was quite common from the 11th to the 13th century. It provided protection and defense for the head of important families and his supporters against enemies.

Transept. Transverse nave in a cruciform church, crossing the main nave at the level of the presbytery.

Trefoil. Three-lobed opening or arch (☞).

Tribune. Area consisting of the presbytery (☞) and apse (☞) of a church. In a Roman basilica the tribune was the semi-circular area where the judges sat; in early Christian churches it indicated the seats behind the main altar where the bishop and clergy sat.

Triptych. ☞ Polyptych.

Truss. A triangular load-bearing structure used to support the roofs of churches and other buildings. The beams are usually made of wood, though they may also be steel or concrete.

Tympanum. Vertical triangular space, plain

or with relief decoration, between the slopes of a roof and the horizontal cornice of a temple or other building with a pediment.

Urn. The ashes of the deceased are kept in a funerary urn after cremation. Also a container for relics of a saint.

Vault. Arched roof of a building or part of a building. Various forms exist: 1) barrel vault - an extreme development of the Roman arch (weight was carried equally by both walls); 2) cross vault where two barrel vaults cross and are divided into four segments with weight-bearing ribs each supported by a pilaster. Where the ribs meet at the apex is a keystone; 3) fan vaulting - rising from a polygonal structure and consisting of a concave cone radiating from each support; 4) domi-cal vault - rising above a square structure an consisting of a section of a sphere whose d ameter is equal to the diagonal of the squar covered.

Via Crucis. The fourteen Stations of th Cross representing the most importar events in the passion and death of Christ.

Wunderkammer. During the Renaissanc wealthy and learned men collected works c art, natural phenomena and scientific an tecnical objects in a study or series of room The collection was not governed by any stri criteria and was intended to reflect the owr er's encyclopedic knowledge. Examples exis in the 'studiolo' of Francesco de' Medici an the Wunderkammern of various aristocra in central and northern Europe.

Index Of Artists

GENERAL INDEX

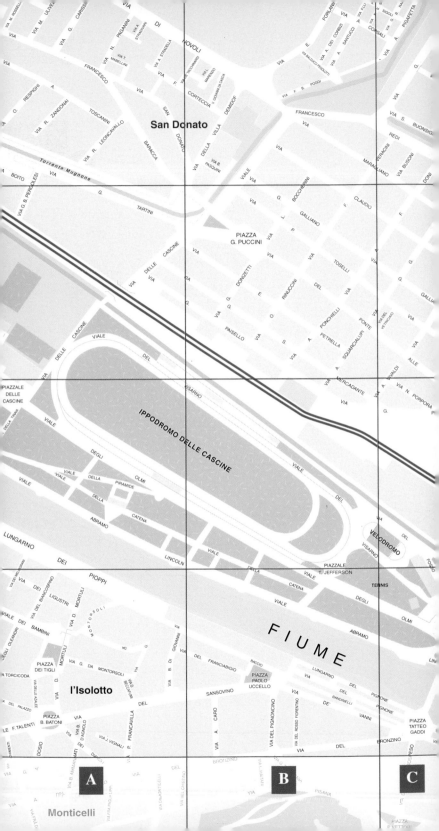

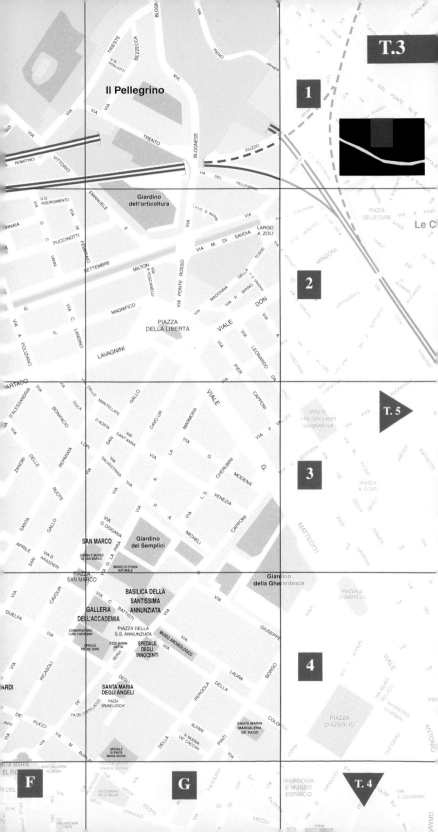

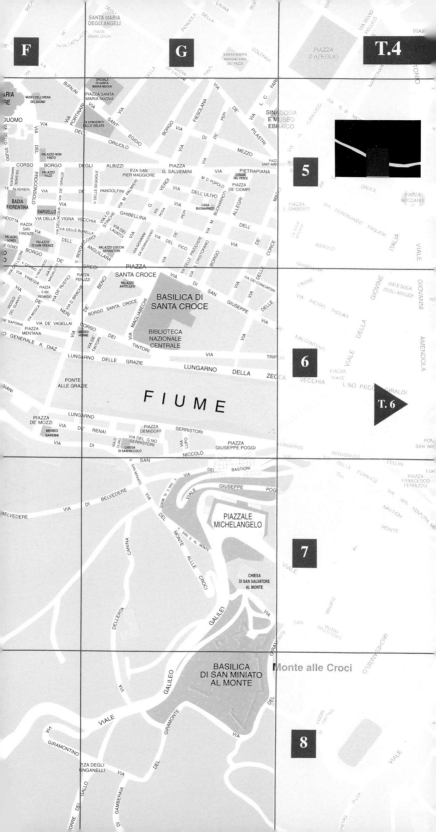

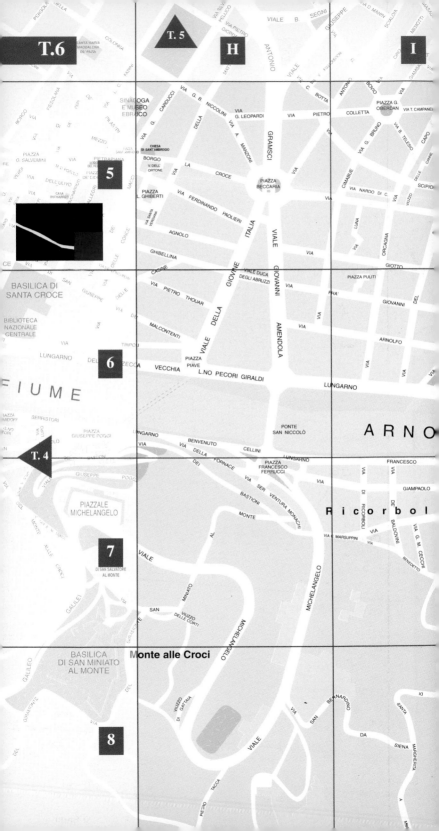

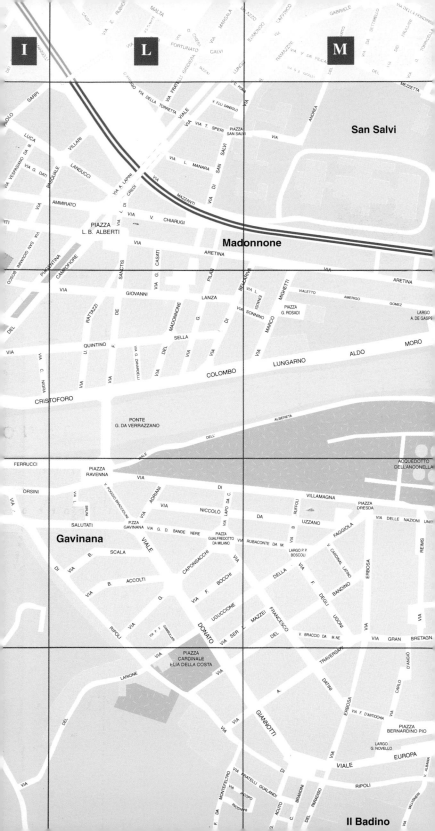

Street Index

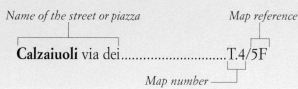

How to use

Name of the street or piazza   *Map reference*

Calzaiuoli via dei T.4/5F

Map number